Tyndale Old Te
Commentaries

Volume 12

Ezra and Nehemiah

Tyndale Old Testament Commentaries

Volume 12

SERIES EDITOR: DAVID G. FIRTH
CONSULTING EDITOR: TREMPER LONGMAN III

Ezra and Nehemiah

An Introduction and Commentary

Geert W. Lorein

An imprint of InterVarsity Press
Downers Grove. Illinois

InterVarsity Press, USA
P.O. Box 1400 | Downers Grove, IL 60515-1426
ivpress.com | email@ivpress.com

Inter-Varsity Press, England
SPCK Group, Studio 101, The Record Hall, 16–16A Baldwin's Gardens
London EC1N 7RJ, England
ivpbooks.com | ivp@ivpbooks.com

InterVarsity Press® is the publishing division of InterVarsity Christian Fellowship/USA®. For more information, visit intervarsity.org.

Inter-Varsity Press, England, originated within the Inter-Varsity Fellowship, now the Universities and Colleges Christian Fellowship, a student movement connecting Christian Unions in universities and colleges throughout Great Britain, and a member movement of the International Fellowship of Evangelical Students. That historic association is maintained, and all senior IVP staff and committee members subscribe to the UCCF Basis of Faith. Website: www.uccf.org.uk.

Unless otherwise noted, Scripture quotations are either taken from the English Standard Version or are the author's own translation.

First published 2024

USA ISBN 978-1-5140-0540-8 (print) | USA ISBN 978-1-5140-0541-5 (digital)

UK ISBN 978-1-78974-412-5 (print) | UK ISBN 978-1-78974-413-2 (digital)

Typeset in Great Britain by Avocet Typeset, Bideford, Devon

Printed in the United States of America ♾

Library of Congress Cataloging-in-Publication Data
A catalog record for this book is available from the Library of Congress.

British Library Cataloguing-in-Publication Data
A catalogue record for this book is available from the British Library.

32 31 30 29 28 27 26 25 24 | 12 11 10 9 8 7 6 5 4 3 2 1

CONTENTS

GENERAL PREFACE

The decision to completely revise the Tyndale Old Testament Commentaries is an indication of the important role that the series has played since its opening volumes were released in the mid 1960s. They represented at that time, and have continued to represent, commentary writing that was committed both to the importance of the text of the Bible as Scripture and a desire to engage with as full a range of interpretative issues as possible without being lost in the minutiae of scholarly debate. The commentaries aimed to explain the biblical text to a generation of readers confronting models of critical scholarship and new discoveries from the Ancient Near East while remembering that the Old Testament is not simply another text from the ancient world. Although no uniform process of exegesis was required, all the original contributors were united in their conviction that the Old Testament remains the word of God for us today. That the original volumes fulfilled this role is evident from the way in which they continue to be used in so many parts of the world.

A crucial element of the original series was that it should offer an up-to-date reading of the text, and it is precisely for this reason that new volumes are required. The questions confronting readers in the first half of the twenty-first century are not necessarily those from the second half of the twentieth. Discoveries from the Ancient Near East continue to shed new light on the Old Testament, while emphases in exegesis have changed markedly. While remaining true to the goals of the initial volumes, the need for contemporary study of the text requires that the series as a whole be updated. This updating is not simply a matter of commissioning new volumes to replace the old. We have also taken the opportunity to update the format of the series to reflect a key emphasis from linguistics, which is that texts communicate in larger blocks rather than in shorter segments such as individual verses. Because of this, the treatment of each section of the text includes three segments. First, a short note on *Context* is offered, placing the passage under consideration in its literary setting within the book as well as noting any historical issues crucial to interpretation. The *Comment* segment then follows the traditional structure of the commentary, offering exegesis of the various components of a passage. Finally, a brief comment is made on *Meaning*, by which is meant the message that the passage seeks to communicate within the book, highlighting its key theological themes. This section brings together the detail of the *Comment* to show how the passage under consideration seeks to communicate as a whole.

Our prayer is that these new volumes will continue the rich heritage of the Tyndale Old Testament Commentaries and that they will continue to witness to the God who is made known in the text.

David G. Firth, Series Editor
Tremper Longman III, Consulting Editor

AUTHOR'S PREFACE

The book of Ezra–Nehemiah (in this commentary Ezra–Nehemiah will be considered as one single book: see Introduction 3b, 'One book or two?') is not a management manual or merely a history of the sixth and fifth centuries BC. Broader than that, it helps us to understand how we as believers can live with God, Scripture, our own faith community and the society around us. Indeed, 'we as believers' – not only church leaders, but all believers who want to take seriously their responsibility in reverence for God.

I consider it a privilege and an honour to have been invited to contribute to the Tyndale Old Testament Commentaries and to have the possibility to serve the church worldwide in this way, using my experience not only in Hebrew prose, in the Aramaic and in the Persian period, but also in Church and State (or larger: law, belief and society) issues. I thank the Evangelische Theologische Faculteit, Leuven, for leaving me 'free' for some months at the end of my presidency of the Federal Synod of Protestant-Evangelical Churches in Belgium in order to finish work on this commentary.

Although it turned out to be a good thing that I had already written a commentary on Ezra–Nehemiah in Dutch (in *Geschriften over de Perzische tijd*, in De Brug, 2010), in the end every element has been pondered again and the extent of this one is almost double that of its predecessor. It remains, nonetheless, a commentary that tries to explain how the text should be understood in its historical context and how it can be applied in our actual context. Apart from some occasional remarks, the history of exegesis is not treated. The whole commentary should be useful for people who do not know Hebrew and Aramaic. I could not, however, restrain myself from putting in the footnotes some philological details whose consequences do not appear sufficiently in the English comments, and also for those readers who have some knowledge of Hebrew but cannot afford technical commentaries on every Bible book. Although my work was always based on the original texts, it is presented as a commentary on the English Standard Version, which in my opinion offers the best mix of trustworthiness and comprehensibility among current English translations. (The differences, however, are not so important among the most used English translations. They differ much less from one another than those in Dutch, my mother tongue.)

This is also the place to thank those who have read the text before its publication: my wife as its first reader, who checked whether I had written things that might be misunderstood; the second reader, my colleague Prof. M. I. Webber, who checked my English (and suggested many clarifications); and as a third reader, Dr D. G. Firth, who was my guide on behalf of the commentary series and suggested many improvements in view of its target group.

Geert W. Lorein
Leuven, Boxing Day, 2022

ABBREVIATIONS

See also Introduction 2c, 'Distances (and other measures)'.

ACEBT	Amsterdamse Cahiers voor Exegese en bijbelse Theologie
AD	Year of the Christian era
AGJU	Arbeiten zur Geschichte des antiken Judentums und des Urchristentums
Ant.	*Jewish Antiquities*: Flavius Josephus' description of the Antiquities (history) of the Jews
AOAT	Alter Orient und Altes Testament
BC	Year before the Christian era
BEATAJ	Beiträge zur Erforschung des Alten Testaments und des antiken Judentum
BST	Bible Speaks Today
BWANT	Beiträge zur Wissenschaft vom Alten und Neuen Testament
BZABR	Beihefte zur Zeitschrift für altorientalische und biblische Rechtsgeschichte
BZAW	Beihefte zur Zeitschrift für die alttestamentliche Wissenschaft
CBET	Contributions to Biblical Exegesis and Theology
cf.	compare
CHANE	Culture and History of the Ancient Near East
CRINT	Compendia Rerum Iudaicarum ad Novum Testamentum

DCLS	Deuterocanonical and Cognate Literature Studies
EAEH	M. Avi-Yonah and E. Stern (eds.), *Encyclopedia of Archaeological Excavations in the Holy Land* (Oxford: Oxford University Press, 1975–78; Hebrew orig.)
EJL	Early Judaism and Its Literature
ET	English translation(s) (e.g. in case of divergent verse numberings)
Ezra-Neh.	Ezra–Nehemiah
FAT	Forschungen zum Alten Testament
FRLANT	Forschungen zur Religion und Literatur des Alten und Neuen Testaments
GKC	*Gesenius' Hebrew Grammar*, ed. E. Kautzsch, tr. A. E. Cowley, 2nd edn (Oxford: Clarendon, 1910)
HALOT	L. Koehler and W. Baumgartner, *The Hebrew and Aramaic Lexicon of the Old Testament* (Leiden: Brill, 1994–2000)
Hebr.	Hebrew
JBL	*Journal of Biblical Literature*
JSHRZ	Jüdische Schriften aus hellenistisch-römischer Zeit
JSJSup	Supplements to the Journal for the Study of Judaism
JSOT	*Journal for the Study of the Old Testament*
JSOTSup	Journal for the Study of the Old Testament Supplement Series
JSPSup	Journal for the Study of the Pseudepigrapha Supplement Series
LHB/OTS	The Library of Hebrew Bible/Old Testament Studies
LSTS	The Library of Second Temple Studies
MS(s)	Manuscript(s)
NIDOTTE	W. A. VanGemeren (ed.), *New International Dictionary of Old Testament Theology and Exegesis*, 5 vols. (Grand Rapids: Zondervan, 1997)
OBO	Orbis Biblicus et Orientalis
OLA	Orientalia Lovaniensia Analecta
op. cit.	In the work already cited
SBL	Society of Biblical Literature
SBLDS	Society of Biblical Literature Dissertation Series

SCS	Septuagint and Cognate Studies
STDJ	Studies on the Texts of the Desert of Judah
TAVO	Tübinger Atlas des Vorderen Orients
v(v).	Verse(s)
VTSup	Supplements to Vetus Testamentum
WAW	Writings from the Ancient World
WUNT	Wissenschaftliche Untersuchungen zum Neuen Testament
ZAW	*Zeitschrift für die alttestamentliche Wissenschaft*

Bible versions

AV	The Authorized Version of the Bible (The King James Bible), the rights in which are vested in the Crown, reproduced by permission of the Crown's Patentee, Cambridge University Press.
ESV	The ESV Bible (The Holy Bible, English Standard Version), copyright © 2001 by Crossway, a publishing ministry of Good News Publishers. Used by permission. All rights reserved.
LXX	Septuagint (pre-Christian Greek translation of the Old Testament).
NAB	The *New American Bible with Revised New Testament and Revised Psalms*, copyright © 1991, 1986, 1970 Confraternity of Christian Doctrine, Washington, D.C. and used by permission of the copyright owner. All rights reserved.
NASB	The NEW AMERICAN STANDARD BIBLE®, Copyright © 1960, 1962, 1963, 1968, 1971, 1972, 1973, 1975, 1977, 1995 by The Lockman Foundation. Used by permission.
NET	The NET Bible, New English Translation, is copyright © 1996 by Biblical Studies Press, LLC. NET Bible is a registered trademark.
NIV	The Holy Bible, New International Version (Anglicized edition). Copyright © 1979, 1984, 2011 by Biblica. Used by permission of Hodder & Stoughton Ltd, an Hachette UK company. All

NRSV   The New Revised Standard Version of the Bible, Anglicized Edition, copyright © 1989, 1995 by the Division of Christian Education of the National Council of the Churches of Christ in the USA. Used by permission. All rights reserved.

RSV   The Revised Standard Version of the Bible, copyright © 1946, 1952 and 1971 by the Division of Christian Education of the National Council of the Churches of Christ in the USA. Used by permission. All rights reserved.

TLB   The Living Bible © 1971. Used by permission of Tyndale House Publishers.

Vulg.   Vulgate (Jerome's Latin translation of the Old Testament).

BIBLIOGRAPHY[1]

Achenbach, R. (2000), 'Die Titel der persischen
  Verwaltungsbeamten in Esra 4,9b (MT*)', *Zeitschrift für
  Althebräistik* 13: 134–144.
Adams, S. L. (2014), *Social and Economic Life in Second Temple Judea*
  (Louisville: Westminster John Knox).
Alonso Schökel, L. (1988), *A Manual of Hebrew Poetics*, Subsidia
  Biblica 11 (Rome: Pontificio Istituto Biblico).
Altmann, P. (2015), 'Ancient Comparisons, Modern Models, and
  Ezra–Nehemiah: Triangulating the Sources for Insights on the
  Economy of Persian Period Yehud', in M. L. Miller, E. Ben Zvi
  and G. N. Knoppers (eds.), *The Economy of Ancient Judah in Its
  Historical Context* (Winona Lake: Eisenbrauns), pp. 103–120.
—— (2016), *Economics in Persian-Period Biblical Texts: Their Interactions
  with Economic Developments in the Persian Period and Earlier Biblical
  Traditions*, FAT 109 (Tübingen: Mohr Siebeck).
Amigues, S. (2003), 'Pour la table du Grand Roi', *Journal des Savants*
  1: 3–59.
Averbeck, R. E. (1997a), 'מִנְחָה', in *NIDOTTE* 2.978–990.
—— (1997b), 'Offerings and Sacrifices', in *NIDOTTE* 4.996–1022.
Avigad, N. (1976), 'Bullae and Seals from a Post-Exilic Judean
  Archive /בולות וחותמות מתוך ארכיון ממלכתי מימי שיבת ציון', *Qedem*
  4: 1–36, א.-לב.

---

1   Titles in **bold** are commentaries on Ezra-Neh.

Avishur, Y. and M. Heltzer (2009), 'Sheshbazzar and Zerubbabel and Their Activities in the Last Third of the VI Century B.C.', *Transeuphratène* 38: 98–117.

Avi-Yonah, M. (1974), 'Historical Geography', in S. Safrai and M. Stern (eds.), *The Jewish People in the First Century: Historical Geography, Political History, Social, Cultural and Religious Life and Institutions*, CRINT 1.1 (Assen: Van Gorcum), pp. 78–116.

Badian, E. (1993), *From Plataea to Potidaea: Studies in the History and Historiography of the Pentecontaetia* (Baltimore: Johns Hopkins University Press).

Balzaretti, C. (1999), *Esdra–Neemia*, I libri biblici, Primo Testamento 23 (Milano: Paoline).

——(2013), *The Syriac Version of Ezra–Nehemiah: Manuscripts and Editions, Translation Technique and Its Use in Textual Criticism*, tr. M. Tait, Biblica et Orientalia 51 (Roma: Gregorian & Biblical).

Bänziger, T. (2014), *"Jauchzen und Weinen": Ambivalente Restauration in Jehud; Theologische Konzepte der Wiederherstellung in Esra-Nehemia* (Zürich: Theologischer).

——(2023), 'Esra–Nehemia', in W. Hilbrands and H. J. Koorevaar (eds.), *Einleitung in das Alte Testament: Ein historisch-kanonischer Ansatz* (Gießen: Brunnen), pp. 1175–1192.

Batten, L. W. (1913), *A Critical and Exegetical Commentary on the Books of Ezra and Nehemiah*, International Critical Commentary (Edinburgh: T&T Clark).

Bauckham, R. (2013), 'The Latin Vision of Ezra: A New Translation and Introduction', in R. Bauckham, J. R. Davila and A. Panayatov (eds.), *Old Testament Pseudepigrapha: More Noncanonical Scriptures* (Grand Rapids: Eerdmans), pp. 498–528.

Bauer, H. and P. Leander (1927), *Grammatik des Biblisch-Aramäischen* (Halle: Niemeyer).

Baumgartner, W. and W. Rudolph (1976), דניאל עזרא נחמיה *Daniel, Esra, Nehemia*, Biblia Hebraica Stuttgartensia 14 (Stuttgart: Württembergische Bibelanstalt).

Becker, U. (2015), 'Die Perser im Esra- und Nehemiabuch', *ZAW* 127: 607–627.

Becking, B. (2010), 'Drought, Hunger and Redistribution: A Social-Economic Reading of Nehemiah 5', in P. R. Davies and

D. V. Edelman (eds.), *The Historian and the Bible*, Festschrift for L. L. Grabbe, LHB/OTS 530 (New York and London: T&T Clark), pp. 137–149.

—— (2018), *Ezra–Nehemiah*, **Historical Commentary on the Old Testament (Leuven: Peeters).**

Beckwith, R. T. (1996), *Calendar and Chronology, Jewish and Christian: Biblical, Intertestamental and Patristic Studies*, AGJU 33 (Leiden: Brill).

Bedford, P. R. (2002), 'Diaspora: Homeland Relations in Ezra–Nehemiah', *Vetus Testamentum* 52: 147–165.

Begg, C. (1988), 'Ben Sirach's Non-mention of Ezra', *Biblische Notizen* 42: 14–18.

Ben-Dov, M. (2002), *Historical Atlas of Jerusalem*, tr. D. Louvish (London: Continuum; Hebrew orig. 2000).

Bengtson, H. (1977), *Griechische Geschichte von den Anfängen bis in die römische Kaiserzeit*, 5th edn (Munich: Beck).

Ben-Gurion, D. (1974), 'Cyrus, King of Persia', in *Commémoration Cyrus*, vol. 1: *Hommage universel*, Acta Iranica 1 (Tehran and Liège: Bibliothèque Pahlavi), pp. 127–134.

Berger, P. R. (1975), 'Der Kyros-Zylinder mit dem Zusatzfragment BIN II Nr. 32 und die akkadischen Personennamen im Danielbuch', *Zeitschrift für Assyriologie* 64: 192–234.

Bergren, T. A. (1998), 'Ezra and Nehemiah Square Off in the Apocrypha and Pseudepigrapha', in M. E. Stone and T. A. Bergren (eds.), *Biblical Figures outside the Bible* (Harrisburg: Trinity), pp. 340–365.

—— (2013), 'Fifth Ezra: A New Translation and Introduction', in R. Bauckham, J. R. Davila and A. Panayatov (eds.), *Old Testament Pseudepigrapha: More Noncanonical Scriptures* (Grand Rapids: Eerdmans), pp. 467–497.

Berman, J. A. (2017), *Inconsistency in the Torah: Ancient Literary Convention and the Limits of Source Criticism* (Oxford: Oxford University Press).

Bévenot, H. (1931), *Die beiden Makkabäerbücher*, Die Heilige Schrift des Alten Testamentes 4.4 (Bonn: Hanstein).

Bickerman, E. J. (1978), 'The Generations of Ezra and Nehemiah', *Proceedings of the American Academy for Jewish Research* 45: 1–28.

Bird, M. F. (2012), *1 Esdras: Introduction and Commentary on the Greek*

Text in Codex Vaticanus, Septuagint Commentary Series (Leiden: Brill).

Bivar, A. D. H. (1985), 'Achaemenid Coins, Weights and Measures', in I. Gershevitch (ed.), *The Cambridge History of Iran*, vol. 2: *The Median and Achaemenian Periods* (Cambridge: Cambridge University Press), pp. 610–639.

Bleibtrau, E. (2001), 'Achaimenidische Kunst', in W. Seipel (ed.), *7000 Jahre persische Kunst: Meisterwerke aus dem Iranischen Nationalmuseum in Teheran* (Bonn: Kunst- und Ausstellungshalle), pp. 187–220.

Blenkinsopp, J. (1987), 'The Mission of Udjahorresnet and Those of Ezra and Nehemiah', *JBL* 106: 409–421.

—— (1989), 'A Theological Reading of Ezra–Nehemiah', *Proceedings of the Irish Biblical Association* 12: 26–36.

—— (2017), 'The Sectarian Element in Early Judaism', in J. Blenkinsopp, *Essays on Judaism in the Pre-Hellenistic Period*, BZAW 495 (Berlin: de Gruyter), pp. 192–206.

Boda, M. J. (2010), *1–2 Chronicles*, Cornerstone Bible Commentary (Carol Stream: Tyndale House).

Bodi, D. (2008), 'Néhémie ch. 3 et la charte des bâtisseurs d'une tablette néo-babylonienne de l'époque perse', *Transeuphratène* 35: 55–70.

Bogaert, P. M. (1984), 'Une version longue inédite de la "Visio beati Esdrae" dans le légendier de Teano (Barberini Lat. 2318)', *Revue Bénédictine* 94: 50–70.

—— (2000), 'Les Livres d'Esdras et leur numérotation dans l'histoire du canon de la Bible latine', *Revue Bénédictine* 110: 5–26.

Boucharlat, R. (1997), 'Susa under Achaemenid Rule', in J. Curtis (ed.), *Mesopotamia and Iran in the Persian Period: Conquest and Imperialism 539–331 BC* (London: British Museum), pp. 54–67.

Briant, P. (2001), *Bulletin d'histoire achéménide*, vol. 2 (Paris: Thotm).

—— (2002), *From Cyrus to Alexander: A History of the Persian Empire*, tr. P. T. Daniels (Winona Lake: Eisenbrauns; French orig. 1996).

Bringmann, K. (2005), *Geschichte der Juden im Altertum: Vom babylonischen Exil bis zur arabischen Eroberung* (Stuttgart: Klett-Cotta).

Broshi, M. (1975), 'La Population de l'ancienne Jérusalem', *Revue Biblique* 82: 5–14.

Brosius, M. (1996), *Women in Ancient Persia* (Oxford: Oxford
University Press).

Brown, A. P., II (2005a), 'Chronological Anomalies in the Book of
Ezra', *Bibliotheca Sacra* 162: 33–49.

——(2005b), 'Nehemiah and Narrative Order in the Book of
Ezra', *Bibliotheca Sacra* 162: 175–194.

**Brown, R. (1998), *The Message of Nehemiah*, BST (Leicester:
Inter-Varsity Press).**

Carpenter, E. and M. A. Grisanti (1997), 'שׁקק', in *NIDOTTE*
3.1270.

Carter, C. E. (1999), *The Emergence of Yehud: A Social and Demographic
Study*, JSOTSup 294 (Sheffield: Sheffield Academic).

Cassuto, U. (1961), *A Commentary on the Book of Genesis*, vol. 1: *From
Adam to Noah: Genesis I – VI 8*, tr. I. Abrahams (Jerusalem:
Magnes; Hebrew orig. 1944).

Chapple, A. (2011), 'Getting *Romans* to the Right Romans:
Phoebe and the Delivery of Paul's Letter', *Tyndale Bulletin* 62:
195–214.

Charles, R. H. (1913), 'The Assumption of Moses', in R. H. Charles
(ed.), *The Apocrypha and Pseudepigrapha of the Old Testament*, vol. 2:
Pseudepigrapha (Oxford: Clarendon), pp. 407–424.

Clines, D. J. A. (1981), 'Nehemiah 10 as an Example of Early
Jewish Biblical Exegesis', *JSOT* 21: 111–117.

——(ed.) (2009), *The Concise Dictionary of Classical Hebrew* (Sheffield:
Sheffield Phoenix).

Cogan, M. (2006), 'Raising the Walls of Jerusalem (Nehemiah
3:1–21): The View from Dur-Sharrukin', *Israel Exploration
Journal* 56: 84–95.

Cole, R. A. (1973), *Exodus*, Tyndale Old Testament Commentaries
(London: Tyndale).

Cook, J. A. (2012), *Time and the Biblical Hebrew Verb*, Linguistic
Studies in Ancient West Semitic 7 (Winona Lake: Eisenbrauns).

Courey, D. J. (2015), *What Has Wittenberg to Do with Azusa? Luther's
Theology of the Cross and Pentecostal Triumphalism* (London:
Bloomsbury T&T Clark).

Cowley, A. (1923), *Aramaic Papyri of the Fifth Century* (Oxford:
Clarendon).

Dallaire, H. (2014), *The Syntax of Volitives in Biblical Hebrew and*

Amarna Canaanite Prose, Linguistic Studies in Ancient West Semitic 9 (Winona Lake: Eisenbrauns).

Dalley, S. (2003), 'The Transition from Neo-Assyrians to Neo-Babylonians: Break or Continuity?', *Eretz-Israel* 27: 25*–28*.

Dalman, G. (1928), *Arbeit und Sitte in Palästina*, vol. 1: *Jahreslauf und Tageslauf* (Gütersloh: Bertelsmann).

—— (1932), *Arbeit und Sitte in Palästina*, vol 2: *Der Ackerbau* (Gütersloh: Bertelsmann).

—— (1933), *Arbeit und Sitte in Palästina*, vol. 3: *Von der Ernte zum Mehl* (Gütersloh: Bertelsmann).

—— (1935), *Arbeit und Sitte in Palästina*, vol. 4: *Brot, Öl und Wein* (Gütersloh: Bertelsmann).

—— (1937), *Arbeit und Sitte in Palästina*, vol. 5: *Webstoff, Spinnen, Weben, Kleidung* (Gütersloh: Bertelsmann).

—— (1939), *Arbeit und Sitte in Palästina*, vol. 6: *Zeltleben, Vieh- und Milchwirtschaft, Jagd, Fischfang* (Gütersloh: Bertelsmann).

Dandama(y)ev, M. A.[2] (1989), *A Political History of the Achaemenid Empire*, tr. W. J. Vogelsang (Leiden: Brill).

—— (2004), 'Twin Towns and Ethnic Minorities in First-Millennium Babylonia', in R. Rollinger and C. Ulf (eds.), *Commerce and Monetary Systems in the Ancient World*, Oriens et Occidens 6 (Wiesbaden: Steiner), pp. 137–151.

—— (2006), 'Neo-Babylonian and Achaemenid State Administration in Mesopotamia', in O. Lipschits and M. Oeming (eds.), *Judah and the Judeans in the Persian Period* (Winona Lake: Eisenbrauns), pp. 373–398.

de Bruin, C. C. (1993), *De Statenbijbel en zijn voorgangers: Nederlandse bijbelvertalingen vanaf de Reformatie tot 1637*, ed. F. G. M. Broeyer, 2nd edn (Haarlem: Nederlands Bijbelgenootschap; Brussels: Belgisch Bijbelgenootschap).

De Fraine, J. (1961), *Esdras en Nehemias*, De Boeken van het Oude Testament (Roermond and Maaseik: Romen).

Deines, R. (2001), 'The Pharisees between "Judaisms" and "Common Judaism"', in D. A. Carson, P. T. O'Brien and M. A. Seifrid (eds.), *Justification and Variegated Nomism*, vol. 1: *The*

---

2   The transcription of the name of this author varies.

Complexities of Second Temple Judaism, WUNT 2.140 (Tübingen: Mohr Siebeck), pp. 443–504.

—— (2013), *Acts of God in History: Studies towards Recovering a Theological Historiography* (Tübingen: Mohr Siebeck).

Delitzsch, F. (1871), *The Psalms*, vol. 3, Biblical Commentary on the Old Testament, tr. F. Bolton (Edinburgh: T&T Clark; German orig., 2nd edn 1867).

Denis, A.-M. (1970), *Introduction aux pseudépigraphes grecs d'Ancien Testament*, Studia in Veteris Testamenti Pseudepigrapha 1 (Leiden: Brill).

Depuydt, L. (1995a), 'The Date of Death of Artaxerxes I', *Die Welt des Orients* 26: 86–96.

—— (1995b), 'Evidence for Accession Dating under the Achaemenids', *Journal of the American Oriental Society* 115: 193–204.

De Schaepdrijver, S. (2013), *De Groote Oorlog: Het koninkrijk België tijdens de Eerste Wereldoorlog* (Antwerpen: Houtekiet).

deSilva, D. A. (2018), *Introducing the Apocrypha: Message, Context, and Significance*, 2nd edn (Grand Rapids: Baker).

De Vaux, R. (1958), *Les Institutions de l'Ancien Testament* (Paris: Cerf).

Donaldson, T. L. (2007), *Judaism and the Gentiles: Jewish Patterns of Universalism (to 135 CE)* (Waco: Baylor University Press).

Drioton, E. and J. Vandier (1989), *L'Égypte: Des origines à la conquête d'Alexandre*, 7th edn (Paris: PUF).

Duggan, M. W. (2001), *The Covenant Renewal in Ezra–Nehemiah (Neh 7:72B – 10:40): An Exegetical, Literary, and Theological Study*, SBLDS 164 (Atlanta: SBL).

—— (2006), 'Ezra 9:6–15: A Penitential Prayer within Its Literary Setting', in M. J. Boda, D. K. Falk and R. A. Werline (eds.), *Seeking the Favor of God*, vol. 1: *The Origins of Penitential Prayer in Second Temple Judaism*, SBL – EJL 21 (Atlanta: SBL), pp. 165–180.

Duguid, I. (2012), 'Nehemiah: The Best King Judah Never Had', in I. Provan and M. J. Boda (eds.), *Let Us Go up to Zion*, Festschrift for H. G. M. Williamson, VTSup 153 (Leiden: Brill), pp. 261–271.

Dušek, J. (2007), *Les manuscrits araméens du Wadi Daliyeh et la Samarie vers 450–332 av. J.-C.*, CHANE NS 30 (Leiden: Brill).

Eckstein, J. (2018), 'The Idiolect Test and the *Vorlage* of Old Greek

Job: A New Argument for an Old Debate', *Vetus Testamentum* 68: 197–217.

Edelman, D. (2011), 'The Location and Function of the Towers of Hanan'el and the Hundred in Persian-Era Jerusalem', *Zeitschrift des Deutschen Palästina-Vereins* 127: 49–74.

Ellis, E. (1988), 'The Old Testament Canon in the Early Church', in M. J. Mulder (ed.), *Mikra: Text, Translation, Reading and Interpretation of the Hebrew Bible in Ancient Judaism and Early Christianity*, CRINT 2.1 (Assen and Maastricht: Van Gorcum; Philadelphia: Fortress), pp. 653–690.

Erickson, M. J. (1983–85), *Christian Theology* (Grand Rapids: Baker).

Eskenazi, T. C. (2010), 'Revisiting the Composition of Ezra–Nehemiah: A Prolegomenon', in F. R. Ames and C. W. Miller (eds.), *Foster Biblical Scholarship*, Festschrift for K. H. Richards, SBL Biblical Scholarship in North America 24 (Atlanta: SBL), pp. 215–234.

Eskhult, M. (2000), 'Verbal Syntax in Late Biblical Hebrew', in T. Muraoka and J. F. Elwolde (eds.), *Diggers at the Well*, STDJ 36 (Leiden: Brill), pp. 84–93.

Estelle, B. (2006), 'The Use of Deferential Language in the Arsames Correspondence and Biblical Aramaic Compared', *Maarav* 13: 43–74.

Fassberg, S. E. (2013), 'Shifts in Word Order in the Hebrew of the Second Temple Period', in S. E. Fassberg, M. Bar-Asher and R. Clements (eds.), *Hebrew in the Second Temple Period: The Hebrew of the Dead Sea Scrolls and of Other Contemporary Sources*, STDJ 108 (Leiden: Brill), pp. 57–71.

——— (2016), 'What Is *Late Biblical Hebrew*?', *ZAW* 128: 1–15.

Fensham, F. C. (1982), *The Books of Ezra and Nehemiah*, New International Commentary on the Old Testament (Grand Rapids: Eerdmans).

Fiensy, D. A. (1983), 'Revelation of Ezra', in J. H. Charlesworth (ed.), *The Old Testament Pseudepigrapha*, vol. 1: *Apocalyptic Literature and Testaments* (New York: Doubleday), pp. 601–604.

Firth, D. G. (1997), 'The Book of Esther: A Neglected Paradigm for Dealing with the State', *Old Testament Essays* 10: 18–26.

——— (2022), 'Reading Deuteronomy after Joshua: On Reversing the Interpretative Flow', *European Journal of Theology* 31: 6–20.

Fitzpatrick-McKinley, A. (2016), 'Models of Local Political
    Leadership in the Nehemiah Memoir', in D. V. Edelman and
    E. Ben Zvi (eds.), *Leadership, Social Memory and Judean Discourse in
    the Fifth–Second Centuries BCE* (Sheffield: Equinox), pp. 165–199.
Fleishman, J. (2012), 'Nehemiah's Request on Behalf of Jerusalem',
    in I. Kalimi (ed.), *New Perspectives on Ezra–Nehemiah: History and
    Historiography, Text, Literature, and Interpretation* (Winona Lake:
    Eisenbrauns), pp. 241–266.
Ford, W. (2017), 'The Challenge of the Canaanites', *Tyndale Bulletin*
    68: 161–184.
Fried, L. (2018), '150 Men at Nehemiah's Table? The Role of the
    Governor's Meals in the Achaemenid Provincial Economy',
    JBL 137: 821–831.
**Fyall, R. S. (2010), *The Message of Ezra and Haggai: Building
    for God*, BST (Downers Grove: InterVarsity Press).**
Gentry, P. J. and A. M. Fountain (2017), 'Reassessing Jude's Use of
    Enochic Traditions', *Tyndale Bulletin* 68: 261–286.
Gesche, B. (2014), 'Die älteste lateinische Übersetzungen des
    Buches Esdras A: Eine neue Entdeckung, *Vetus Testamentum*
    64: 401–415.
—— (2016), 'Von Nordafrika über Paris nach Stuttgart: Wie
    kommt die verderbte Fassung der Übersetzung von Esdras A'
    in die Vulgata?', in S. Kreuzer, M. Meiser and M. Sigismund
    (eds.), *Die Septuaginta: Orte und Intentionen*, WUNT 361
    (Tübingen: Mohr Siebeck), pp. 117–131.
Geva, H. (2003), 'Western Jerusalem at the End of the First
    Temple Period in Light of the Excavations in the Jewish
    Quarter', in A. G. Vaughn and A. E. Killebrew (eds.), *Jerusalem
    in Bible and Archaeology: The First Temple Period* (Atlanta: SBL),
    pp. 183–208.
Gogel, S. L. (1998), *A Grammar of Epigraphic Hebrew*, SBL Resources
    for Biblical Study 23 (Atlanta: Scholars).
Goitein, S. D. (1970), 'Nicknames as Family Names', *Journal of the
    American Oriental Society* 90: 517–524.
Goswell, G. (2010), 'The Handling of Time in the Book of Ezra–
    Nehemiah', in *Trinity Journal* NS 31: 187–203.
—— (2011), 'The Attitude to the Persians in Ezra–Nehemiah',
    Trinity Journal NS 32: 191–203.

—— (2018), 'Should the Church Be Committed to a Particular Order of the Old Testament Canon?', *Horizons in Biblical Theology* 40: 17–40.

Grant, J. (2001), 'Psalms 73 and 89: The Crisis of Faith!', in C. Bartholomew and A. West (eds.), *Praying by the Book: Reading the Psalms* (Carlisle: Paternoster), pp. 60–86.

Greenfield, J. C. (1981), 'Aramaic Studies and the Bible', in J. A. Emerton (ed.), *Congress Volume*, VTSup 32 (Leiden: Brill), pp. 110–130.

Grojnowski, D. (2015), 'Flavius Josephus, Nehemiah, and a Study in Self-Presentation', *Journal for the Study of Judaism* 46: 345–365.

Grosheide, H. H. (1963), *Ezra–Nehemia*, vol. 1: *Ezra*, Commentaar op het Oude Testament (Kampen: Kok).

Grudem, W. (2009), 'The Perspicuity of Scripture', *Themelios* 34: 288–308.

Hagedorn, A. C. (2015), 'The Biblical Laws of Asylum between Mediterraneanism and Postcolonial Critique', *Zeitschrift für altorientalische und biblische Rechtsgeschichte* 21: 291–307.

Häusl, M. (2013), 'Jerusalem, the Holy City: The Meaning of the City of Jerusalem in the Books of Ezra–Nehemiah', in G. T. M. Prinsloo and C. M. Maier (eds.), *Constructions of Space*, vol. 5: *Place, Space and Identity in the Ancient Mediterranean World*, LHB/OTS 576 (London: Bloomsbury T&T Clark), pp. 87–106.

Heather, P. (2006), *The Fall of the Roman Empire: A New History of Rome and the Barbarians* (New York: Oxford University Press).

Helberg, J. L. (1990), *Die Verbondsvolk se verhouding tot sy land*, Wetenskaplike Bydrae van die PU vir CHO A 76 (Potchefstroom: Potchefstroomse Universiteit vir CHO).

Heltzer, M. (1981), 'The Tell el-Mazār Inscription No. 7 and Some Historical and Literary Problems of the Vth Satrapy', *Transeuphratène* 1: 111–118.

—— (1989), 'The Social and Fiscal Reforms of Nehemia in Judah and the Attitude of the Achaemenid Kings to the Internal Affairs of the Autonomous Provinces', *Apollinaris* 62: 333–354.

—— (1994), 'Neh. 11.24 and the Provincial Representative of the Persian Royal Court', *Transeuphratène* 8: 109–119.

Heltzer, M. and Y. Avishur (2002), 'The Term *sōfēr māhîr* as

Designating a Courtier in the Old Testament and the Aḥiqar Story', *Ugaritische Forschungen* 34: 217–221.

Henkelman, W. F. M. (2021), 'Van Elam naar Perzië: De lange wortels van het Achaemenidenrijk', *Phoenix* 67.1: 8–21.

Hensel, B. (2017), *Juda und Samaria: Zum Verhältnis zweier nachexilischer Jahwismen*, FAT 110 (Tübingen: Mohr Siebeck).

Hofstetter, J. (1972), 'Zu den griechischen Gesandtschaften nach Persien', in G. Walser (ed.), *Beiträge zur Achämenidengeschichte*, Historia Einzelschriften 18 (Wiesbaden: Steiner), pp. 94–107.

Högemann, P. (1992), *Das alte Vorderasien und die Achämeniden: Ein Beitrag zur Herodot-Analyse*, Beihefte zum TAVO B 98 (Wiesbaden: Reichert).

Hölzel, H.-R. (1972), 'Die Rolle des Stammes "*mlk*" und seiner Ableitungen für die Herrschaftsvorstellungen der vorexilischen Zeit', dissertation, Universität Hamburg.

Houtman, C. (1986–89), *Exodus*, vols. 1–2, Commentaar op het Oude Testament (Kampen: Kok).

Howard, D. M., Jr. (1993), *An Introduction to the Old Testament Historical Books* (Chicago: Moody).

Hutter, M. (2009), 'Iranisches Sprachgut in den hebräischen Namenslisten der Bücher Esra und Nehemia', *Kleine Untersuchungen zur Sprache des Alten Testaments und seiner Umwelt* 10: 83–95.

Instone-Brewer, D. (2010), 'The Old Testament Text beyond Qumran' (Cambridge: Tyndale House), <https://instonebrewer.com/publications/OT%20Text%20Beyond%20Qumran+Handout.pdf>

Jaeger, L. (2013), 'La vérité: perspectives philosophiques et théologiques', *Théologie Évangélique* 12.2: 3–32.

Janz, T. (2010), *Deuxième livre d'Esdras*, La Bible d'Alexandrie 11.2 (Paris: Cerf).

Janzen, D. (2002), 'Politics, Settlement, and Temple Community in Persian-Period Yehud', *Catholic Biblical Quarterly* 64: 490–510.

Japhet, S. (1968), 'The Supposed Common Authorship of Chronicles and Ezra–Nehemiah Investigated Anew', *Vetus Testamentum* 18: 330–371.

——— (2011), '1 Esdras: Its Genre, Literary Form, and Goals', in L. S. Fried (ed.), *Was 1 Esdras First? An Investigation into the*

Priority and Nature of 1 Esdras, Ancient Israel and Its Literature 7 (Atlanta: SBL), pp. 209–224.

—— (2016), 'What May Be Learned from Ezra–Nehemiah about the Composition of the Pentateuch?', in J. C. Gertz, B. M. Levinson, D. Rom-Shiloni and K. Schmid (eds.), *The Formation of the Pentateuch: Bridging the Academic Cultures of Europe, Israel, and North America*, FAT 111 (Tübingen: Mohr Siebeck), pp. 543–560.

Jenni, E. (2002), 'Höfliche Bitte im Alten Testament', in A. Lemaire (ed.), *Congress Volume Basel 2001*, VTSup 92 (Leiden: Brill), pp. 1–16.

—— (2009), 'Sprachliche Übertreibungen im Alten Testament', in C. Karrer-Grube, J. Krispenz, T. Krüger, C. Rose and A. Schellenberg (eds.), *Sprachen, Bilder, Klänge: Dimensionen der Theologie im Alten Testament und in seinem Umfeld*, Festschrift for R. Bartelmus, AOAT 359 (Münster: Ugarit), pp. 75–88.

Jeremias, A. (1916), *Das Alte Testament im Lichte des Alten Orients*, 3rd edn (Leipzig: Hinrichs).

Jobes, K. and M. Silva (2015), *Invitation to the Septuagint*, 2nd edn (Grand Rapids: Baker).

Joüon, P. and T. Muraoka (2006), *A Grammar of Biblical Hebrew*, Subsidia Biblica 27, 2nd edn (Roma: Pontificio Istituto Biblico).

Kaiser, W. C., Jr. and M. Silva (2007), *Introduction to Biblical Hermeneutics: The Search for Meaning*, 2nd edn (Grand Rapids: Zondervan).

Kamesar, A. (1993), *Jerome, Greek Scholarship, and the Hebrew Bible: A Study of the* Quaestiones Hebraicae in Genesim (Oxford: Clarendon).

Karrer, C. (2021), 'Beter dan een koning? Leiderschap in Juda volgens het rapport van Nehemia', in J. Dubbink (ed.), *Ezra & Nehemia*, ACEBT 34 (Amsterdam: Societas Hebraica Amstelodamensis), pp. 105–116.

Käser, A. (2023), 'Narrativik', in W. Hilbrands and H. J. Koorevaar (eds.), *Einleitung in das Alte Testament: Ein historisch-kanonischer Ansatz* (Gießen: Brunnen), pp. 257–271.

Keel, O. (1972), *Die Welt der altorientalischen Bildsymbolik und das Alte Testament* (Zürich: Benziger; Neukirchen: Neukirchener).

Keil, C. F. (1873), *The Books of Ezra, Nehemiah, and Esther*,

tr. S. Taylor, *Biblical Commentary on the Old Testament*
(Edinburgh: T&T Clark; German orig. 1870).

Kellermann, U. (1967), *Nehemia: Quellen, Überlieferung und Geschichte*,
BZAW 102 (Berlin: Töpelmann).

Kent, R. G. (1953), *Old Persian: Grammar, Texts, Lexicon*, 2nd edn
(New Haven: American Oriental Society).

Kessler, J. (1992), 'The Second Year of Darius and the Prophet
Haggai', *Transeuphratène* 5: 63–84.

**Kidner, D. (1979), *Ezra and Nehemiah*, Tyndale Old
Testament Commentaries (Leicester: Inter-Varsity Press).**

Kiel, Y. (2017), 'Reinventing Mosaic Torah in Ezra–Nehemiah in
the Light of the Law (*dāta*) of Ahura Mazda and Zarathustra',
JBL 136: 323–345.

Kitchen, K. A. (2003), *On the Reliability of the Old Testament* (Grand
Rapids: Eerdmans).

Klement, H. H. (2011), 'Rhetorical, Theological and Chronological
Features of Ezra–Nehemiah', in J. A. Grant, A. Lo and
G. J. Wenham (eds.), *A God of Faithfulness*, Festschrift for
J. G. McConville, LHB/OTS 538 (New York and London:
T&T Clark), pp. 61–78.

Knoppers, G. N. (2009), 'Beyond Jerusalem and Judah: The
Mission of Ezra in the Province of Transeuphrates', *Eretz-Israel*
29: 78*–87*.

Konkel, A. H. (1997), 'נֵכָר', in *NIDOTTE* 3.108–109.

Koopmans, J. J. (1957), *Arameese Grammatica (voor het Oud-
Testamentisch Aramees)*, 2nd edn (Leiden: NINO).

Kraft, R. A. (1979), '"Ezra" Materials in Judaism and Christianity',
in W. Haase (ed.), *Aufstieg und Niedergang der römischen Welt II*,
vol. 19.1, *Religion (Judentum: Allgemeines; palästinisches Judentum)*,
Festschrift for J. Vogt (Berlin: de Gruyter), pp. 119–136.

Kreissig, H. (1973), *Die sozialökonomische Situation in Juda zur
Achämenidenzeit*, Schriften zur Geschichte und Kultur des alten
Orients 7 (Berlin: Akademie).

Kroeze, J. H. (2008), 'The So-Called Nominative Uses of את:
A Semantic Solution', *Journal for Semitics* 17: 484–516.

Kumon, H. (2016), 'The Semantic Map of Subordination and Its
Application to Aramaic די in Ezra', in *Journal of Northwest Semitic
Languages* 42: 61–82.

Lalleman, H. (2004), *Celebrating the Law? Rethinking Old Testament Ethics* (Milton Keynes: Paternoster).

Lanni, A. (2006), *Law and Justice in the Courts of Classical Athens* (Cambridge: Cambridge University Press).

Laperrousaz, E.-M. (1994), 'L'Étendue de Jérusalem à l'époque perse', in E.-M. Laperrousaz and A. Lemaire (eds.), *La Palestine à l'époque perse* (Paris: Cerf), pp. 123–156.

Lau, P. H. W. (2009), 'Gentile Incorporation into Israel in Ezra–Nehemiah?', *Biblica* 90: 356–373.

Lee, A. C. H. and G. G. Harper (2019), 'Dodging the Question? The Rhetorical Function of the מה־זאת עשית Formula in the Book of Genesis', *Tyndale Bulletin* 70: 161–183.

Leithwood, K., D. Jantzi and R. Steinbach (1999), *Changing Leadership for Changing Times* (Maidenhead: Open University Press).

Lemaire, A. (1990), 'Populations et territoires de la Palestine à l'époque perse', *Transeuphratène* 3: 31–74.

—— (1994), 'Histoire et administration de la Palestine à l'époque perse', in E.-M. Laperrousaz and A. Lemaire (eds.), *La Palestine à l'époque perse* (Paris: Cerf), pp. 11–53.

—— (1995), 'Ashdodien et Judéen à l'époque perse: Ne 13,24', in K. Van Lerberghe and A. Schoors (eds.), *Immigration and Emigration within the Ancient Near East*, Festschrift for E. Lipiński, OLA 65 (Leuven: Peeters), pp. 153–163.

—— (1996), 'Zorobabel et la Judée à la lumière de l'épigraphie (fin du VIᵉ s. av. J.-C.)', *Revue Biblique* 103: 48–57.

—— (2001), 'Épigraphie et religion en Palestine', *Transeuphratène* 22: 97–113.

—— (2015), *Levantine Epigraphy and History in the Achaemenid Period (539–322 BCE)*, Schweich Lectures (Oxford: Oxford University Press).

—— (2017), 'Unité et diversité des Judéens à l'époque achéménide d'après les données épigraphiques', *Transeuphratène* 49: 163–186.

Leonhardt-Balzer, J. (2005), *Apokalypsen und Testamenten: Fragen Esras*, JSHRZ NS 1 (Gütersloh: Gütersloher).

Lettinga, J. P. and H. von Siebenthal (2016), *Grammatik des biblischen Hebräisch*, 2nd edn (Gießen: Brunnen; Basel: Immanuel).

Levin, Y. (2007), 'The Southern Frontier of *Yehud* and the Creation of Idumea', in Y. Levin (ed.), *A Time of Change: Judah and Its*

Neighbours in the Persian and Early Hellenistic Periods, LSTS 65 (London: T&T Clark), pp. 239–252.

Lindenberger, J. M. (2003), *Ancient Aramaic and Hebrew Letters*, WAW 14, 2nd edn (Atlanta: SBL).

Lipiński, E. (1975), *Studies in Aramaic Inscriptions and Onomastics*, vol. 1, OLA 1 (Leuven: Leuven University Press).

—— (1994), *Studies in Aramaic Inscriptions and Onomastics*, vol. 2, OLA 57 (Leuven: Peeters).

—— (2000), *The Aramaeans: Their Ancient History, Culture, Religion*, OLA 100 (Leuven: Peeters).

—— (2001), *Semitic Languages: Outline of a Comparative Grammar*, OLA 80, 2nd edn (Leuven: Peeters).

—— (2006), *On the Skirts of Canaan in the Iron Age*, OLA 153 (Leuven: Peeters).

—— (2007), 'Silver of Ishtar of Arbela and of Hadad', in M. Lubetski (ed.), *New Seals and Inscriptions*, Hebrew Bible Monographs 8 (Sheffield: Phoenix), pp. 185–200.

—— (2016), *Studies in Aramaic Inscriptions and Onomastics*, vol. 4, OLA 250 (Leuven: Peeters).

—— (2018), *A History of the Kingdom of Israel*, OLA 275 (Leuven: Peeters).

Lippert, S. (2017), 'La Codification des lois en Égypte à l'époque perse', in D. Jaillard and C. Nihan (eds.), *Writing Laws in Antiquity / L'Écriture du droit dans l'Antiquité*, BZABR 19 (Wiesbaden: Harrassowitz), pp. 78–98.

Lipschits, O. (2012), 'Nehemiah 3: Sources, Composition, and Purpose', in I. Kalimi (ed.), *New Perspectives on Ezra–Nehemiah: History and Historiography, Text, Literature, and Interpretation* (Winona Lake: Eisenbrauns), pp. 73–99.

Loiseau, A.-F. (2016), *L'Influence de l'araméen sur les traducteurs de la LXX principalement, sur les traducteurs grecs postérieurs, ainsi que sur les scribes de la Vorlage de la LXX*, SCS 65 (Atlanta: SBL).

Lorein, G. W. (2003), *The Antichrist Theme in the Intertestamental Period*, JSPSup 44 (London and New York: T&T Clark).

—— (2008), 'De verhouding tussen aannemer en bewoners tijdens verbouwingswerken: Leiders en gemeenschap in Ezra 7 – Nehemia 13', in P. Boersema, J. Hoek, M.-J. Paul and M. Verhoeff (eds.), *Gezag in beweging: Kerkelijk leiderschap tussen tekst en context* (Heerenveen: Protestantse Pers), pp. 144–157.

—— **(2010a), 'Ezra–Nehemia', in G. W. Lorein and W. H. Rose, *Geschriften over de Perzische tijd*, De Brug 11 (Heerenveen: Groen), pp. 93–189.**

—— (2010b), 'Maleachi', in G. W. Lorein and W. H. Rose, *Geschriften over de Perzische tijd*, De Brug 11 (Heerenveen: Groen), pp. 331–354.

—— (2011a), 'Dealing with Scripture and Circumstances in Nehemiah 9 – 10', in S. Riecker and J. Steinberg (eds.), *Das heilige Herz der Tora*, Festschrift for H. Koorevaar (Aachen: Shaker), pp. 61–77.

—— (2011b), 'The Holy Spirit at Qumran', in D. G. Firth and P. D. Wegner (eds.), *Presence, Power and Promise: The Role of the Spirit of God in the Old Testament* (Nottingham: Apollos), pp. 371–395.

—— (2014), 'The Latin Versions of the Old Testament from Jerome to the *Editio Clementina*', in A. Houtman, E. van Staalduine-Sulman and H.-M. Kirn (eds.), *A Jewish Targum in a Christian World*, Jewish and Christian Perspectives 27 (Leiden: Brill), pp. 125–145.

—— (2016), 'Entwicklungen zwischen dem Alten und dem Neuen Testament', in H. J. Koorevaar and M.-J. Paul (eds.), *Theologie des Alten Testaments: Die bleibende Botschaft der hebräischen Bibel* (Giessen: Brunnen), pp. 301–323.

—— (2018), 'The Land in a Time of Exile: Promises and Duties', in H. J. Koorevaar and M.-J. Paul (eds.), *The Earth and the Land: Studies about the Value of the Land of Israel in the Old Testament and Afterwards*, Edition Israelogie 11 (Berlin: Lang), pp. 248–273.

—— (2020), '"Religion Never Stands above the Law": The Relation between the State and Faith Groups as Illustrated in Belgium', *International Journal for Religious Freedom* 13: 11–20.

—— (2021a), 'Fidus Interpres: The Translation of Biblical Hebrew Prose', in J. Kok and M. Webber (eds.), *Off the Beaten Path*, Festschrift for G. Vleugels, Beiträge zum Verstehen der Bibel 48 (Zürich: Lit), pp. 14–29.

—— (2021b), 'Nehemia 3: Individueel engagement ter afscherming van Jeruzalem', in J. Dubbink (ed.), *Ezra & Nehemia*, ACEBT

34 (Amsterdam: Societas Hebraica Amstelodamensis), pp. 69–82.

—— (2021c), 'Le Régime des cultes en Flandres: enjeux et débats; l'*episkopos* en tant que contrôleur ou en tant que protecteur', *Commentaires de la Chaire Droit & Religions (UCLouvain)* no. 2021/4, <http://belgianlawreligion.unblog.fr/2021/04/27/le-regime-des-cultes-en-flandres-enjeux-et-debats/>

—— (2021d), 'The Relationship of the Believer to Society: Different Approaches in the Earliest Interpretations of the Old Testament', *European Journal of Theology* 30: 248–274.

—— (2022), 'Knowing God in the Intertestamental Period', in A. J. Beck, J. de Kock and S. C. van den Heuvel (eds.), *The Vitality of Evangelical Theology* (Leuven: Peeters), pp. 25–39.

—— (2023a), 'Esther', in W. Hilbrands and H. J. Koorevaar (eds.), *Einleitung in das Alte Testament: Ein historisch-kanonischer Ansatz* (Gießen: Brunnen), pp. 1161–1174.

—— (2023b), 'Das Ineinander von Geschichte, Text und Theologie', in W. Hilbrands and H. J. Koorevaar (eds.), *Einleitung in das Alte Testament: Ein historisch-kanonischer Ansatz* (Gießen: Brunnen), pp. 57–71.

Lorein, G. W., and E. van Staalduine-Sulman (2005), 'A Song of David for Each Day: The Provenance of the *Songs of David*', *Revue de Qumran* 22.85: 33–59.

Lust, J. (2003), 'Septuagint and Canon', in J.-M. Auwers and H. J. de Jonge, *The Biblical Canons*, Bibliotheca Ephemeridum Theologicarum Lovaniensium 163 (Leuven: Peeters), pp. 39–55.

Maarsingh, B. (1985), *Ezechiël*, vol. 1, De Prediking van het Oude Testament (Nijkerk: Callenbach).

Maciariello, J. (2003), 'Lessons in Leadership and Management from Nehemiah', *Theology Today* 60: 397–407.

Mahieu, B. (2012), *Between Rome and Jerusalem: Herod the Great and His Sons in Their Struggle for Recognition – A Chronological Investigation of the Period 40 BC–39 AD, with a Time Setting of New Testament Events*, OLA 208 (Leuven: Peeters).

Malamat, A. (2001), *History of Biblical Israel: Major Problems and Minor Issues*, CHANE 7 (Leiden: Brill).

Maloney, R. P. (1974), 'Usury and Restrictions on Interest-Taking in the Ancient Near East', *Catholic Biblical Quarterly* 36: 1–20.

Marcus, D. (2006), עזרא ונחמיה : *Ezra and Nehemiah*, Biblia
Hebraica Quinta 20 (Stuttgart: Deutsche Bibelgesellschaft).

Mason, S. (2008), *Flavius Josephus: Translation and Commentary*,
vol. 1B: *Judean War 2* (Leiden: Brill).

Mathewson, S. (2002), *The Art of Preaching Old Testament Narrative*
(Grand Rapids: Baker; Carlisle: Paternoster).

Mathys, H.-P. (2015), '"Erinnere dich meiner, mein Gott, mir zum
Guten" (Neh 13,31)', *Theologische Zeitschrift* 71: 326–362.

Meinhold, A. (2001), 'Serubbabel, der Tempel und die Provinz
Jehud', in C. Hardmeier (ed.), *Steine, Bilde, Texte: Historische
Evidenz ausserbiblischer und biblischer Quellen*, Arbeiten zur Bibel
und ihrer Geschichte 5 (Leipzig: Evangelische Verlagsanstalt),
pp. 193–217.

Meyer, E. (1896), *Die Entstehung des Judenthums: Eine historische
Untersuchung* (Halle: Niemeyer).

Meyer, R. (1969, 1972, 1982), *Hebräische Grammatik*, 3rd edn (Berlin:
de Gruyter).

Millard, A. (1976), 'Assyrian Royal Names in Biblical Hebrew',
Journal of Semitic Studies 21: 1–14.

—— (1997), 'Nebuchadnezzar', in *NIDOTTE* 4.972–974.

—— (2001), 'Where Was Abraham's Ur?', *Biblical Archaeology Review*
27.3: 52–53, 57.

—— (2012), 'Writing and Prophecy', in M. J. Boda and
J. G. McConville (eds.), *Dictionary of the Old Testament Prophets*
(Downers Grove: InterVarsity Press), pp. 883–888.

—— (2023), 'Schriftlichkeit im Alten Testament und Alten
Vorderen Orient', in W. Hilbrands and H. J. Koorevaar (eds.),
Einleitung in das Alte Testament: Ein historisch-kanonischer Ansatz
(Gießen: Brunnen), pp. 207–218.

Min, K. (2004), *The Levitical Authorship of Ezra-Nehemiah*, JSOTSup
409 (London: T&T Clark).

Mitchell, T. C. (1991), 'The Babylonian Exile and the Restoration
of the Jews in Palestine (586–c.500 BC)', in J. Boardman,
I. E. S. Edwards, N. G. L. Hammond and E. Sollberger (eds.),
*The Assyrian and Babylonian Empires and Other States of the Near
East, from the Eighth to the Sixth Centuries BC*, Cambridge Ancient
History 3.2, 2nd edn (Cambridge: Cambridge University Press),
pp. 410–460.

Moffat, D. P. (2013), 'The Metaphor at Stake in Ezra 9:8', in *Vetus Testamentum* 63: 290–298.

Mor, M. (2011), 'The Building of the Samaritan Temple and the Samaritan Governors. Again', in J. Zsengellér (ed.), *Samaria, Samarians, Samaritans: Studies on Bible, History and Linguistics*, Studia Judaica 66; Studia Samaritana 6 (Berlin: de Gruyter), pp. 89–108.

Muraoka, T. (2012), *An Introduction to Egyptian Aramaic*, Lehrbücher orientalischer Sprachen 3.1 (Münster: Ugarit).

—— (2020), *A Biblical Aramaic Reader*, 2nd edn (Leuven: Peeters).

Myers, J. M. (1974), *I and II Esdras*, Anchor Bible 42 (Garden City: Doubleday).

Najman, H. (2003), *Seconding Sinai: The Development of Mosaic Discourse in Second Temple Judaism*, JSJSup 77 (Leiden: Brill).

Negev, A. (ed.) (1970), *Dictionnaire archéologique de la Bible* (Paris: Hazan; English orig. 1970).

Noonan, B. J. (2011), 'Did Nehemiah Own Tyrian Goods? Trade between Judea and Phoenicia During the Achaemenid Period', *JBL* 13: 281–298.

Noordtzij, A. (1939), *De boeken Ezra en Nehemia*, Korte Verklaring der Heilige Schrift (Kampen: Kok).

Nuchelmans, J. (1979), 'Parthenon', in J. Nuchelmans et al. (eds.), *Woordenboek der Oudheid*, vol. 2: *Helius–Plutus* (Bussum: Romen), coll. 2144–2145.

Oegema, G. S. (2001), *Apokalypsen*, JSHRZ 6 1.5 (Gütersloh: Gütersloher).

Oeming, M. (2006), '"See, We Are Serving Today" (Nehemiah 9:36): Nehemiah 9 as a Theological Interpretation of the Persian Period', in O. Lipschits and M. Oeming (eds.), *Judah and the Judeans in the Persian Period* (Winona Lake: Eisenbrauns), pp. 571–588.

Ossendrijver, M. (2018), 'Babylonian Scholarship and the Calendar During the Reign of Xerxes', in C. Waerzeggers and M. Seire (eds.), *Xerxes and Babylonia: The Cuneiform Evidence*, OLA 277 (Leuven: Peeters), pp. 135–163.

Parker, R. A. and W. H. Dubberstein (1956), *Babylonian Chronology 626 B.C. – A.D. 75*, Brown University Studies 19, 3rd edn (Providence: Brown University Press).

Pastor, J. (1997), *Land and Economy in Ancient Palestine* (Abingdon: Routledge).

Pike, D. M. (2017), 'The Word of the LORD and the Teacher of Righteousness in the Qumran Texts', in D. W. Parry, S. D. Ricks and A. C. Skinner (eds.), *The Prophetic Voice at Qumran*, STDJ 120 (Leiden: Brill), pp. 97–114.

Polak, F. H. (2006), 'Sociolinguistics and the Judean Speech Community in the Achaemenid Period', in O. Lipschits and M. Oeming (eds.), *Judah and the Judeans in the Persian Period* (Winona Lake: Eisenbrauns), pp. 589–628.

Porten, B. (2002), 'Theme and Structure of Ezra 1 – 6: From Literature to History', *Transeuphratène* 23: 27–49.

—— (2003), 'Elephantine and the Bible', in L. H. Schiffman (ed.), *Semitic Papyrology in Context: A Climate of Creativity*, Festschrift for B. A. Levine, CHANE 14 (Leiden: Brill), pp. 51–84.

Posener, G. (1936), *La Première domination perse en Égypte: Recueil d'inscriptions hiéroglyphiques*, Bibliothèque d'études 11 (Cairo: Institut français d'archéologie orientale).

Pummer, R. (2010), 'Samaritanism: A Jewish Sect or an Independent Form of Yahwism?', in M. Mor and F. V. Reiterer (eds.), *Samaritans: Past and Present – Current Studies*, Studia Judaica 53; Studia Samaritana 5 (Berlin: de Gruyter), pp. 1–24.

—— (2018), 'Samaritan Studies: Recent Research Results', in M. Kartveit and G. N. Knoppers (eds.), *The Bible, Qumran, and the Samaritans*, Studia Judaica 104; Studia Samaritana 10 (Berlin: de Gruyter), pp. 57–77.

Raaflaub, K. A. (2004), 'Archaic Greek Aristocrats as Carriers of Cultural Interaction', in R. Rollinger and C. Ulf (eds.), *Commerce and Monetary Systems in the Ancient World: Means of Transmission and Cultural Interaction* (Stuttgart: Steiner), pp. 197–217.

Reich, R., E. Shukron and O. Lernau (2007), 'Recent Discoveries in the City of David', *Israel Exploration Journal* 57: 153–169.

Reinmuth, T. (2002), *Der Bericht Nehemias: Zur literarischen Eigenart, traditionsgeschichtlichen Prägung und innerbiblischen Rezeption des Ich-Berichts Nehemias*, OBO 183 (Fribourg: Universitätsverlag).

Reiterer, F. V. (2013), 'Ein unkonventioneller Umgang mit der biblischen Autorität: Siras Art in hellenistischer Umgebung aus seiner Bibel zu denken und zu sprechen', in I. Kalimi,

T. Nicklas and G. G. Xeravits (eds.), *Scriptural Authority in Early Judaism and Ancient Christianity*, Deuterocanonical and Cognate Literature Studies 16 (Berlin: de Gruyter), pp. 129–166.

Rendtorff, R. (1997), 'Nehemiah 9: An Important Witness of Theological Reflection', in M. Cogan, B. L. Eichler and J. H. Tigay (eds.), *Tehillah le-Mosheh*, Festschrift for M. Greenberg (Winona Lake: Eisenbrauns), pp. 112–117.

Ritmeyer, L. and K. (2014), *Jerusalem in the Time of Nehemiah*, 2nd edn (Jerusalem: Carta).

Ron, Z. (2020), 'Naming Nehemiah', *Jewish Bible Quarterly* 48: 157–162.

Schaeder, H. H. (1930), *Esra der Schreiber*, Beiträge zur historischen Theologie 5 (Tübingen: Mohr).

Schaper, J. (2000), *Priester und Leviten im achämenidischen Juda: Studien zur Kult- und Sozialgeschichte Israels in persischer Zeit*, FAT 31 (Tübingen: Mohr Siebeck).

Schaudig, H. (2019), 'The Text of the Cyrus Cylinder', in R. Shayegan (ed.), *Cyrus the Great: Life and Lore*, Ilex Foundation Series 21 (Cambridge: Harvard University Press), pp. 16–25.

Schmökel, H. (1957), *Keilschriftforschung und alte Geschichte Vorderasiens*, Handbuch der Orientalistik 2.3 (Leiden: Brill).

Schneemelcher, W. (1966), 'Esra', in T. Klauser (ed.), *Reallexikon für Antike und Christentum*, vol. 6: *Erfüllung – Exitus illustrium virorum* (Stuttgart: Hiersemann), coll. 595–612.

Schnittjer, G. E. (2016), 'The Bad Ending of Ezra–Nehemiah', *Bibliotheca Sacra* 173: 32–56.

Schorch, S. (2013), 'Which Kind of Authority? The Authority of the Torah During the Hellenistic and the Roman Periods', in I. Kalimi, T. Nicklas and G. G. Xeravits (eds.), *Scriptural Authority in Early Judaism and Ancient Christianity*, DCLS 16 (Berlin: de Gruyter), pp. 1–15.

Schwiderski, D. (2000), *Handbuch der nordwestsemitischen Briefformulars: Ein Beitrag zur Echtheit-Frage der aramäischen Briefe des Esrabuches*, BZAW 295 (Berlin: de Gruyter).

Scott, R. B. Y. (1952), 'Meteorological Phenomena and Terminology in the Old Testament', *ZAW* 64: 11–25.

Segert, S. (1975), *Altaramäische Grammatik* (Leipzig: Enzyklopädie).

Shea, W. H. (1991), 'Darius the Mede in His Persian-Babylonian Setting', *Andrews University Seminary Studies* 29: 235–257.

Shepherd, D. (2005), 'Prophetaphobia: Fear and False Prophecy in Nehemiah vi', *Vetus Testamentum* 55: 232–250.

Shepherd, M. B. (2009), *Daniel in the Context of the Hebrew Bible*, Studies in Biblical Literature 123 (New York: Lang).

Silver, M. (2004) 'Modern Ancients', in R. Rollinger and C. Ulf (eds.), *Commerce and Monetary Systems in the Ancient World: Means of Transmission and Cultural Interaction*, Oriens et Occidens 6 (Wiesbaden: Steiner), pp. 65–87.

Simons, J. (1952), *Jerusalem in the Old Testament* (Leiden: Brill).

Ska, J.-L. (2001), '"Persian Imperial Authorization": Some Question Marks', in J. W. Watts (ed.), *Persia and Torah: The Theory of Imperial Authorization of the Pentateuch*, SBL Symposium Series 17 (Atlanta: SBL), pp. 161–182.

Smith-Christopher, D. L. (2001), 'Prayers and Dreams: Power and Diaspora Identities in the Social Setting of the Daniel Tales', in J. J. Collins and P. W. Flint (eds.), *The Book of Daniel: Composition and Reception*, VTSup 83 (Leiden: Brill), pp. 266–290.

—— (2002), *A Biblical Theology of Exile* (Minneapolis: Fortress).

Snell, D. C. (1997), *Life in the Ancient Near East, 3100–332 B.C.E.* (New Haven: Yale University Press).

—— (2001), *Flight and Freedom in the Ancient Near East*, CHANE 8 (Leiden: Brill).

Snyman, S. D. (2006), 'Wie en wat word veroordeel – en waarom? Nogeens Maleagi 2:10–16', *In die Skriflig* 40: 19–33.

Stadelmann, H. (1990), 'Die Reform Esras und der Kanon', in G. Maier (ed.), *Der Kanon der Bibel* (Giessen: Brunnen; Wuppertal: Brockhaus), pp. 52–69.

Steinberg, J. (2004), 'Die *Ketuvim*: Ihr Aufbau und ihre Botschaft', dissertation, Evangelische Theologische Faculteit, Leuven.

Steiner, R. C. (2001), 'The *mbqr* at Qumran, the *episkopos* in the Athenian Empire, and the Meaning of *lbqr'* in Ezra 7:14: On the Relation of Ezra's Mission to the Persian Legal Project', *JBL* 120: 623–646.

—— (2006), 'Bishlam's Archival Search Report in Nehemiah's Archive: Multiple Introduction and Reverse Chronological

Order as Clues to the Origin of the Aramaic Letters in Ezra
4 – 6', *JBL* 125: 641–685.

—— (2007), 'Why Bishlam (Ezra 4:7) Cannot Rest "In Peace": On
the Aramaic and Hebrew Sound Changes That Conspired to
Blot Out the Remembrance of Bel-Shalam the Archivist', *JBL*
126: 392–401.

Steinmann, A. E. (2008), 'A Chronological Note: The Return of
the Exiles under Sheshbazzar and Zerubbabel (Ezra 1 – 2)',
Journal of the Evangelical Theological Society 51: 513–522.

—— **(2010), *Ezra and Nehemiah*, Concordia Commentary
(St Louis: Concordia).**

—— (2011), *From Abraham to Paul: A Biblical Chronology* (St Louis:
Concordia).

Stern, E. (1982), *Material Culture of the Land of the Bible in the Persian
Period 538–332 B.C.* (Warminster: Aris & Phillips).

Stiegler, S. (1994), *Die nachexilische JHWH-Gemeinde in Jerusalem*,
BEATAJ 34 (Frankfurt: Lang).

Stolper, M. W. (1997), 'Flogging and Plucking', in *Recherches récentes
sur l'Empire achéménide*, Topoi: Orient-Occident Sup. 1 (Lyon:
Maison de l'Orient méditerranéen), pp. 347–350.

Stone, M. (1995), 'A New Edition and Translation of the Questions
of Ezra', in Z. Zevit, S. Gitin and M. Sokoloff (eds.), *Solving
Riddles and Untying Knots*, Festschrift for J. C. Greenfield
(Winona Lake: Eisenbrauns), pp. 293–316.

Stordalen, T. (2001), 'Law or Prophecy? On the Order of the
Canonical Books', *Tidsskrift for Teologi og Kirke* 72: 131–150.

Stronk, J. P. (2007), 'Ctesias of Cnidus, a Reappraisal', *Mnemosyne*
60: 25–58.

Tavernier, J. (2007), *Iranica in the Achaemenid Period (ca. 550–330 B.C.):
Lexicon of Old Iranian Proper Names and Loanwords, Attested in
Non-Iranian Texts*, OLA 158 (Leuven: Peeters).

Thompson, J. A. (1974), *Deuteronomy*, Tyndale Old Testament
Commentaries (Leicester: IVP).

Thompson, M. D. (2012), 'The Divine Investment in Truth:
Toward a Theological Account of Biblical Inerrancy', in
J. K. Hoffmeier and D. R. Magary (eds.), *Do Historical Matters
Matter to Faith? A Critical Appraisal of Modern and Postmodern
Approaches to Scripture* (Wheaton: Crossway), pp. 71–97.

Throntveit, M. A. (1992), *Ezra–Nehemiah*, **Interpretation (Louisville: John Knox).**

Tov, E. (2004), *Scribal Practices and Approaches Reflected in the Texts Found in the Judean Desert*, Studies on the Texts of the Desert of Judah 54 (Leiden: Brill).

—— (2020), 'Protomasorético, premasorético, semimasorético y masorético: un estudio sobre terminología y teoría textual', *DavarLogos* 19: 1–26.

Trimp, C. (1961), *Om de oeconomie van het welbehagen: Een analyse van de idee der 'Heilsgeschichte' in de 'Kirchliche Dogmatik' van Karl Barth* (Goes: Oosterbaan & Le Cointre).

Tromp, J. (1993), *The Assumption of Moses: A Critical Edition with Commentary*, Studia in Veteris Testamenti Pseudepigrapha 10 (Leiden: Brill).

Tuplin, C. (1987), 'The Administration of the Achaemenid Empire', in I. Carradice (ed.), *Coinage and Administration in the Athenian and Persian Empires*, British Archaeological Reports International Series 343 (Oxford: British Archaeological Reports), pp. 109–166.

—— (1998), 'The Seasonal Migration of Achaemenid Kings: A Report on Old and New Evidence', in M. Brosius and A. Kuhrt (eds.), *Studies in Persian History*, in Memory of D. M. Lewis, Achaemenid History 11 (Leiden: NINO), pp. 63–114.

—— (2015), 'The Justice of Darius: Reflections on the Achaemenid Empire as a Rule-Bound Environment', in A. Fitzpatrick-McKinley (ed.), *Assessing Biblical and Classical Sources for the Reconstruction of Persian Influence, History and Culture*, Classica et Orientalia 10 (Wiesbaden: Harrassowitz), pp. 73–126.

—— (2017), 'Serving the Satrap: Lower-Rank Officials Viewed through Greek and Aramaic Sources', in B. Jacobs, W. Henkelman and M. W. Stolper (eds.), *Die Verwaltung im Achämenidenreich: Imperiale Muster und Strukturen*, Classica et Orientalia 17 (Wiesbaden: Harrassowitz), pp. 613–676.

Uffenheimer, B. (1996), 'Zerubbabel: The Messianic Hope of the Returnees', *Jewish Bible Quarterly* 24: 221–228.

Ulrich, D. R. (2021), *Now and Not Yet: Theology and Mission in Ezra–Nehemiah* **(London: Apollos).**

Ussishkin, D. (2006), 'The Borders and *De Facto* Size of Jerusalem in the Persian Period', in O. Lipschits and M. Oeming (eds.), *Judah and the Judeans in the Persian Period* (Winona Lake: Eisenbrauns), pp. 147–166.

—— (2012), 'On Nehemiah's City Wall and the Size of Jerusalem During the Persian Period: An Archaeologist's View', in I. Kalimi (ed.), *New Perspectives on Ezra–Nehemiah: History and Historiography, Text, Literature, and Interpretation* (Winona Lake: Eisenbrauns), pp. 101–130.

van Bekkum, K. (2018), '"How the Mighty Have Fallen": *Sola Scriptura* and the Historical Debate on David as a Southern Levantine Warlord', in H. Burger, A. Huijgen and E. Peels (eds.), Sola Scriptura: *Biblical and Theological Perspectives on Scripture, Authority, and Hermeneutics,* Studies in Reformed Theology 32 (Leiden: Brill), pp. 159–182.

Van Dam, C. (1997a), 'אורים', in *NIDOTTE* 1.329–331.

—— (1997b), 'פרץ', in *NIDOTTE* 3.691–694.

Vanderhooft, D. S. (1999), *The Neo-Babylonian Empire and Babylon in the Latter Prophets,* Harvard Semitic Monographs 59 (Atlanta: Scholars).

VanderKam, J. C. (2004), *From Joshua to Caiaphas: High Priests after the Exile* (Minneapolis: Fortress; Assen: van Gorcum).

van der Kooij, A. (1991a), 'On the Ending of the Book of 1 Esdras', in C. E. Cox (ed.), *VII Congress of the International Organization for Septuagint and Cognate Studies* (Atlanta: Scholars), pp. 37–49.

—— (1991b), 'Zur Frage des Anfangs des 1. Esrabuches', *ZAW* 103: 239–252.

—— (1998), 'The Canonization of Ancient Books Kept in the Temple of Jerusalem', in A. van der Kooij and K. van der Toorn (eds.), *Canonization and Decanonization,* Studies in the History of Religion 82 (Leiden: Brill), pp. 17–40.

—— (2009), 'The Public Reading of Scriptures at Feasts', in C. Tuckett (ed.), *Feasts and Festivals,* CBET 53 (Leuven: Peeters), pp. 27–44.

—— (2012), 'Preservation and Promulgation: The Dead Sea Scrolls and the Textual History of the Hebrew Bible', in N. Dávid, A. Lange, K. De Troyer and S. Tzoref (eds.), *The*

Hebrew Bible in Light of the Dead Sea Scrolls, FRLANT 239
(Göttingen: Vandenhoeck & Ruprecht), pp. 29–40.

—— (2015), 'Leading Scholars and the Interpretation of
Scripture: The Case of LXX Haggai 2.1–9', in M. C. A. Korpel
and L. L. Grabbe (eds.), *Open-Mindedness in the Bible and
Beyond*, Festschrift for B. Becking, LHB/OTS 616 (London:
Bloomsbury T&T Clark), pp. 139–150.

—— (2016), '"Do You Understand What You Are Reading" (Acts
8:30): On Septuagint Hermeneutics and the Book of Isaiah', in
S. Kreuzer, M. Meiser and M. Sigismund (eds.), *Die Septuaginta:
Orte und Intentionen*, WUNT 361 (Tübingen: Mohr Siebeck),
pp. 655–668.

van der Merwe, C. H. J. (1990), ''n Basiese kennis van Bybelse
Hebreeus kan ook bruikbaar wees! 'n Beskrywing van enkele
maklik herkenbare Hebreeuse partikel wat dikwels nie tot
hulle reg kom in vertalings en kommentare nie', *Nederlands
Gereformeerde Teologiese Tydskrif* 31: 134–146.

van der Veen, P. (2003), 'Beschriftete Siegel als Beweis für das
biblische Israel? Gedalja und Seine Mörder par exemple (Eine
Antwort an Bob Becking)', in F. Ninow (ed.), *Wort und Stein:
Studien zur Theologie und Archäologie*, Festschrift for U. Worschech
(Frankfurt am Main: Lang), pp. 238–259.

—— (2007), 'Gedaliah ben Aḥiqam', in M. Lubetski (ed.), *New
Seals and Inscriptions*, Hebrew Bible Monographs 8 (Sheffield:
Phoenix), pp. 55–70.

van der Woude, A. S. (1982a), 'Geschiedenis van Israël en zijn
godsdienst vanaf de tijd van de babylonische ballingschap tot
de komst van Alexander de Grote', in A. S. van der Woude
(ed.), *Bijbels Handboek*, vol. 2A: *Het Oude Testament* (Kampen:
Kok), pp. 141–171.

—— (1982b), *Haggai, Maleachi*, De Prediking van het Oude
Testament (Nijkerk: Callenbach).

—— (1983), 'Geschiedenis en godsdienst van het palestijnse
Jodendom vanaf Alexander de Grote tot aan de komst van
de Romeinen', in A. S. van der Woude (ed.), *Bijbels Handboek*,
vol. 2B: *Tussen Oude en Nieuwe Testament* (Kampen: Kok), pp. 5–89.

—— (1984), *Zacharia*, De Prediking van het Oude Testament
(Nijkerk: Callenbach).

—— (1985), *Jona, Nahum*, De Prediking van het Oude Testament, 2nd edn (Nijkerk: Callenbach).

—— (1992), 'Pluriformity and Uniformity: Reflections on the Transmission of the Text of the Old Testament', in J. N. Bremmer and F. García Martínez (eds.), *Sacred History and Sacred Texts in Early Judaism*, CBET 5 (Kampen: Kok), pp. 151–169.

van Eecken, H. (2002), 'Het verbond met Levi: Een exegetisch en bijbels-theologisch onderzoek naar Numeri 25', thesis, Theologische Universiteit Apeldoorn.

Van Hoonacker, A. (1891), 'Zorobabel et le second temple', *Le Muséon* 10: 72–96, 232–260, 379–397, 489–515, 634–644.

van Leeuwen, C. (1968), *Hosea*, De Prediking van het Oude Testament (Nijkerk: Callenbach).

van Nes, H. and E. van Staalduine-Sulman (2014), 'The "Jewish" Rabbinic Bibles versus the "Christian" Polyglot Bibles', in A. Houtman, E. van Staalduine-Sulman and H.-M. Kirn (eds.), *A Jewish Targum in a Christian World*, Jewish and Christian Perspectives 27 (Leiden: Brill), pp. 185–207.

Veenhof, K. R. (2001), *Geschichte des alten Orients bis zur Zeit Alexanders des Großen*, tr. H. Weippert, Grundrisse zum Alten Testament 11 (Göttingen: Vandenhoeck & Ruprecht).

Vermeylen, J. (2006), 'The Gracious God, Sinners and Foreigners: How Nehemiah 9 Interprets the History of Israel', in N. Calduch-Benages and J. Liesen (eds.), *History and Identity: How Israel's Later Authors Viewed Its Earlier History* (Berlin: de Gruyter), pp. 77–114.

Vogt, E. (1971), *Lexicon linguae Aramaicae Veteris Testamenti documentis antiquis illustratum* (Roma: Pontificium Institutum Biblicum).

vom Orde, K. (1997), *Die Bücher Esra und Nehemia*, Wuppertaler Studienbibel (Wuppertal: Brockhaus).

von Soden, W. (1994), *The Ancient Orient: An Introduction to the Study of the Ancient Near East*, tr. D. G. Schley (Grand Rapids: Eerdmans).

Vriezen, T. C. and A. S. van der Woude (2005), *Ancient Israelite and Early Jewish Literature*, tr. B. Doyle (Leiden: Brill; Dutch orig. 2000).

Wahl, O. (1977), *Apocalypsis Esdrae; Apocalypsis Sedrach; Visio beati*

Esdrae, Pseudepigrapha Veteris Testamenti Graeca 4 (Leiden: Brill).

Waltke, B. K. and M. O'Connor (1990), *An Introduction to Biblical Hebrew Syntax* (Winona Lake: Eisenbrauns).

Washburn, D. L. (2002), *A Catalog of Biblical Passages in the Dead Sea Scrolls*, Text-Critical Studies 2 (Atlanta: SBL).

Waters, M. (2021), 'The Far Side of the Long Sixth Century: Mesopotamian Political Influences on Early Achaemenid Persia', in P. Barmash and M. W. Hamilton (eds.), *In the Shadow of Empire: Israel and Judah in the Long Sixth Century BCE*, Archaeology and Biblical Studies 30 (Atlanta: SBL), pp. 139–160.

Wegner, P. D. (2013), 'Current Trends in Old Testament Textual Criticism', *Bulletin for Biblical Research* 23: 461–480.

Werline, R. A. (1998), *Penitential Prayer in Second Temple Judaism: The Development of a Religious Institution*, SBL Early Judaism and Its Literature 13 (Atlanta: SBL).

Whybray, R. N. (2002), *The Good Life in the Old Testament* (London and New York: T&T Clark).

Wiesehöfer, J. (2008), 'Gerechtigkeit und Recht im achaimenidischen Iran', in H. Barta, R. Rollinger and M. Lang (eds.), *Recht und Religion: Menschliche und göttliche Gerechtigkeitsvorstellungen in den antiken Welten*, Philippika 24 (Wiesbaden: Harrassowitz), pp. 191–203.

Williams, G. R. (2002), 'Contextual Influences in Readings of Nehemiah 5: A Case Study', *Tyndale Bulletin* 53: 57–74.

Williamson, H. G. M. (1977), *Israel in the Book of Chronicles* (Cambridge: Cambridge University Press).

—— **(1985), *Ezra, Nehemiah*, Word Biblical Commentary (Waco: Word).**

—— (1988), 'The Governors of Judah under the Persians', *Tyndale Bulletin* 39: 59–82.

—— (1991), 'Ezra and Nehemiah in the Light of the Texts from Persepolis', *Bulletin for Biblical Research* 1: 41–61.

—— (1998), 'Judah and the Jews', in M. Brosius and A. Kuhrt (eds.), *Studies in Persian History*, in Memory of D. M. Lewis, Achaemenid History 11 (Leiden: NINO), pp. 145–163.

—— (2008), 'The Aramaic Documents in Ezra Revisited', *Journal of Theological Studies* NS 59: 41–62.

Wiseman, D. J. (1985), *Nebuchadrezzar and Babylon*, Schweich Lectures 1983 (Oxford: Oxford University Press).

—— (1991), 'Babylonia 605–539 BC', in J. Boardman, I. E. S. Edwards, N. G. L. Hammond and E. Sollberger (eds.), *The Assyrian and Babylonian Empires and Other States of the Near East, from the Eighth to the Sixth Centuries BC*, Cambridge Ancient History 3.2, 2nd edn (Cambridge: Cambridge University Press), pp. 229–251.

Wiseman, P. J. (1977), *Clues to Creation in Genesis*, ed. D. J. Wiseman (London: Marshall, Morgan & Scott; orig. 1936 and 1948).

Wong, G. C. I. (1995), 'A Note on "Joy" in Nehemiah viii 10', *Vetus Testamentum* 45: 383–386.

Wright, J. L. (2010), 'Commensal Politics in Ancient Western Asia: The Background to Nehemiah's Feasting', in *ZAW* 122: 212–233, 333–352.

Wunsch, C. (2002), 'Debt, Interest, Pledge and Forfeiture in the Neo-Babylonian and Early Achaemenid Period: The Evidence from Private Archives', in M. Hudson and M. Van De Mieroop (eds.), *Debt and Economic Renewal in the Ancient Near East*, Series sponsored by the Institute for the Study of Long-Term Economic Trends and the International Scholars Conference on Ancient Near Eastern Economies 3 (Baltimore: CDL), pp. 221–253.

Wursten, D. (2021), 'NBV21: Hoe vroom moet een vertaling zijn?', *Met andere woorden* 40.2: 56–61.

Würthwein, E. (1973), *Der Text des Alten Testaments: Eine Einführung in die Biblia Hebraica*, 4th edn (Stuttgart: Deutsche Bibelgesellschaft).

Xeravits, G. G. and P. Porzig (2015), *Einführung in die Qumranliteratur: Die Handschriften vom Toten Meer* (Berlin: de Gruyter).

Yamauchi, E. M. (1988), 'Ezra–Nehemiah', in F. E. Gaebelein (ed.), *The Expositor's Bible Commentary*, vol. 4 (Grand Rapids: Zondervan), pp. 563–771.

—— (1990), *Persia and the Bible* (Grand Rapids: Baker).

—— (2002), 'The Eastern Jewish Diaspora', in M. Chavalas and K. L. Younger (eds.), *Mesopotamia and the Bible*, JSOTSup 341 (Sheffield: Sheffield Academic), pp. 356–377.

Younger, K. L. (2004), 'The Repopulation of Samaria (2 Kings 17:24, 27–31) in Light of Recent Study', in J. K. Hoffmeier and A. Millard (eds.), *The Future of Biblical Archaeology: Reassessing Methodologies and Assumptions* (Grand Rapids: Eerdmans), pp. 254–280.

Zadok, R. (2012), 'Some Issues in Ezra–Nehemiah', in I. Kalimi (ed.), *New Perspectives on Ezra–Nehemiah: History and Historiography, Text, Literature, and Interpretation* (Winona Lake: Eisenbrauns), pp. 151–181.

Zehnder, M. (2005), *Umgang mit Fremden in Israel und Assyrien: Ein Beitrag zur Anthropologie des 'Fremden' im Licht antiker Quellen*, BWANT 168 (Stuttgart: Kohlhammer).

—— (2018), 'Mass-Migration to the Western World in Light of the Hebrew Bible: The Challenge of Complexity', *European Journal of Theology* 27: 4–17.

Zenger, E. (2003), 'Der Psalter im Horizont von Tora und Prophetie: Kanongeschichtliche und kanonhermeneutische Perspektiven', in J.-M. Auwers and H. J. de Jonge (eds.), *The Biblical Canons*, Bibliotheca Ephemeridum Theologicarum Lovaniensium 163 (Leuven: Peeters), pp. 111–134.

Zevit, Z. (2009), 'Is There an Archaeological Case for Phantom Settlements in the Persian Period?', *Palestine Exploration Quarterly* 141: 124–137.

Ziegert (2023), 'Geschichte des hebräischen Textes', in W. Hilbrands and H. J. Koorevaar (eds.), *Einleitung in das Alte Testament: Ein historisch-kanonischer Ansatz* (Gießen: Brunnen), pp. 101–127.

Zillessen, A. (1904), 'Miszellen', *ZAW* 24: 143–144.

Zorell, F. (1968), *Lexicon Hebraicum et Aramaicum Veteris Testamenti* (Roma: Pontificium Institutum Biblicum).

INTRODUCTION

1. Genre

a. *The genre of Ezra-Neh.*

The question about the genre of a text is most important for our reading of that text. We read a letter from the tax services with a different mode (or code) of interpretation from that we use to read an invitation from the local football club. So the answer to the question of genre will define our idea of the relationship between the text and history. Is it a representation of history, or has it only had its origin in a specific cultural context? For the answer, we need to determine in the first place how the text presents itself. Poetic exaggeration and symbolic theatre may exist, but when the text seems to present real situations, we must read it that way. Of course, that is not very easy, because its historical and social background is not ours. What was easy for the first readers to understand demands a lot of reconstruction in contemporary historiography. For example, when we read through Ezra-Neh. without former knowledge, we have the impression of a rather compact history, but when we read it in a more informed way, we shall understand that more than a century is covered. This implies also that even though we say that the decision about the genre is of first importance, different levels must be studied at the same time.[1]

Of course, you can read the text also in a different way, and circular reasoning (cf. Williamson 2008: 45–46) can play a role. Someone who, at every point where two different interpretations can be chosen, opts for the interpretation that implies historical mistakes and theological deception, will obviously conclude that Ezra-Neh. is historically unreliable and theologically tendentious. Of course, Ezra-Neh. is theologically tendentious, but not in the sense that the truth would be violated. One who reads in a canonical context, and looks for readings that are historically reliable as well as theologically consistent, can be successful without too much effort. Does this prove mathematically that Ezra-Neh. is historically reliable and rightfully belongs to the biblical canon? No, that is not the case; always a choice will need to be made between believing acceptance and deconstructive declining. What van Bekkum (2018: 177) says about the books of Samuel can also be applied to Ezra-Neh.:

> Taking the biblical text seriously, implies that the historical constraints and claims that are offered by the text, need to be considered carefully … But in addition, this also involves the text's theological claims … Is this story-line that has convinced so many generations and religious groups, to be trusted or not? The last decades of history of research show that scholars cannot avoid it to consider their own presuppositions and theological attitude … In this way, a reluctant application of *sola scriptura* – understood as an effort to interpret all the data on their own terms – touches upon its theological meaning, that is, the nature of scripture as divine revelation.

---

1   By way of analogy: if we understand well the historical – or rather, the 'non-historical' – introduction of the book of Judith, we shall also understand that the genre of Judith is not historical but meta-historical (see Lorein 2003: 57–64).

In more sophisticated literary terms, we still need to decide whether Ezra-Neh. is 'historiography' or a 'story'. In historiography a nation holds a central place, in a longer series of events, with an interpretation by the author. The story, by contrast, speaks about only a few people, around a specific question, but in more detail, normally well formulated. Both can be 'historical'. Both have literary qualities (at least in the neutral sense of the word 'quality'), such as selection, arrangement and rhetorical devices (Kaiser and Silva 2007: 123–124). It is clear that in Ezra-Neh. we have to do with historiography without an elevated literary style (but with a tight structure).

b. The genre of commentary writing

The genre of Ezra-Neh. is not the only genre important for this commentary. We need also to speak about the genre of 'commentary' and the writer's theological bias. I have a Free Evangelical background, moved towards a Reformed Evangelical viewpoint. I have been active for many years in the field of relations between Church and State but have been influenced in those activities by my reading of the biblical writings about the Persian period.

The Bible translator cannot skip passages but has the possibility of translating texts without understanding them. The Bible commentator has the privilege of skipping problems for which he or she does not have an answer (giving the message that there is no problem, while in reality having no solution). In this commentary I try to handle all levels of the text: linguistic, historical, literary (not only for aesthetical reasons, but also because literary devices tell us something about the author's intentions) and theological, with a mention of where a problem remains without a solution. Sidestepping a problem by positing that the text is simply wrong is not a genuine solution. Issues in the Hebrew and Aramaic will mostly be hidden in this commentary based on the English text, by default the English Standard Version. Some important details about Hebrew/Aramaic text and grammar are briefly referred to in footnotes. It has been rather difficult to discuss language issues based on differences among the standard English Bible translations, because they are much nearer to one another than Bible translations in Dutch (my mother tongue). In a Dutch commentary, you need to explain the differences between the translations by explaining the Hebrew (Aramaic) behind them.

This means that the text as such, as well as references to the *hors-texte* (see 2a, 'Rootedness'), is taken seriously; this is the right combination for a Bible commentary, whatever literature-only or history-only adepts may think about it. What is not treated is the way people have read Ezra-Neh., especially not after Antiquity. Presentation of the viewpoints of other commentators and discussions with them will remain absent. In the same vein, in general no problems will be discussed that are based just on wrong interpretations.

A problem with writing Bible commentaries is that a commentator in the twenty-first century cannot be original, especially not with the principles mentioned earlier. Even though the church needs a fresh commentary for each generation, originality is difficult and at best restricted to some specific issues. The influence of earlier commentators is always there and of course their right comments are repeated. For a long time, commentaries did not cite every source. In view of recent problems that some commentators have faced regarding plagiarism, this commentary is quite large in citing, even though I am not sure that Grosheide (1963), Fensham (1982), Yamauchi (1988) and my predecessor in this series, Kidner (1979), have at every passage received the honours due to them. With ingredients coming from several places, the cooking has been mine.

2. Historical background

a. Rootedness

Having concluded that Ezra-Neh. is a form of historiography (see 1a, 'The genre of Ezra-Neh.'), we must now give attention to the importance of its historical rootedness.

God is transcendent and sovereign, but has revealed himself in history – and this not only in some 'main events' such as creation, incarnation and resurrection where he would have invaded 'vertically from above':[2] it has pleased him to act *constantly* in history and to reveal himself in language (Thompson 2012: 92–93). That

---

2 Translated from the German expression *senkrecht von oben*.

is what we find represented in Scripture. Therefore it is important to know as much as we can about the historical background, of the events themselves as well as of the author (Lorein 2023b: 63). There is really something outside the text[3] (Trimp 1961: 166, 196, 200–210; Deines 2013: 21; Jaeger 2013: 3–5)! The Bible is not just offering some testimonies of religiously sensitive persons: 'While God has spoken in the past in many parts and in many ways to our fathers by the prophets, in these last days he has spoken to us by a Son' (Heb. 1:1–2a, my translation).

This historicity does not imply that the author was unbiased or averse to any interpretation (Kaiser and Silva 2007: 133). Nor does it imply that the interpretation is immediately crystal clear (Grudem 2009). Some elements of knowledge have escaped us in the course of history; on the other hand, new findings can give new light to the interpretation, and perhaps even to the application, which has to be in correspondence with new evolutions in society in any case.

This importance of the historical background is also illustrated within Ezra-Neh., as becomes clear by the many biblical references in the prayer of Nehemiah 9.

b. Julian dates

Before turning to the historical background as such, we must discuss the problem of dates. If, for example, the date of 12 October 539 BC is given, we must realize that an office calendar on the wall never indicated that that specific day was 12 October and still less that it was the year 539 BC. We nevertheless use these Julian dates to give an idea of the time of year and the period in history. Indeed, we refer to 'Julian' dates because, for dates before the Gregorian adaptation (15 October 1582), months (and days, with some adaptation) were expressed according to the system developed under Julius Caesar and adjusted by Augustus. The Christian era was based on the

---

3 Contra the thesis of Jacques Derrida (1930–2004) – as it is generally understood – that there is nothing outside the text ('Il n'y a pas de hors-texte') and Roland Barthes' (1915–80) book *La mort de l'auteur* (1968; 'The Death of the Author').

calculations of Dionysius Exiguus in AD 525, who seems to have
been quite right (Mahieu 2012).

The Julian calendar is also used for dates 'Before Christ'. This
can cause some problems (the Julian year is a little bit too long when
compared with the solar year; cf. Ossendrijver 2018: 149 n. 46), but
considering the degree of precision with which we work, this does
not play a role. Indeed, the precision is reassuring for the period
under study, but it is not extreme; for historical reconstruction, it
is more than sufficient.[4] Mentioning the dates in the calendrical
systems used during the events under discussion would be too complicated, because no system existed for the days, and there was no
uniformity regarding the months and eras: the Seleucid era started
only in 312 BC; earlier, a new 'era' started with every new king.
Thanks to the work of Parker and Dubberstein,[5] based on dispersed
historical and astronomical information, it is possible to translate
the chronological indications into our habitual system.

c. Distances (and other measures)

Not only the situation in time but also the situation in space has
its challenges. Distances mentioned in ancient sources are quite
imprecise, so calculating distances between different locations
depends on the identification with current locations. Modern authors
are not able to measure every distance themselves and, even if they
could, would not always take the shortest way, nor would they necessarily be able to do so given the terrain or circumstances on the
ground. This means that in practice there are two main sources for
calculating distances (and so mentioning them in commentaries):
(1) publications about geography and (2) measuring on maps. Who
can guarantee, however, that the authors of geographical publications
did not use method (2) themselves? And how much rounding off has
taken place among older sources, using other units of measurement

---

4   E.g., if we can discuss whether a specific event took place on 11 or 12
    September 515 BC, is this an indication of the precision of our
    knowledge or of its lack of precision?
5   Parker and Dubberstein: 1956. For some corrections, see Ossendrijver
    2018: 139–147.

or investigating other problems? Maps are often at a scale that does not permit precise calculations. Printing is less precise than we would like. And there is also a problem of a different nature: 5 miles is a distance you can cover in a few minutes by car or in half an hour by bike, but for which you need two hours if walking.

The publishing house asked me to use miles in this commentary. For the hundreds of millions of people who read English but were not raised with miles, Table I.1 shows the conversions, rounded off, of course, for the reasons already mentioned.

Table I.1: Conversions for measurements

1 mile = 1.6 km
1 acre = 0.4 ha
1 yard = 0.9 m
1 inch = 2.5 cm

And to be complete:

1 troy oz = 31.1 g
1 grain = 64.8 mg
1 lb = 453 g
1 gal. = 4.55 l

d. Setting

Even though the Persian Empire (for its organization, see 2f, 'Organization of the Persian Empire') is always present in the background, Ezra-Neh. is almost completely situated in Jerusalem (aside Neh. 1:10 – 2:10), as the capital of Judah. Neighbouring provinces were Samaria in the north, Ammon across the Jordan, Moab on the other side of the Dead Sea, Idumea in the south, Ashdod in the north-west and Dor in the north-east (see Fig. I.1).[6]

---

6 Most places not 100% sure and/or situated approximately: see pp. 6–7 (Introduction 2c, 'Distances [and other measures]'), 75-77 (Ezra 2:20–35), 86–87 (3:7), 171–175 (Neh. 3:2–19), 192 (6:2), 236–238 (11:25–36), 242 (12:27–29). My thanks to Miss Esther Lorein for technical assistance.

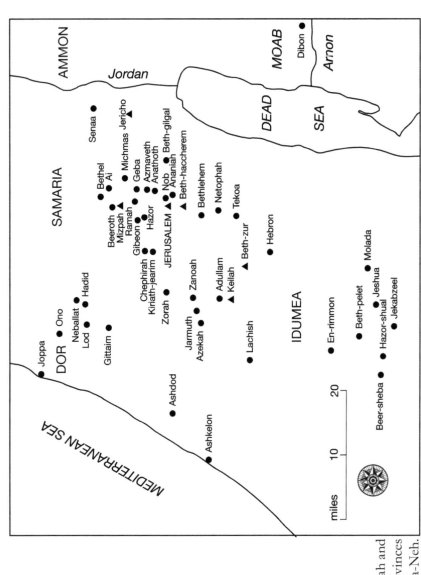

Figure I.1: Judah and neighbouring provinces at the time of Ezra-Neh.

Since the beginning of the exile many immigrants had come to Judah from Moab and Edom (Ezek. 35:10–15). They had taken over the houses of the exiles and partly their religion too, without completely setting aside their own national and religious identity. Migration had also taken place in the other direction: Jews were living in Ammon (and could have informed those in Judah: see Neh. 4:12; Heltzer 1981: 117). We must also be aware of the fact that many Judeans had not gone into exile but had just stayed in Judah: the land was not empty (Lorein 2018: 249).

What is described in Ezra-Neh. seems to be compact, but nevertheless covers a long period of time; this must have been clear to the original reader (as well as to present-day informed readers). Indeed, Ezra-Neh. spans the period from 538 to 425 BC (with the lists continuing to about 395 BC; see Neh. 11:22; 12:11). The number of verses is not equally divided over the number of years – as is quite normal – but here an important hiatus exists, not between the book of Ezra and the book of Nehemiah, but between Ezra 6 and Ezra 7, as Bänziger (2023: 1179) has visualized (see Fig. I.2).

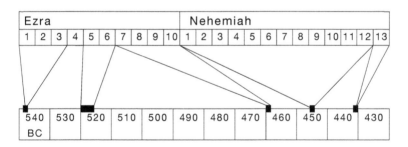

Figure I.2: Relationship between chapters and years.
Used with kind permission from the editor Dr W. Hilbrands

We could set this schematically as follows (the lines in italics denote events not mentioned in Ezra-Neh., but which put these books into their historical context):

538–537: approval for and execution of the return from exile: Ezra 1
536: start of the reconstruction of the temple: Ezra 3
    interruption of the reconstruction of the temple: Ezra 4:1–5, 24
520–515: restart and completion of the reconstruction of the temple:
    Ezra 5 – 6
519: Udjahorresnet, Cambyses' chief physician, makes his entreaty
509: The Romans opt for a system with two consuls each year
496: birth of the Greek tragedy writer Sophocles
490: battle between Persian and Greek armies at Marathon
485: opposition to the reconstruction of the walls: Ezra 4:6
480: battle between Persian and Greek armies at Salamis
479: battle between Persian and Greek armies at Plataeae
469: birth of the Greek philosopher Socrates
460: opposition to the reconstruction of the walls: Ezra 4:7
458–457: Ezra's first appearance: Ezra 7 – 10
shortly before 448: opposition to the reconstruction of the walls:
    Ezra 4:8–23
446: report to Nehemiah: Neh. 1
445–433: Nehemiah's first appearance: Neh. 2 – 12
445–444: Ezra's second appearance: Neh. 8 – 12
430–425: Nehemiah's second appearance: Neh. 13

e. Persian kings
i. Cyrus
Cyrus[7] ('[a god] protects, bestows care' – if Elamite; Henkelman
2021: 18–19) started his career as vassal of Media (560–558), but he
was already mentioned in Isaiah 44:28 – 45:1 (and referred to in
Isa. 45:13). In 550 BC he united Medes and Persians and replaced
his suzerain as king (Briant 2002: 33). From that moment on he
had the power to take over the Babylonian Empire, which happened effectively by the capture of Babylon on 12 October 539
(Dan. 5:30). This conquest was considered important enough to
start a new era and thus Cyrus' first regnal year (after the partial

---

7 To be precise: Cyrus II, because from 610 to 585 his grandfather Cyrus
   had already reigned over Anshan (Briant 2002: 13–18). We will follow
   common usage in just saying 'Cyrus'.

accession year) started on 24 March 538 (Kessler 1992: 79). It was
the start of the Persian Empire, stretching from the frontiers
with Egypt and Greece to the frontier with India. While many
structures and functionaries were taken over (Greenfield 1981:
116), we see also discontinuity: a different language system (no
longer Akkadian as the main language, but Old Persian as the
language of the royal family, Akkadian and Elamite to stress
the continuity with earlier empires, and Aramaic as a common
language[8]), a different worldview and a different attitude to
submitted nations. So we read in the Cyrus Cylinder (shortly after
539 BC; l.32): 'I returned the gods who had been there [Babylon]
to their own places and I let them dwell again in eternal abodes. I
gathered all their inhabitants and returned them to their places.'[9]
Although he speaks here about 'gods' (plural), his familiarity with
Zoroastrianism (in the large sense; rather called Mazdeism for this
period) may have led him to some sympathy for the Jews because
of their shared monotheism, even though Cyrus' theology is not
clear.

According to Daniel 6 (where he is mentioned with his Median
throne name: 'King Darius'; Shea 1991), Cyrus recognizes God as
the living, eternal God who is able to rescue. This must be situated
sometime during the last days of the year 539 BC. It seems logical
to see a relation between Daniel's prayer and Gabriel's message
in Daniel 9 on the one hand, and the king's decree on the other,
in the sense that Daniel would have made suggestions to King
Cyrus (cf. Dan. 6:28[10]); but this hypothesis depends on the possibilities of communication between Daniel, who had remained in the
region of Babel, and the king, who apparently (see Ezra 6:1–2) was

---

8 Aramaic language with its practical advantages was also used in the
Babylonian Empire (Dandamayev 2004: 149), but only in the Persian
Empire was this done officially (Segert 1975: 41).

9 My translation; the Akkadian reads: 'DIĜIR^MEŠ a-ši-ib ŠÀ-bi-šú-nu a-na
áš-ri-šu-nu ú-tir-ma ú-šar-ma-a šu-bat da-rí-a- ta kul-lat ÙĜ^MEŠ-šú-nu
ú-pa-aḫ-ḫi-ra-am-ma ú-te-er da-ád-mi-šú-un' (Schaudig
2019: 20).

10 Or Dan. 6:29 in the numbering of the Aramaic text.

in Ecbatana during the summer[11] of 538 when he gave permission to the Jews to turn back to Judah. The permitted return became reality in 537 (Ezra 1:5–11). Also during his days (in 536) the building of the temple was started (Ezra 3) and interrupted (Ezra 4:1–5, 24). He died in 530 in battle.

ii. Cambyses

Cambyses reigned from 530 to 522. He is not mentioned in the Bible. It was during his reign that the Persian Empire had its largest extent.

iii. Darius

Darius was born in 550 as the son of a satrap of royal descent. He became king in 522. It was during his reign that the temple at Jerusalem was rebuilt (Ezra 5 – 6). Darius entered European history by his attempt to conquer Greece (Marathon, 12 September 490). He died in 486. Haggai's activity is completely situated during Darius' reign (Hag. 1:1, 15; 2:10); Zechariah's partly (Zech. 1:1, 7; 7:1).

iv. Xerxes

Xerxes (Old Persian Hshayārshā, Hebr. Ahashverosh, Greek Xerxes; Lorein 2023a: 1163) was Darius' successor in November 486. The resistance to the reconstruction of the walls of Jerusalem mentioned in Ezra 4:6 occurred in about 485. He continued the war with Greece (Salamis, 28 September 480; Plataeae, 27 August 479). The year after (478), Esther entered his life (Esth. 2:16). Zechariah 9 – 14 must be situated in his reign. Xerxes (as well as Darius earlier) started inscriptions with 'A great god is Ahura Mazda, the greatest of the gods' (and described himself as 'the great king').[12] It must be clear that this does not imply that Xerxes was monotheistic or that everyone in the society was Zoroastrian (Mazdean). He was

---

11   Persian kings had different capitals for different seasons and moved constantly from one capital to another, visiting the regions in between on the same occasion; for further references see Lorein 2023a: 1164.

12   Translations mine; the Old Persian reads: 'Baga vazraka Auramazdā hya maθišta baganām' (Kent 1953: 135, 146, 152) and 'xšāyaθiya vazraka' (Kent 1953: 116, 134, 148–150, 152).

murdered together with the royal prince in August 465 by his chief
bodyguard, who wanted to succeed him.

v. Artaxerxes

Artaxerxes I (Old Persian Artaxshachā, 'dominion through truth',
Hebr. Artahshasth, Greek Artaxerxes; Hutter 2009: 85) succeeded
his father immediately (Briant 2002: 566). The resistance to the
reconstruction of the walls of Jerusalem mentioned in Ezra 4:7
occurred in about 460. In 458, Ezra came to Jerusalem (Ezra 7:21–
26) and stayed there for a rather limited time (he is not mentioned
in the book of Ezra any more after 457). Shortly before 448 the
resistance to building the walls mentioned in Ezra 4:8–23 occurred
(cf. Ezra 4:8). Nehemiah was informed about the situation at Jerusalem in 446 (Neh. 1) and travelled there in 445 (Neh. 2:5–8). Ezra
came back to Jerusalem (Neh. 8:2) in the same year. Nehemiah
stayed there from 445 to 433 (Neh. 2 – 12), Ezra until 444 (Neh.
8 – 12). Between 433 and about 430, Nehemiah was again at the
king's palace. He came back to Jerusalem in about 430 (Neh. 13).
Artaxerxes died in 424 (Depuydt 1995a).

vi. Darius II

Darius II reigned from 424 to 405. Perhaps he is mentioned in
Nehemiah 12:22.

Later Persian kings are not mentioned in the Bible. The Persian
Empire ended with Alexander the Great's victories over the last
Persian king, Darius III (Ipsos in 333 and Gaugamela in 331). At
that moment, the Hellenistic-Roman period started, which in a
certain sense continues until this day, for example through its influ-
ence on the organization of the Christian church. The Eastern
Roman Empire ended in AD 1453 with the fall of Constantinople/
Byzantium. Scholars fleeing from Byzantium greatly influenced the
Western Renaissance. In other aspects too, the institutions of the
Roman Empire had an enduring influence.

f. Organization of the Persian Empire

The lack of details concerning the organization of the Persian
Empire in Ezra-Neh. corresponds with the Persian ideal of a meagre

state: neither good infrastructure, nor education nor health care for
its citizens was the goal of the Achaemenids; rather, it focused on
the amalgamation of bullion in their palaces (Smith-Christopher
2001: 278–279).

The organization of the empire as represented in the Bible is
correct, if we understand the difficulty of translating the term *peḥâ*:
it can be translated by 'governor' of a province, but also by 'satrap',
head of the larger entity of the satrapy. The empire extended from
India (the Indus region, i.e. present-day Pakistan) to 'Cush', often
translated by Ethiopia but better by Nubia: the south of present-day
Egypt and the north of present-day Sudan (Ethiopia is still more
– and too far – to the south).

The satrapy to which the province of Judah belonged is called
'Across the River',[13] that is, on the other side of the Euphrates,
with a Greek based term 'Trans-Euphrates'. On which side of the
Euphrates? On the western side: in the days of the Persian Empire
the world was viewed from the Persian mainland. Of course, when
we are looking from Europe or Africa, Judah is on *this* side of the
Euphrates, and the translators of the Authorized Version have
integrated this in their 'on this side the river', a rare place where
they opted for a target-culture-based translation. The situation is
still more complicated as probably some parts of Northern Mesopotamia (so to the *east* of the Euphrates) were also part of it, in
total stretching from the northern border of Syria (Harran, Latin
Carrhae) to the desert in the south (Herodotus 3.91). The capital
was probably Damascus (Briant 2002: 585). Judah's dependence on
Samaria was a temporary situation when Nehemiah arrived. Most
of the time Judah was a unit on the same level, as already in the
Babylonian period. The province was partitioned in (at least) five
districts: Jerusalem, Beth-haccherem, Mizpah, Beth-zur and Keilah.

---

13   If this were an introduction to Persian constitutional law and not a
     commentary on Ezra-Neh., all this should be nuanced, because the
     Persian Empire was not a post-revolutionary clear-cut state, but an
     amalgam of regions with different histories and customs, also on the
     level of relationships with the central authorities (see e.g. Högemann
     1992).

g. The documents

For a long time, critical orthodoxy in biblical scholarship doubted the historicity of the official documents represented in Ezra, but especially since the work of Schaeder (1930; already announced with Meyer 1896) the edicts were generally considered as genuine (possibly with redactional adaptations) with the following arguments: (1) the language of the edicts corresponded to what was to be expected for the period of Aramaic in question (orthography, prepositions, adverbs, expressions); (2) the form of the edict was right; (3) there were no conflicts with historical data. The Elephantine papyri, known since the beginning of the twentieth century, confirmed this.

Another round was started by Schwiderski (2000: 375–382), who sought to prove that the formal features are typical for the Hellenistic-Roman period. This brought Williamson (2008; an earlier reaction by Porten 2003: 51–62) to a new overview, the arguments of which are as follows:

(1) If the documents had indeed been forgeries, they would have followed the usual forms more strictly. (2) The occurrence of words not used in later texts points to an early date. (3) The description of the treasury in Ezra 6:1 is in accordance with what has been found at Persepolis. (4) Jewish material in the documents might have been based on the input of Jewish officials at the Persian court. (5) The orthography of *dî* (with *d* instead of the older *zî*) occurs already in 437; moreover, orthography could have been adapted in the transmission history. (6) The orthography of the suffixes *-hom* (and *-kom*) instead of *-hôn* (and *-kôn*) in the documents indicates that they are older than the narrative. (7) The orthography *Haphel* (instead of *Aphel*) points to an early date. (8) Some words (in Ezra 4:8–9, 13, 20; 5:8, 14; 6:12, 13; 7:21, 23, 24) are no longer used in later times. (9) The adverbs *kᵉ'an* / *kᵉ'et* / *kᵉ'enet* as a transition marker within the body of the letter is typically Achaemenid, not later (then *dî* is used). (10) The preposition *lᵉ* is already used in the fifth century; moreover, it can easily have replaced the prepositions *'al* and *'el* in the transmission history. (11) The word *šᵉlām* was not used as a greeting in full form, but was already used as an abbreviation in the fifth century; indeed, in Ezra we do not have the full texts, but only the body and summaries of the other parts of the documents.

(12) The same applies to the form of address: not the full form, only a summary. Such a summary would not have been used if the text had been a forgery.

This leads to the conclusion that the documents represent genuine historical texts, rather than being productions of a late redactor.

h. Ezra

Ezra and Nehemiah were great personalities. This may be denied by a strand of modern sociology that represents the progress of history as determined by waves of structures. Indeed, progress without the support of the community would be very limited, but on the other hand great personalities function as catalysts.

Even though Ezra is not mentioned in contemporary historical sources, his historical existence is scarcely doubted.

Ezra (short for Azariah, 'the LORD has helped', a very common name) was born into a priestly family (Ezra 7:1–5) about the year 500 (Yamauchi 2002: 371). Besides being a priest, he was also educated as a scribe (Ezra 7:6, 11). Probably, he was a civil servant of the Persian Empire as advisor for Jewish affairs. As such he mastered the Aramaic language, the language of the Persian Empire for international relationships. In this same period, Aramaic became an important language for the Jewish communities (Lemaire 2015: 43–45). In the Babylonian Talmud (Sanhedrin 21b–22a; with reference to Ezra 4:7, which is not about Ezra's days!), Ezra is also said to have introduced the Aramaic variant of the North-Western Semitic alphabet for the Hebrew language.

According to Ezra 7:9, he started his journey to Jerusalem as a visiting commissioner on 8 April 458; he arrived on 4 August 458. No earlier mention of Ezra occurs: he does not play any role in the first chapters of the book called by his name. The reason and goal of his action can be concluded only from what he actually did at Jerusalem. Possibly a relation existed with a threat that had arisen in Egypt, which might have made it necessary for the king to undertake a positive action towards Judah, to have more loyal Jews on the Egyptian border (Bringmann 2005: 43). He came back to Jerusalem in 445 as priest and scribe, collaborating with Nehemiah. According to Josephus, *Jewish Antiquities* 11.158, he died at an advanced age and was buried in Jerusalem (later traditions situate his grave on the banks of the Tigris – Becking 2018: 16).

Ezra gives a rather happy impression, confident that he will be successful.

i. Nehemiah

Apparently, nobody has ever doubted that Nehemiah was a historical figure.

Nehemiah ('the LORD comforts') was probably born later than Ezra (about 480, or even 470 – thus Bickerman 1978: 24), in a well-to-do family (Heltzer 1989: 334). He had become 'cupbearer' at the Persian court, a most important function. Literally the cupbearer is the one who causes to drink, but his function was not limited to filling the king's glass. Rather he should be compared to a butler, responsible for the king's well-being (also as his taster) and for deciding who at which moment could approach the king (see Xenophon, *Cyropaedia* 1.3.8–11; cf. Yamauchi 1990: 259; Briant 2002: 264). Some have concluded from this position that he was a eunuch in the sexual sense of the word, but this was only a necessary condition for non-nobility functionaries in the king's harem (Heltzer 1989: 334; Yamauchi 1990: 260–264; Briant 2002: 977). It must be remarked, however, that nowhere in the book of Nehemiah is mention made of spouse or children (but this applies to other biblical protagonists) and Nehemiah regularly (Neh. 5:19; 13:14, 22, 31) prays for remembrance (but that is not a coercive argument either). Indeed, generally, eunuchs in the sexual sense had no access to the congregation (Deut. 23:1), but God is gracious towards those who serve him (Isa. 56:3–5; alluded to in Wisdom of Solomon 3:14: 'And the eunuch who has not wrought lawlessness with his hand, nor imagined wicked things against the Lord, to him will be given a peculiar favour for his faithfulness and a very delightful portion in the sanctuary of the Lord' [my translation]).

Informed by his brother about the situation in Jerusalem at the end of 446, he wanted to rebuild the city of his ancestors (Neh. 1). In a first phase, the king allowed him a secondment; shortly afterwards he became governor of the province of Judah (Neh. 5:14), and this remained the case until 433.

With the same commitment with which he had served the Persian king, and with the management competences he had acquired, he started his work in Jerusalem. In the first place he reconstructed the city walls, but also made efforts to rearrange society. From 433 onwards (Neh. 13:6) he stayed again at the Persian court, probably until 430 (cf. Neh. 13:7). According to Josephus, *Jewish Antiquities* 11.183, Nehemiah too grew quite old.[14]

In his whole career he was aware of his dependence on God, with whom he could not assert any right (Neh. 5:19; 13:14, 22, 31). He was a man of principle and very prudent, despite his privileged political status; stern with himself and with others; anxious to serve his countrymen (Josephus, *Ant.* 11.183); loyal towards the Persian authorities, but having some trouble with the priests. Finally, his achievements were more important than Ezra's (but certainly not in every aspect: see Neh. 13), also because at the right moment he could rely on Ezra (Neh. 8). Of course, as governor he held a higher position than Ezra did as visiting commissioner (Steiner 2001: 628–629). The 'statesman' (thus van der Woude 1982a: 159) Nehemiah has gained more sympathy from most commentators. This did not help his reputation in Antiquity, however: it is Ezra who is mentioned most in post-biblical Jewish literature (see 4f, 'The afterlife of Ezra-Neh. in Antiquity').

j. Relationship between Ezra and Nehemiah

As explained at 2h, 'Ezra', and 2i, 'Nehemiah', this commentary situates Ezra's activity in Jerusalem in two shifts starting in 458 and 445, the second one together with Nehemiah, and Nehemiah's activity in Jerusalem also in two shifts, from 445 to 433 and a shorter one starting in 430. This expresses an order (Ezra first, Nehemiah later) and a period of common presence in Jerusalem, starting in 445.

Although no inherent problem hinders this chronological presentation, some commentaries reject it, supposing that Nehemiah arrived earlier in Jerusalem than Ezra. In the first instance, such a reconstruction is based on a harmless identification of the King Artaxerxes mentioned in Ezra 7:7 as Artaxerxes II Mnemon,

---

14   See also 3a, 'Components and redaction'.

who reigned from 404 to 358. As no 'number' (II) is mentioned in the Bible – the order numbers did not even exist: they are a (very practical) invention of modern historians – this seems a valid option, making Ezra arrive in Jerusalem in 398. On the other hand, it requires a series of textual changes further on, which makes this interpretation unacceptable. Another hypothesis supposes that what is received in the text as the *seventh* year of Artaxerxes I (no change as far as the person of the king is concerned) is a transmission error for the thirty-seventh year. We must agree that numbers are quite liable to copying errors, but nothing invites us to doubt the text and this reconstruction is hindered by the fact that the number occurs in both Ezra 7:7 and Ezra 7:8 and that it does not lead to a tidier presentation of history. Both hypotheses lead to completely new interpretations (where Ezra arrives at Jerusalem [much] later than Nehemiah), which do not explain the text as it stands but a reconstructed text. This reconstruction would represent a more rectilinear evolution of Judean society, but real life does not present rectilinear evolutions very often. In this commentary we try to understand and explain the text as it has been handed down to us, and not as it could possibly be reimagined. Therefore, together with the Jewish tradition, we stay with the position that Ezra arrived in 458, and had a part in Nehemiah's initiatives in Nehemiah 8 – 12, as becomes very clear in Nehemiah 12:36–38. No rearrangement is necessary, even though the return of Ezra in Nehemiah 8 finds no explanation within the text and the collaboration between Nehemiah and Ezra is left without any details – they do nevertheless work together in Nehemiah 8:9; 12:31–43.

One problem remains to be discussed: how do we reconstruct the relation between the end of Ezra's activity in Ezra 10 and the start of Nehemiah's activity in Nehemiah 1? In order to solve this problem, we must try to understand the relation between three elements: (1) the book of Ezra does not mention him any more after the year 457 (Ezra 10); (2) what has been described in Ezra 4:8–23 (introduced at that specific place because of the general theme of opposition against the reconstruction activities) must be situated between Ezra 10 and Nehemiah 1; (3) Nehemiah starts his activity in Nehemiah 1. This is the general order, but do we have a direct relation between (1) and (2) or between (2) and (3)?

In the option of a strong relationship between (1) and (2), it is supposed that Ezra tried to rebuild the city in 456 on his own initiative, but that the king gave in to the complaints of the Samarians,[15] not wanting to have still more trouble in Judah than he had already had with Ezra's difficult decision about the marriages. Two problems with this hypothesis must be mentioned. In the first place, the king had given significant resources to Ezra (Ezra 7:13–26), so why should he have been angry about Ezra's elaboration of these competences? Second, why was Nehemiah so upset, when nothing structurally had changed in Jerusalem for ten years?

It is therefore easier to relate Ezra 4:8–23 to the message to Nehemiah. In this hypothesis the building activities had started again (directed by Nehemiah's brother Hanani? – thus De Fraine 1961: 42) some years before the facts of Nehemiah 1, were stopped by the action of the Samarians, and this sad situation was reported to Nehemiah in Nehemiah 1, who understandably was upset. The disadvantage of this hypothesis is that Ezra 4:12 makes one more easily (but not necessarily!) think of Ezra; the great advantage is that the king's reaction in Ezra 4:17–22 is easier to understand some years after his order in Ezra 7:13–26, and Nehemiah's reaction is easier to understand if he has been informed about rather recent developments. The 'stop' (Ezra 4:21) and 'go' (Neh. 2:6) policy of King Artaxerxes was probably influenced by the general position of his empire, which indeed had become more favourable after the Peace of Callias at the end of 449 (see Ezra 4:8). Nehemiah makes use of this change, and the king has no further problem granting Nehemiah's request in Nehemiah 2.

k. Jerusalem

Some discussion exists about the extent of Jerusalem in Nehemiah's day. Although the story can be understood with different solutions to this question in mind, the arguments for a large city are mentioned here.

Jerusalem seems to have contained up to 12,000 inhabitants and so a small city would be too small (even though a large city would be

---

15   For the Samarians, see 21, 'Samarians/Samaritans – Judeans/Jews'.

quite large; Laperrousaz 1994: 125–127); the number of gates (Neh. 2 – 3) is functional only with a large city (Simons 1952: 440); to take the Valley Gate as a starting point for the processions (Neh. 12; Simons 1952: 447) fits better with a large city; the word 'Valley' must refer to the Hinnom Valley, south of the city (Ussishkin 2012: 124).

Nevertheless, arguments for a small city also exist: the population had diminished considerably by the exile (that is true: see Lorein 2018: 249; but that had been almost a century and a half earlier!); according to other calculations, Jerusalem seems to have contained only 4,800 inhabitants (Broshi 1975: 6, 9, 11; or even only 1,500, according to Carter 1999: 201). The argument that within fifty-two days (Neh. 6:15) only a previously existing wall can be repaired is used on both sides, but there are doubts as to whether a wall existed at the western edge of the City of David (Ussishkin 2012: 115, 122); on the other hand, while it should no longer be doubted that walls existed on the south-western hill, no proof is seen that these walls were rebuilt in Persian times (only in the Hasmonean period; Geva 2003: 188, 208). In any case, at the time of the exile, the walls were not destroyed mechanically, only damaged (Laperrousaz 1994: 123–125). We cannot reach certainty in this matter, but the reconstruction best honouring the different elements indicates a large city, partly used, especially near to the walls (Neh. 7:3; Laperrousaz 1994: 128). After all, this summary is also found in Nehemiah 7:4. This is often the case in walled cities, both in Antiquity (e.g. Trier) and in the Middle Ages (e.g. Constantinople, Leuven) (Ussishkin 2006: 161–162). This brings us to the map shown in Figure I.3. Note that a large city (150 acres) is much larger than a small city (37 acres), but the wall of a large city (2½ miles) is not very much longer than the wall of a small city (2 miles) (Lorein 2021b: 78). We dare to part from the majority of today's students and propose this reconstruction,[16] not with the conviction that it is exact, but in order to give an idea of what is described in Nehemiah 2; 3; 12.

---

16   Mainly based on Simons (1952), Edelman (2011) and the Ritmeyers (2014). The western wall of the 'small city' is still more approximate than the other elements. Unless otherwise indicated, references are to Nehemiah. Thanks to Ms Olga Bernaerts for technical assistance.

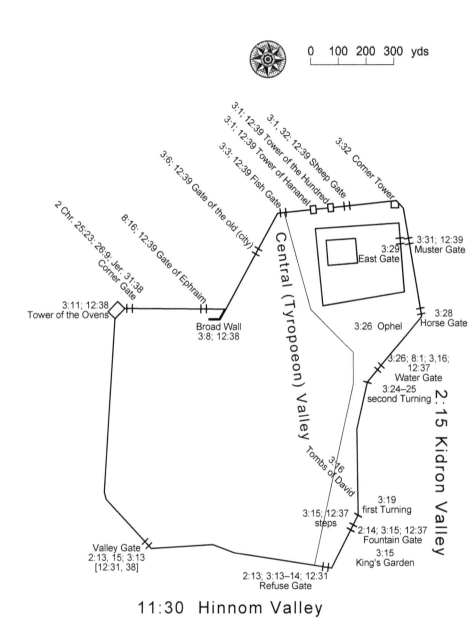

Figure I.3: Jerusalem at the time of Ezra-Neh.

l. Samarians/Samaritans – Judeans/Jews

Two other points of discussion concern the choice between 'Samarians' and 'Samaritans' and 'Judeans' and 'Jews'. We shall approach the problem by starting with the first-mentioned group. They have a long history. From the moment of the division of the kingdom after Solomon's death (930 BC), the Northern Kingdom stuck less to the guidelines of Scripture than the Southern Kingdom. This does not apply to every individual: throughout the centuries believers in the Northern Kingdom continued to be oriented on Jerusalem in religious matters. Some even moved to the Southern Kingdom. After the end of the Northern Kingdom (722), other peoples were displaced from different areas in the Assyrian Empire to the territory of the former Northern Kingdom, plainly according to Assyrian policy. These new settlers came with their own religion, although at a given moment they were eager to know Yahwism as an addition, which led to a mixed religion (cf. 2 Kgs 17:24–41). In Ezra 4 we see the distance between Samarians and Judeans/Jews; we see it again in Nehemiah 4 and 6. At the end of the fourth century, as the result of a conflict within the Jerusalem priesthood, many priests went to the North and a temple was built[17] on Mount Gerizim, while, on the other hand, doctrine was heavily influenced by more conservative Judaism (Josephus, *Ant.* 11.306–312, 322–324[18]). From that period on we speak about Samaritans (instead of Samarians). A period of flourishing followed for the Samaritans, who considered themselves Israelites (Pummer 2010: 17), always in conflict with the Jews (Josephus, *Ant.* 12.156). In the time of Antiochus IV Epiphanes, they presented themselves as distinct from the Jews (Josephus, *Ant.* 12.257–261). The Maccabean king John Hyrcanus destroyed the Gerizim temple in 128 (Josephus, *Ant.* 13.256), which made the rupture irreparable. It is this situation that we meet in the

---

17   Or rather renewed? In that case the earlier 'religious construction' (not necessarily a real 'temple') had already been built in the fifth century, by the 'Samarians' (Pummer 2018: 58, 60).

18   Flavius Josephus puts both developments together. For an overview of related archaeological and chronological problems, see Mor 2011: 90–99.

New Testament: Jews did not want to visit Samaria (Luke 17:11; John 4:4) and Samaritans did not want Jerusalem to be mentioned (Luke 9:51–56). This history (which is more complicated than sketched here) implies that a theological distance between Samarians and Judeans, between Samaritans and Jews, always existed, even if for different reasons in the course of history.

We have already used the term 'Jews' in the previous paragraph, in opposition to 'Samaritans', considering both as religious terms, while 'Samarians' rather indicates inhabitants of Samaria and 'Judeans' inhabitants of Judah. Although the reason for making a choice is the same for both pairs of terms, the actual use is not completely parallel, because we restrict the use of 'Samaritans' to the later phase and see already 'Jews' at work outside Judah (or even inside but with the accent on their religion) in the periods of exile and return, that is to say, also in times when we choose to use 'Samarians'.

m. Other Bible passages about the same period [19]
i. Chronicles
The final verses of Chronicles, 2 Chronicles 36:22–23, must be considered to have been written in order to lead easily to the already existing text of Ezra-Neh. See also 3c, 'Relationship between Ezra-Neh. and Chronicles'.

ii. Esther
The events of the book of Esther must be situated during the reign of Xerxes, who is mentioned briefly in Ezra 4:6. This reminds us of the fact that many Jews had not returned but had stayed in the land of exile (and from that moment on we should speak of 'diaspora').

iii. Isaiah
In Isaiah 44:28b and 45:13 the events of Ezra-Neh. are prophesied.

---

19 Following the order of the ESV.

iv. Jeremiah
Ezra 1:1 refers to the fulfilment of what was prophesied by Jeremiah
in Jeremiah 29:10. In Ezra 1:7–11 the return of the utensils is realized, as prophesied in Jeremiah 27:22. See for both instances the
commentary on Ezra 1:1 for details.

v. Daniel
During the spring of 538, Daniel understands that a return to Jerusalem is possible, but that Israel is not worthy of it (Dan. 9). For
the possible relation between Daniel's prayer (see especially Dan.
9:17–19) and Gabriel's message on the one hand and King Cyrus'
decree on the other, see 2e, 'Persian kings: Cyrus'.
     The vision of Daniel 10 – 12 was revealed on 23 April 536 (Dan.
10:4); the rebuilding of the temple started on 29 April 536 (see
Context for Ezra 3:7–13). In the same days as the return from exile
becomes functional, the huge vision about what will happen until
the end is revealed.

vi. Haggai
Haggai is active in the year 520, during the reign of Darius (Ezra
5:1; 6:14), in the time when the reconstruction of the temple was
interrupted (cf. Ezra 4:24). See also *Context* for Ezra 5:1 – 6:15.

vii. Zechariah
Zechariah worked together with Haggai to encourage the people
to rebuild the temple (Ezra 5:1; 6:14), which led to the dedication in
515 (Ezra 6:13–18), during the reign of Darius (Zech. 1:1, 7).
     Zechariah delivered his fasting sermon (Zech. 7 – 8) on
7 December 518, during the reign of Darius. The third part of the
book of Zechariah (Zech. 9 – 14) can be situated during the last
years of the reign of Darius and the first half of the reign of Xerxes,
in the gap between Ezra 6 and Ezra 7.
     Zechariah is also mentioned in Nehemiah 12:16. See also *Context*
for Ezra 5:1 – 6:15.

viii. Malachi
Malachi's activity can be situated about 430, in the time when
Nehemiah had gone back to the Persian court (Neh. 13:6), but

the promise to pay the tithes again had already been made (Neh. 10:37b–39a).

n. Ezra's Law

In Ezra 7:14 we read: *For you* [Ezra] *are sent by the king … to make enquiries about Judah and Jerusalem according to the Law of your God, which is in your hand.* Ezra had God's Law at his disposal and the king knew this. In other words, the Law existed already; Ezra did not need to write it (or to have it written).

We must speak, however, about the *Reichsautorisation* ('imperial authorization') theory, which has had a large impact on research about Ezra. It posits that (1) Artaxerxes elevated local legislation to the status of having imperial authority, and that (2) this would have urged Ezra to create a standard legislation for the Jewish community. He would have done so on the basis of documents at the disposal of priests and elders and so the Pentateuch was patched out.

Ska (2001) notices some flaws with the second aspect of this hypothesis: the Pentateuch is quite a long text (cf. Japhet 2016: 556: the book of Ezra-Neh. apparently knows the totality of the Pentateuch), with not only juridical aspects but even elements that might predispose the Persians against it (Gen. 15:18; Deut. 17:14–20; contacts with foreign nations), is written in Hebrew (and not in Aramaic) and nowhere mentions the importance of the Persian government. Moreover, even the juridical parts of the Pentateuch are not legislation, but rather sapient principles 'providing a sense of justice and righteousness' (Shepherd 2009: 16; see *Meaning* for Neh. 9:1 – 10:39). Instruction and scribal authorship as found in the Pentateuch already existed earlier in the Ancient Near East (Kiel 2017: 326). As far as the first aspect is concerned, no basis can be found for the surmised central archive with general validity, and in its strictest form the theory implies creating contradicting laws (Wiesehöfer 2008: 199–202).

Of course, this does not exclude the existence in Ezra's day of other biblical books (Ezra 1:1; elsewhere references are made to many other traditions,[20] but these references cannot prove that

---

20 See 2m, 'Other Bible passages about the same period'.

the *books* existed already). But apparently the Jewish 'law' (and other local legislation) obtained a certain status in Artaxerxes' day (Wiesehöfer 2008: 200–201).

Here we need to examine the terms and concepts in the different languages and cultures involved. The Aramaic word behind the translation 'law' in Ezra 7:12, 14, 21, 25, 26 is *dāt*. When we keep in mind that the word *tôrâ* is not used in Aramaic,[21] this choice is not strange: the Old Persian word *dāta* means 'what has been set down'[22] (Kiel 2017: 325; a merger with 'what has been given' cannot be excluded: Tuplin 2015: 73). For the Persians of Ezra's day, their law/religion had been set down by the god Ahura Mazda, as revealed through Zarathustra (Kiel 2017: 338, 343–344), and led to benevolent justice, so that the one who respected it and worshipped Ahura Mazda 'becomes both happy during life and blessed after death' (Xerxes, Persepolis Text h ll.54–56).[23] Recognizing parallels between Iranian religion and the Jewish one (Kiel 2017: 327), King Artaxerxes had parallel ideas about Ezra's law/religion. This means that the Jewish law was not considered as Persian imperial law, and in that way did not need to be written in Ezra's day in order to be Persia-proof. Even though the Persians sustained local codification, at least in Egypt and perhaps in Anatolia (Tuplin 2015: 85–86, 102–104; Kiel 2017: 324–325; Lippert 2017: 78–79, 84–87), this does not *prove* the *Reichsautorisation* theory in its strictest form (Tuplin 2015: 84). What might have been an innovation for the Jewish community was the idea that the Pentateuch was a formal unity (Kiel 2017: 323, 325, 327–329) – and so here can be found the origin of the preponderance of the Pentateuch in Jewish thinking – but this idea might have existed earlier too.

This new term, *dāt*, had a disadvantage: it was easily (and correctly) understood as 'law' (which in Greek was rendered by *nomos*, so in the New Testament) and through this translation the aspect of

---

21   In the third-century legal document from Egypt, edited by Cowley 1923: no. 82 l. 10, a homonym must be meant.

22   Cf. the etymology of English 'law' and German *Gesetz*.

23   My translation; the Old Persian reads: 'hauv utā jīva šiyāta bavatiy utā marta artāvā bavatiy'(Kent 1953: 151).

'instruction', the proper meaning of *tôrâ*, was not visible any more. This created the risk that the Torah was no longer considered as the base for teaching how to live and believe, but only as a list of rules (Becker 2015: 623). This risk, however, always existed and was not a necessary consequence of this change. Besides, the handling of the 'law' as providing principles ('cases of justice'; von Soden 1994: 131) applies to the Code of Hammurabi too (Lorein 2011a: 74–75; Tuplin 2015: 91). On the other hand, in a pluralistic society (be it in the Roman Empire or in our own day), positive law has its advantages, because it leaves the judge less room for a free interpretation (Lorein 2011a: 76). The use of *lex* in Latin Bible translations and theology was quite specific, as this word used to refer to a specific law ('statute'), but the word that normally was used to group all specific laws, namely *ius*, meant also 'right' and so in any case could not be used as equivalent to 'Torah'.

o. Some historical subjects treated in the commentary
Below is an overview of some specific historical subjects for which one might expect an explanation in this introduction but which receive some elucidation at the appropriate place in the commentary.

i. Zerubbabel
See on Ezra 2:2.

ii. Musical instruments
For the clarion (trumpet) and the cymbals, see on Ezra 3:10. For the harp and the lyre, see on Nehemiah 12:27.

iii. Parallels in ancient history
See on Ezra 3:12; *Context* for Nehemiah 3:1–22; Nehemiah 7:3; *Meaning* for Nehemiah 7:4–5; *Meaning* for Nehemiah 9:1 – 10:39; Nehemiah 12:27–29.

iv. Udjahorresnet
See on Nehemiah 13:31b.

3. Authorship

a. *Components and redaction*

Although we are unable to dissect the text exactly, we can observe three components in Ezra-Neh.: Ezra's files, Nehemiah's files and redactional material. Ezra's and Nehemiah's files both consisted of official documents and personal memoirs (with reference to Ezra or Nehemiah using 'I', the first-person singular pronoun). Nehemiah's memoirs are marked by a specific language register, probably influenced by the knowledge of other languages than Hebrew.

The possibility that the final redaction was done by Ezra is ruled out by the fact that some lists (cf. Neh. 11:22; 12:11) continue up to the early years of the fourth century, which for him would suppose an age of 110 years. Even though Klement (2011: 67) rightly observes that for the text of Nehemiah 12:11 Jaddua must have been alive to have been mentioned in this list but not necessarily already functioning as a high priest, it would be strange to mention him before it was certain that he would become the new high priest. On the other hand, Nehemiah would have been 'only' ninety years old (or even eighty, if Bickerman 1978: 24 is right)[24] and in 2 Maccabees 2:13 he is mentioned as responsible for collecting what could be considered to be the complete canon of the Old Testament. That makes him a candidate for the redaction of Ezra-Neh. This would involve the insertion of the different sources (memoirs and documents) in a historical overview, not only for Ezra 7 – Neh. 13, but also for Ezra 1 – 6.

Even though it is not necessary to think of Nehemiah as the final redactor, the redaction must have taken place in the same period.

b. *One book or two?*

But perhaps we proceeded too quickly in the previous paragraph and the question should have been raised about the relation between

---

24 Once people had passed the age of children's diseases, they could become very old in well-to-do circles. See on Ezra 3:12, n. 36.

the book of Ezra and the book of Nehemiah. Or should we simply speak about the book Ezra-Neh.? We shall consider internal and external arguments.

i. Internal arguments

In the first place we mention common structural elements: the Persian Empire as background, the importance of the temple, walls and community and their advancement, some key terms such as 'go up' (*'ālâ*) and 'build' (*bānâ*). On the other hand, these elements can be considered as obviously used in two books with kindred subject matters, without any interdependence.

Ezra would have a priestly perspective, Nehemiah a lay perspective. That is correct, but it describes the persons, not the books.

Double use of the same list in Ezra 2 and Nehemiah 7 can be seen as an indication that we have to do with two books (Reinmuth 2002: 13). For an approach that explains the presence of the list in two places, see *Context* for Nehemiah 7:6–73a.

It is correct to observe that Haggai is mentioned in Ezra (5:1; 6:14), not in Nehemiah, but that is limited to the first part of Ezra, that is, at the place where Haggai chronologically can be expected.

Both Ezra 6:14 and Nehemiah 12:47 give a larger context, but that does not prove that they belong to one single book.

The intention of Ezra 7:10, 25 is realized in Nehemiah 8:1–8, which unites the two books (Steinberg 2004: 172).

For the idea 'to gather', Ezra 7:28; 8:15; 10:1, 7, 9 uses the Hebrew *qābaṣ*, while in Nehemiah 8:1, 13; 9:1 the word *'āsaf* is used.[25] An indication of two different books, or mere coincidence?

The prayers of Ezra 9 and Nehemiah 9 can easily be compared. Does this imply that we have to do with kinds of doublets in two different Bible books, or do they point to consistency in theology? Another obvious comparison would be with Daniel 9, but nobody proposes grouping these three texts into one Bible book.

Ezra 9:9 joins the second part of Ezra with its first part (Duggan 2006: 177), but that is in any case within the same book.

---

25   The situation is a little bit more complicated: except in the memoir texts ('I') in Ezra 7:28; 8:15, the Niphal is always used for both verbs.

The recurring subject of relationships with foreign wives in Ezra 9 – 10, Nehemiah 10:30 and Nehemiah 13:23–29 can be explained in different ways, but the fact that the matter is treated twice in the book of Nehemiah, on different occasions, proves that the occurrence may just follow the flow of history.

The fact that the relationship between Ezra 10 and Nehemiah 1 is not explained does not make things easy (see 2j, 'Relationship between Ezra and Nehemiah'), but the transition between Ezra 6 and Ezra 7 is not any clearer.

Nehemiah 1:1 clearly indicates a break, but Proverbs 30 and Proverbs 31 start with the same construction ('The words of . . .') and no-one considers Proverbs 30 and Proverbs 31 as separated books.

In Nehemiah, only 6:6–7 quotes an official document, while in Ezra many documents are quoted, not only cited. If Nehemiah was the final redactor, this may be explained by his relative distance from the documents: what he had seen himself he did not deem necessary to quote (cf. Steinberg 2004: 171).

Schnittjer (2016: 36–37) points to a common redactional style (maximal use of sources, minimal editing) as an argument that it is one single book.

For Becking (2018: 3–7), these arguments lead to the conclusion that we have two books, in the first place Nehemiah, quite reliable, and in the second place Ezra, with Ezra 7 – 10 as a fictional prequel and Ezra 1 – 6 as a largely fictional prequel to Ezra 7 – 10.

These internal elements do not lead to an inevitable conclusion.

ii. External arguments

When we go to the different editions of the Hebrew text, the reworkings and the translations, we must keep in mind the basic question of whether these can say anything about the original situation.

First Esdras (or 3 Ezra) is a reworking of 2 Chronicles 35 – 36; Ezra; Nehemiah 7:73b – 8:12. This can be seen, however, rather as an argument for the unity of Chronicles and Ezra-Neh. (see 3c, 'Relationship between Ezra-Neh. and Chronicles', and 4e, 'Translations').

Josephus, *Contra Apionem* 1.40, does not mention individual books, but the number of books within each category is too limited to consider Ezra and Nehemiah as separate books.

No Targum (Aramaic translation) of Ezra-Neh. exists. Of course, Ezra was not translated into Aramaic because it partly was written in Aramaic, and the fact that Nehemiah was not translated either proves that they formed one single book in the minds of those responsible for the Targum (cf. Dan., for which a Targum does not exist either).

Iulius Africanus referred in his *Chronographiae*, the first Christian world history (AD 221), to Nehemiah's request to the king (Neh. 2:1–9) with 'as we read in Ezra's book'.[26] The same occurred in Jewish sources (Ron 2020: 157).

The canon lists mentioned by Eusebius (*Historia ecclesiastica* 4.25–26) both suppose one single book for the Hebrew, although Origen himself apparently knew them as two books.

Jerome wrote only one single Prologue for the twenty-three chapters of Ezra-Neh., with the explicit mention that for the Hebrews Ezra and Nehemiah are contained in one single volume. Nevertheless, the break between Ezra and Nehemiah is indicated in the main medieval Latin manuscript, the Codex Amiatinus (from AD 716; Lorein 2014: 129), but without passing to a new page (Codex Amiatinus 738v). The official Roman Catholic edition of the Vulgate (AD 1592; Lorein 2014: 134) has at Nehemiah 1:1 'The book of Nehemiah that is also called the second of Ezra',[27] but that represents the insights of its day, not Jerome's interpretation (contra Steinmann 2010: 13).

The oldest manuscripts of the LXX put the twenty-three chapters together (Janz 2010: 31, 33–34).

The manuscripts of the Syriac translation (Peshitta) have a colophon only at the end of Nehemiah, with the mention that the book of Ezra the scribe ends there (Balzaretti 2013: 14).

The Babylonian Talmud (Sanhedrin 93b) mentions Nehemiah as main author but says that the book of Nehemiah was for a long time integrated in the book of Ezra because Nehemiah boasted

---

26 Quoted by Jerome, in his commentary on Dan. 9:24 (2.162–163). My translation; the Latin reads: 'sicut in Ezrae libro legimus'.

27 My translation; the Latin reads: 'Liber Nehemiae qui et Esdrae secundus dicitur.'

about his deeds (which must be denied: see 2i, 'Nehemiah'). Baba
Batra 14b leaves no doubt: one single book.

The Masoretes counted Nehemiah 3:22 as the middle verse and
mentioned the number of verses only at the end of Nehemiah. This
makes clear that they considered Ezra-Neh. as one single book.

The First Rabbinic Bible (1517) has them as one book, but the
Second (1525), which led to the *Textus Receptus*, the basic Hebrew
edition for centuries, splits it up under Christian influence (van Nes
and van Staalduine-Sulman 2014: 201–202).

iii. Conclusion

Even though there are no compulsory internal elements, historically
the two books were mostly grouped together, perhaps because the
unity, as demonstrated in the Analysis (see pp. 59–61), was observed
with some variation by most readers. This structure, indeed, reckons
with an overall unity as well as with different parts. The split might
have occurred to maintain the number of Esdras books mentioned
in the lists of the LXX, after having left 1 Esdras behind, perhaps
under the influence of Isidore of Seville (Bogaert 2000: 13, 22–23;
Balzaretti 2013: 16).

c. Relationship between Ezra-Neh. and Chronicles

In 1832, Leopold Zunz proposed the thesis that Chronicles and
Ezra-Neh. were redacted by one and the same person and together
formed the Chronicler's history. This viewpoint determined
research about and commentaries on Ezra-Neh. during most of
the twentieth century. It may be clear that Ezra-Neh. stands nearer
to Chronicles than to the book(s)[28] of Kings, on a linguistic level
as well as for attention given to typical aspects. But the setting
in the same period can well lead to common features without
necessarily leading to one single redactor. Research by S. Japhet
(1968) and H. G. M. Williamson (1977) highlighted the differences
between Chronicles and Ezra-Neh. and their proposal met with
large agreement (Bänziger 2023: 1182).

---

28 Only for practical reasons was the book of Kings written on two
    different scrolls: a still larger scroll would have been impracticable.

Nevertheless, since both Ezra 1:1–3a and 2 Chronicles 36:22–23 contain the edict for return, there is an obvious relationship, but in which direction? Both options are defended. Probably the Chronicler ended his writings in order to make this ending at the same time a transition. But this overlap would not have been necessary if Chronicles and Ezra-Neh. were a single work (Kidner 1979: 137).

Jerome put Ezra-Neh. between Chronicles and Esther; this order is also found in most manuscripts depending on the Carolingian/Alcuinian renaissance. In the Codex Amiatinus, however, we find Ezra-Neh. between Esther and 1 and 2 Maccabees (in other words, as the last 'canonical' book, just as in the Hebrew Codex Leningradensis). The Paris Bibles have 'our' order (but of course including the deuterocanonical writings; Lorein 2014: 137–138).

4. Languages, text and canon

a. Languages
Most of Ezra-Neh. is written in Hebrew. Because of the quoted documents, Ezra 4:8 – 6:18 and 7:12–26 are written in Aramaic.

i. Hebrew
Even though in the classification Archaic, Classical or Late Biblical Hebrew the existence (or definition) of the first category must be doubted, it is clear that the Hebrew of Ezra-Neh. belongs to the category of Late Biblical Hebrew. This has implications mainly for verbal categories, where some rules are less strict. This can lead to less clear situations, but it is not really problematic in Ezra-Neh. (cf. Neh. 2:3, 18; Polak 2006: 614–615; Fassberg 2016: 11–12). Other peculiarities are interesting for students of Hebrew but do not influence interpretation or translation.

ii. Aramaic
Aramaic is related to Hebrew. It started as the language of the Arameans in the interior of Syria but launched its international career because it used an alphabet instead of the extremely complicated system of cuneiform Akkadian. The alphabet system is the same for both Aramaic and Hebrew and the form eventually became the same too. Use of Aramaic continued in the Persian

period (although the Persian writing system – though not really alphabetical – was much easier than cuneiform Akkadian) and it was the language used for official communication between the central government and different parts of the empire. In the Bible, other than a few words in Genesis and Jeremiah, some parts of Ezra and almost six chapters of Daniel were written in this language. Through its international status it also became a common language for Jews up to and through the Middle Ages.

Even though most Old Testament scholars are less equipped for Aramaic than for Hebrew, Aramaic is not a badly documented, studied or understood language. In that sense, Ezra-Neh. being partly written in Aramaic is not a problematic issue.

For the language of the documents, see 2g, 'The documents'.

b. Establishing the text

The text is barely present at Qumran: 4QEzra (the Ezra manuscript found in the fourth cave discovered at Qumran; technically 4Q117) has only Ezra 4:2–6, 9–11 (the first passage in Hebrew, the second in Aramaic; both passages very fragmentary) and 5:17 – 6:5 (also Aramaic; also fragmentary, but less so; the differences with the Masoretic text consist of grammatical variants). An expression of Ezra 9:14 is recycled in the Community Rule (1QS IV, 13–14), confirming that the book was known at Qumran. The so-called XQNeh is a forgery.[29] Is such a limited presence normal for this category of Bible books? The Qumran Community indeed gave most attention to the Pentateuch, Psalms, Isaiah and the Minor Prophets, not to historical texts (see Washburn 2002).

In the great medieval standard edition, the Aleppo Codex, Ezra-Neh. did not survive the 1947 riots (Würthwein 1973: 39).

The Codex Leningradensis (AD 1008) is complete and thus presents also Ezra-Neh., as the last book of the Writings, after the book of Daniel (Marcus 2006: 5*).

---

29 See 'Museum of the Bible: Dead Sea Scroll Collection – Scientific Research and Analysis', Final Report 2019, <https://d2f7x7uhr2xem7. cloudfront.net/sixteen_by_nine/MOTB-DSS-Report-FINAL-web. pdf>.

Of course, some text-critical issues do exist, but generally the text is not problematic. Where the Hebrew manuscripts do not help, assistance is sought in the versions (see 4e, 'Translations').

In order to facilitate consultation of and reference to the biblical text, it has been divided into chapters and verses. While the verses as such were clearly delineated by the Masoretes, the chapter division was introduced by Stephan Langton at the beginning of the thirteenth century. This made it possible to number also the verses, a system that found its application in the sixteenth century (Lorein 2014: 138). Unfortunately, the chapter division was not perfect and this has produced some problems, for example with the strange verse Nehemiah 7:73.[30] English versions never change this at 8:1, but differ in putting verse 73b together with Nehemiah 7 or with Nehemiah 8. Another problem turns up at Nehemiah 9:38, which could be better considered as 10:1, but in all English versions occurs as 9:38. For those who work with sources other than those written in English, the presentation in Table I.2 might be helpful.

ESV	7:73a	7:73b	8:1–18	9:38	10:1–39
Vulgate[31]	7:73	8:1a	8:1b–18	9:38	10:1–39
Hebrew[32]	7:72a	7:72b	8:1–18	10:1	10:2–40
Dutch HSV	7:73	8:1	8:2–19	9:38	10:1–39

Table I.2: Versification differences in Nehemiah across the versions

c. Replacing Nehemiah 8?
Some exegetes assume that a deviation of an ordinary chronological sequence has very often occurred and rearrange entire books. According to several authors (e.g. Williamson 1985: 127,

---

30   This verse is numbered 73 only when Ezra 2:66 is transferred to the list of Neh. 7 as Neh. 7:68, although without basis for this in the transmitted Hebrew text.

31   Normally presenting the most original chapter division and verse numbering.

32   BHQ; also Dutch NBV21, French Segond 21, German Zürcher.

308–310; vom Orde 1997: 128, 230–231), the confession of the officials in Ezra 9 occurred because of the acceptance of the Law in Nehemiah 8 (for different results of this rearrangement, see Brown 2005b: 180). Indeed, a thematic (instead of chronological) arrangement is possible,[33] but then some indication for that device must be found, which is missing here. If we regroup the chapters in Ezra's first period of activity, we must apply an amputation in Nehemiah 8:10 (Nehemiah could not be active there); if we regroup the chapters in Nehemiah's period of activity, it is strange that the question of Ezra 9:1 (rather societal than theological) is asked to Ezra, not to Nehemiah. It must be observed also that Nehemiah 8 does not say that it describes Ezra's first reading of the Law (Bänziger 2014: 53–54) and/or that the Law had never been read before (Brown 2005b: 181). Moreover, such a rearrangement is never found either in Hebrew manuscripts or in the ancient versions (Brown 2005b: 182). In short, there is no need to rearrange (e.g. because of historical impossibilities) and neither is there reason to do so (e.g. by a mention of changing chronological perspective).

d. Canonicity
i. From inspiration to canon
We have an established text (see 4b, 'Establishing the text'). In which sense is this text 'canonical'? To arrive at this point, we must start with the fundamental confession that God exists and has revealed himself. This revelation did not immediately and not necessarily lead to a written expression, but writing did exist from the earliest times.[34] Even though writing cannot represent every aspect of spoken language, the two go together: the written form preserves the spoken word, the spoken word actualizes the written

---

33 A rearrangement does appear in Ezra 4 (see there), but then indications are available. See e.g. Ezra 4:6–23, where the mention of the kings' names in vv. 6 and 7 and the use of 'Then' in v. 24 make it clear that this section is a digression.

34 For a defence of a very early date, see Wiseman 1977: 24–25, 56–57.

word.[35] Writing is not secondary in the sense of being less important:
God himself has written (Exod. 34:1) and we may trust that in Scripture this has happened in a sufficient way (van der Kooij 1998: 38;
Reiterer 2013: 132–133). Does this mean that biblical authors knew
at the moment of writing that they were writing canonical lines? We
may trust that such an author was aware of a special state of inspiration, but it is more complicated than that: the final redaction of a
Bible book is rarely done by the main person of the book, and it is
only from that point that we can really speak about a 'text' (Wegner
2013: 462). These texts, started by people with divine inspiration
and finalized in book form, were considered to be canonical and
were reliably deposited in the temple (the first components in the
tabernacle: Deut. 17:18; 31:24–26) (van der Woude 1992: 162; van der
Kooij 1998: 34–35, 37; Reiterer 2013: 132, 142). After the destruction
of the temple in AD 70 systems for preserving the exact wording
became more important, because the original context disappeared
and the text had to remain unaltered in a foreign environment.[36]

The recognition of inspired writings did not continue for ever. At
a certain moment it stopped. Zechariah 13:2–6 predicts the cessation
of prophecy, albeit without mentioning a specific point in time.
The deuterocanonical literature considered the Old Testament as a
whole (Reiterer 2013: 142–143). The Qumran Community Rule (1QS
IX, 11) confirmed in 105 BC that no prophet was recognized.[37] The

---

35 Millard 2012: 887: 'Ancient ... texts ... were written in order to be read,
    sooner or later, and reading was done aloud.' Cf. Phoebe's role in
    transmitting Paul's letter to the Romans (Chapple 2011).
36 In the same way, Roman law fixes the rules, differently from Ancient
    Near Eastern law that transmits the principles.
37 The Teacher of Righteousness possessed divinely inspired insights into
    the old prophecies, but he did not utter new prophecies; the Qumran
    community recognized the ancient prophets and expected the
    imminent appearance of an eschatological prophet (Pike 2017: 98, 112).
    This applies also to the larger group of the Essenes (Josephus, *Bellum
    judaicum* 2.159): because they have had a long training in studying the
    prophecies, they can say beforehand what will happen; i.e. they are not
    inspired on the spot. Josephus uses the word 'prophet' only for Bible

phenomenon of pseudepigraphical writings can also be considered
as a testimony to the cessation of inspiration (Gentry and Fountain
2017: 277). The idea of 'canonicity' is thus closely connected with
the 'closedness of the canon' (this overview is, of course, limited to
the Old Testament). In the Protestant vision, this is (at least partly)
defined by what was realized by Jerome shortly before AD 390: the
Hebraica veritas, implying not only that the *Hebrew* text is the true
basis for any study and translation, but also that only books acknow-
ledged by the *Jews* (written in Hebrew or Aramaic) could be part of
the canon (Kamesar 1993: 43, 46; Lorein 2014: 126, 135). Moreover,
it is written in our hearts (Jer. 31:33; see also the importance of
the Word in John 17, the chapter on Christian unity). The precise
wording is important for the tradition (Reiterer 2013: 131–133, 138–
139, 142, 161), but *applying* the revelation in our lives is essential.
All further guidance that we think to experience ought to have its
place within the framework of *sola Scriptura* (Courey 2015: 217–225).

ii. Canonical order
So we started with books for which inspiration was recognized
('canonical') and then it was realized that this was a well-defined
group of books ('canon'). At the start, all these books were written
on scrolls and were kept together in a basket with their labels. There
was no need to decide on a specific order until all the Bible books
were gathered in one single codex (cf. Neh. 8:5; Stordalen 2001:
136–137). From that moment on we find different orders, and every
order has its implications for the observed relationships between
the books, but no order seems to be canonical as such (Goswell
2018: 17–22, 25–31; Stordalen 2001: 137).
    In the typically Jewish order, Ezra-Neh. is put at the end. This
is a logical place, at the historical end of the canon and considering
the lack of liturgical connection with other parts of the canon –
the liturgical aspect is most important in the Jewish order (Ellis
1988: 686; Lust 2003: 40; Zenger 2003: 119–123). In the typically
Christian order Ezra-Neh. can be found among the historical

books (with the exception of John Hyrcanus, *Bellum judaicum* 1.68 and
Ant. 13.300) (Mason 2008: 128–129).

books, at the place where it could be expected chronologically, immediately following the Chronicles (Ezra 1:1–3a ‖ 2 Chr. 36:22–23!).

iii. Textual variants[38]

How then should we explain textual variants regarding the canonical text?

Tov (2020: 22–26) has recently offered some overviews with a scale of differences in relation to the Masoretic text. This leads to the conclusion that in 200 BC (the year the overviews start) a standard text existed and that only in the Qumran Community did the text start to vary. Reasons (not for Ezra-Neh., because this Bible book is very poorly represented at Qumran – see 4b, 'Establishing the text' – but in general) may be a lack of capabilities[39] in the Community and the fact that no need of exactitude was felt as long as the Teacher of Righteousness was at their side (van der Woude 1992: 168). This makes Qumran an interesting topic, but shows it is rather marginal, different from the situation at other places in the Judean desert, where a standard Bible text was used (van der Kooij 2012: 39–40). But even at Qumran a copyist could not do whatever he wanted, as corrections in manuscripts demonstrate.[40]

The supposed deviant text behind the LXX translation can indeed be considered helpful for solving problems occurring with the Hebrew (Aramaic) text. The possibility must always be considered, however, that no deviant text is hidden behind the translation, but that the translator, feeling himself responsible to his community for spiritual guidance, made an adaptation in order

---

38   This paragraph contains general observations. For specific observations concerning the text of Ezra-Neh., see 4b, 'Establishing the text', and 4e, 'Translations'.

39   Wegner 2013: 465 mentions also a lack of means during the exile as a possible reason for transmission errors. Of course, this does not apply to a post-exilic book such as Ezra-Neh.

40   G. J. Brooke, lecture, Colloquium Biblicum Lovaniense, 3 August 2022, Leuven.

to safeguard the (his) message of the text (van der Kooij 2016: 659–660, 662, 666) – a device that also can be found in modern translations (Wursten 2021: 59–60). We must also keep in mind that the Septuagint was the very first Bible translation enterprise in world history. So where in the first instance more difficult passages had been left out of the translation process (Eckstein 2018) and the translation took into account in a large measure the circumstances of the community for which the translation was made (van der Kooij 2015: 143–144), gradually the insight grew that a translation should be nearer to the original (rather than a sort of imperialism of the Masoretic text). This implies that it *might* be the case that the LXX suggests a better Hebrew text, but not necessarily so: (1) perhaps it was the LXX that had misread the text (and the LXX has to be corrected through the Hebrew text); (2) perhaps the specific translation style caused theological or linguistic differences; (3) for some Bible books apparently two different redactions of the same material have existed (we have already seen that the final redaction was rarely done by the protagonist), with a different length of text and a different order of the chapters (Jobes and Silva 2015: 161–162), in which case some will opt for the theory of 'equivalent variants', but the Christian church, or at least Jerome and the Reformation, has opted for the *Hebraica veritas*, the conviction that the Hebrew text was in any case the standard canonical text (Lorein 2023b: 58).

Perhaps we must consider a distinction between Bible manuscripts and citations: while Bible manuscripts should be faithful in form, the use of a Bible passage in a new text needs to be faithful in content and might be adapted to take its place in the flow of the new text (cf. Instone-Brewer 2010: 5, 13).

We are *not* speaking about variants that only present modernized orthography or even morphology: these were always allowed (Tov 2004: 25).

e. Translations
In the LXX, the translation of the canonical Ezra-Neh. is called 2 Esdras (Esdras B′); it is a careful and literal translation, to be dated to about 100 BC (Janz 2010: 76, 83, 163). Only in the lists of Nehemiah 11 – 12 do the translators give the impression of

becoming a bit tired. The LXX contains also 1 Esdras (Esdras A'), which cannot be called a translation (see 4f, 'The afterlife of Ezra-Neh. in Antiquity').[41]

Bible books partly written in Aramaic (Ezra 4:6 – 6:18; 7:12–26!) have no Targum (Aramaic explaining translation). This applies to Ezra-Neh. as well as to the book of Daniel.

The Old Latin translation (Vetus Latina) was already a rather faithful representation of the original text, even though it was based on the Greek version (Bogaert 2000: 17; Marcus 2006: 11*).

For Ezra-Neh., as always elsewhere in the Vulgate, Jerome made an excellent translation in 394, not only from Hebrew, but also from Aramaic (Lorein 2014: 126).

The Syriac translation (Peshitta) is, according to Marcus (2006: 12*), 'essentially a literal translation', but Balzaretti (2013: 71–75, 307, 345) says that at many points the translation gives an easier version of the facts, and even posits that everywhere in the book of Nehemiah the person of Ezra is seen as the protagonist, with almost a complete erasure of Nehemiah – a quite important intervention, we might say.

f. The afterlife of Ezra-Neh. in Antiquity[42]
i. Writings named after Ezra
Not only are some verses barely found at Qumran, but no other writings influenced by Ezra-Neh. are there either, probably also because of a dominant interest in eschatological matters based on texts written by prophets[43] (Vriezen and van der Woude 2005: 667; Xeravits and Porzig 2015: 113). Ezra-Neh. shares this destiny with the book of Esther, since 4Q550 is no longer considered parts of a variant of the canonical book (Xeravits and Porzig 2015: 248–250; Lorein 2023a: 1169).

---

41   The B and the A serve as numerals in Greek.

42   I thank the Oudtestamentisch Werkgezelschap for having commented on a presentation of this section during the session at Groningen, 4 October 2022.

43   Not only Isaiah, Jeremiah, Ezekiel and the Twelve Minor Prophets, but also Moses, David and Daniel.

The fact that we barely meet Ezra-Neh. at Qumran or in the Targum does not mean that in Antiquity no attention to this book, or rather to the figure of Ezra, was paid.[44]

First, besides a translation of the canonical Ezra-Neh., the LXX also offers 1 Esdras. This book is a compilation of 2 Chronicles 35:1–19; its own material in 1 Esdras 1:21–22 (Josiah's piety); 2 Chronicles 35:20 – 36:21; Ezra 1:1–11; 4:7–24; its own material in 1 Esdras 3:1 – 5:6 (wisdom contest of the bodyguards, won by Zerubbabel); Ezra 2:1 – 4:5; 5:1 – 10:44; and Neh. 7:73b – 8:12. The material is rearranged around the wisdom contest (1 Esdras 3 – 4), concentrating destruction, return and reconstruction in one tight line in order to highlight Ezra as high priest (although he is never seen as such in the canonical writings), probably in this way legitimizing the hegemony of the high priest at the time of writing, somewhere in the second half of the second century BC (Japhet 2011). In this way, Nehemiah disappears from his normal position and becomes contemporary with Zerubbabel. This creates, of course, chronological and identification problems which will continue during Antiquity, although they apparently did not hinder the author. In spite of some critical comments, we have the complete text of 1 Esdras. The first verse as we know it is also originally the first verse, because a hypothetical earlier verse cannot have contained what is found in 2 Chronicles 34, as reference is made to this chapter in other ways (1 Esdras 1:21 – 22, 31) and as starting with 'And' is possible in Septuagint Greek (van der Kooij 1991b: 240, 249–251). The end of the book is clean on the condition that it is translated as 'to rejoice greatly because they were inspired by the words in which they had been taught and were all together', ending the sentence with a full stop exactly at that point. The hypothesis that 1 Esdras was originally longer than the text we now have cannot be sustained by a reference to Flavius Josephus, because he knew not only 1 Esdras, but also Ezra-Neh. and in that way was not representing just 1 Esdras (van der Kooij 1991a: 41, 44–47). In spite of its problems, the book was appreciated in Christian circles (partly because knowledge of chronology was almost absent in

---

44 As said earlier, Nehemiah suffered a bad reputation, even though wrongly so (2i, 'Nehemiah') – see Heb. 6:10.

Antiquity – here too, Jerome is the blissful exception). Augustine (*De civitate Dei* 18.36), for example,[45] begins by placing Esdras on the same level as the book of Esther, being more historical than prophetical, but then remarks that perhaps the author of Esdras has prophesied about Christ in the wisdom contest of the bodyguards, because he has said that truth is victor above everything (1 Esdras 3:12; 4:35, 38, 41), while we know when we read the gospel (John 14:6) that Christ is the truth.[46] The book of 1 Esdras did not figure in early medieval Bibles, but it was a standard part – for an unknown reason – of the Paris Bibles, whose arrangement had the largest influence on the earliest printed Bibles, in the Old Latin translation (Jerome had not made a translation for the Vulgate, as he did not consider 1 Esdras to be canonical; Gesche 2014: 403). Finally, the Council of Trent moved it to the Appendix of the Apocrypha (Gesche 2016: 119–128). In Orthodox churches it is canonical, as it is found in Septuagint manuscripts (Bird 2012: 27).

At the end of the first century AD, the apocalyptic book of 4 Ezra was written, or at least 4 Ezra 3 – 14, in reaction to the loss of the temple (Becking 2018: 12). Ezra is described as reporting three dialogues and four visions about suffering and the end times. The revelation is situated in the year 557 BC (4 Ezra 3:1), which is problematic because Ezra was born only in 500 BC (see 2h, 'Ezra'). Ezra is said to have dictated again all the canonical books (i.e. also Ezra-Neh.!), because they had been burnt (4 Ezra 14:21–46), and also seventy books that had to be hidden (in Greek *apokrufa*: apocryphal books). It is a witness to the path from Pharisaism to Rabbinic Judaism (without having arrived there yet; Deines 2001: 488), just as are the Targums, but in a completely different style.

Because 4 Ezra 1 – 2 and 4 Ezra 15 – 16 are two Christian additions from, respectively, the mid and the late third century

---

45   For further references, see Myers 1974: 17–18.

46   Compare, however, 1 Esdras 4:40 ('To her [= truth] belongs the strength, the kingdom, the authority and the majesty of all ages'; my translation) with Matt. 6:13 (Majority Text: 'For yours [= the Father's] is the kingdom and the power and the glory, for ever').

AD (Bergren 2013: 473, 488), they are more correctly called 5 Ezra and 6 Ezra, although in '6 Ezra' Ezra is not even mentioned (but the subject matter is the same as in 4 Ezra and the manuscripts do combine the texts; Denis 1970: 93–94; Bergren 2013: 468; deSilva 2018: 384–389). The book was largely cited in Christian works (Bergren 2013: 474–475, 487) but was never considered canonical.

It will be clear by now that the numbering of the different Ezra books is rather complicated and depends on the language tradition in which they are situated (Bogaert 2000). Most important is that in Latin manuscripts the canonical book of Ezra is called 1 Ezra while the canonical book of Nehemiah is called 2 Ezra, and that in Greek manuscripts the whole of the canonical Ezra-Neh. is called 2 Esdras (see Table I.3).[47]

Hebr./Aram.	Greek	Latin[48]	description
Ezra	2 Esdras 1 – 10	1 Ezra	canonical (Ezra)
Neh.	2 Esdras 11 – 23	2 Ezra	canonical (Neh.)
	1 Esdras	3 Ezra	'rewritten Bible'
		4 Ezra	apocalyptic
		5 Ezra	Christian (4 Ezra 1 – 2)
		6 Ezra	Christian (4 Ezra 15 – 16)

Table I.3: Overview of writings named after Ezra books in
different traditions

The Greek Apocalypse of Esdras, also an apocalyptic work – as the title indicates – is about creation, sin and the end times

---

47 Unfortunately, still more numberings do exist (Bogaert 2000: 22; Gesche 2016: 129).

48 To be precise: in the Paris editions, which are the basis for the arrangement in 'our' Bibles (Bogaert 2000: 5; Lorein 2014: 130–131). Earlier Vulgate manuscripts had only one book, as Jerome wanted it (Bogaert 2000: 9–11, 22).

(Oegema 2001: 52). It contains a debate between Ezra and God
about judgment (1:1 – 4:4), a description of hell (4:5 – 6:2) and Ezra's
refusal to die (6:3 – 7:4) (Wahl 1977: 4). The book is difficult to
situate in time and in intellectual background, but a Jewish basis
would have been completed by Christian additions (Wahl 1977:
5–7). Oegema (2001: 50) dates it between the second and fourth
centuries.

The Vision of Ezra survives in Latin and would have been
written in Greek in the second half of the fourth century AD. Its
complete text has become available only quite recently, that is to say,
in 1984 (Bogaert 1984: 50, 52; Bauckham 2013: 508, 510). The visions
describe hell and paradise (Bauckham 2013: 502–505). Despite the
Jewish elements, it is a Christian text (Bogaert 1984: 58).

The Questions of Ezra survived only in Armenian, which makes
a study of this text less obvious. It is a dialogue between Ezra and
the angel of the Lord about the blessing of the righteous and the
punishment of the sinners, with an ascent to heaven. It was probably
written in the train of 4 Ezra, but a more precise date cannot be
given (Leonhardt-Balzer 2005: 7).

The Revelation of Ezra consists of seven (long) verses in Latin
and supposes that a relationship exists between the general quality
of a year and the day of the week on which 1 January comes. It is
clearly Christian: the first day of the week is 'the Lord's Day'. A date
for this writing cannot be given (Fiensy 1983: 601).

From 5 Ezra on, Ezra is presented as a prophet. Steinmann
rightly remarks that these writings, by putting Ezra in the mould
of a prophet, miss the point that '*Ezra is a man of the written revelation of God*', not a prophet (Steinmann 2010: 118; italics original).
Deines (2013: 303) goes in the same direction: 'Ezra's authority
and power … is based on his expertise in the law but no longer
on an intimate knowledge of God or a revelation given to him by
God.'

ii. Other writings in Antiquity referring to Ezra and/or Nehemiah
Ezra and Nehemiah are also mentioned in writings not named
after either of them. The first instance is Sirach 49:13 (written
around 190–180 BC; Lorein 2022: 35), in the 'Praise of the Fathers',
where Nehemiah receives the honour he deserves: 'and also a large

memorial for Nehemiah, who raised for us the fallen walls, set up
gates and bars and raised up our premises' (my translation). In the
two previous verses Zerubbabel and Jeshua (see Ezra 2:2; 3:2, 8;
4:2–3; 5:2; 6:7) are praised. The question is often asked why Ezra is
not mentioned here. Perhaps because Sirach was also hoping for
political reform (Kellermann 1967: 114–115), or because he was not
a builder (as Zerubbabel and Jeshua were; so Begg 1988: 17–18), but
we must keep in mind that in the Praise of the Fathers a selection
was necessary in any case.

Possibly Ezra or Nehemiah is alluded to in the image of the three
returning sheep in 1 Enoch 89:72–73, but that is hypothetical, due
to the allegorical character of this 'Animal Apocalypse' (1 Enoch
85–90; to be dated between 167 and 161 BC: Donaldson 2007: 86–87).
Kellermann (1967: 134) opts for Nehemiah, because he thinks it is
directed against the Samarians, and Ezra had not been engaged in
the battle against the Samarians.

Nehemiah is mentioned again in 2 Maccabees 1:18–36 (dated
to 124 BC; Lorein 2016: 322). It contains a prayer ascribed to
Nehemiah and Jonathan upon the reinstalment of sacrifices at
the temple after the Babylonian exile. This is problematic, because
the offerings had already begun in 537 (Ezra 3:6), the temple was
already dedicated in 515 (Ezra 6:16), Nehemiah arrived in Jerusalem only in 445 (Neh. 2:11) and Jonathan was never high priest.
Probably the author of 2 Maccabees mixed up in the first place the
great Nehemiah with a namesake mentioned in Ezra 2:2 (and in
the parallel Neh. 7:7)[49] and in the second place Johanan, high priest
from 425 to 390, mentioned in Nehemiah 12:22, with Jonathan
(who was never a high priest) mentioned in Nehemiah 12:11 and
Jonathan, high priest from 153 to 143, shortly before the redaction
of 2 Maccabees.

Can the text of 2 Maccabees 2:13–14 ('These things were
narrated also in the archives and the memoirs of Nehemiah; as
well as how he founded a library and collected the books about the

---

49 Bévenot (1931: 173–174) mentions the possibility of a new purification
    by Nehemiah, but admits that most probably it was in the first place
    about Ezra.

kings and the prophets, and those of David, and letters of kings
about sacred objects'[50]) be interpreted as referring to Nehemiah
who was not only responsible for the redaction of Ezra-Neh., but
who – the Pentateuch already existing – gathered all the books
of the Old Testament (Ziegert 2023: 105–106; van der Kooij 2012:
32–36)?

Another apocalyptic summary of the events from Moses until
the Herods can be found in chapters 2–6 of the Assumption (or
Testament) of Moses, to be dated shortly after AD 6 (Lorein 2003:
135). Since Charles (1913: 417), Daniel is usually supposed to be
the person described as follows: 'the one who is above them will
enter, and he will stretch forth his hands and kneel upon his knees
and pray for them' (4:1; my translation), but Ezra seems to be a
candidate too (cf. Neh. 8:5; Tromp 1993: 175–176; Bergren 1998:
344).

The Hellenistic Jewish philosopher Philo (20 BC – AD 50) does
not mention Ezra or Nehemiah at all. Was this because their story
was too far removed from Egyptian reality and allegorization
was not possible either? The absence of Nehemiah and the rise
of Ezra in post-70 Judaism is also explained by opposition to the
political example of Nehemiah and the need for teaching the Torah
(Kellermann 1967: 146), but that does not explain everything.

Zerubbabel is mentioned in Matthew 1:12 and Luke 3:27, but
without allusion to what is described in Ezra-Neh. There is indeed
a parallel to Ezra 6:10 in 1 Timothy 2:2; to Nehemiah 9:6 in Acts
4:24 and Revelation 10:6; and to Nehemiah 9:26 in Matthew 21:35
and Acts 7:52; but always without necessarily having a relationship
with Ezra-Neh. This is, finally, a poor harvest, especially if we think
of the opportunities of Acts 7 and Hebrews 11.

Flavius Josephus (AD 37–100) retells the story of Ezra-Neh.
in his *Jewish Antiquities* 11.1–183 (AD 94). In general, Josephus

---

50 My translation; the Greek reads: 'Exègounto de kai en tais anagrafais
kai en tois hupomnèmatismois tois kata ton Neemian ta auta kai
hôs kataballomenos bibliothèkèn episunègagen ta peri tôn basileôn
biblia kai profètôn kai ta tou David kai epistolas basileôn peri
anathematôn.'

abbreviates. The value of the details not found also in Scripture and his use of 1 Esdras are difficult to determine; perhaps he was seduced by the better Greek of 1 Esdras (Vriezen and van der Woude 2005: 519), but this has not improved the historical accuracy of Josephus' *Jewish Antiquities* (11.159, 168, 179), situating Nehemiah wrongly in Xerxes' days. *Against Apion* 1.40, however, makes it clear that Josephus knows the right order of the Persian kings, when he is not misled by 1 Esdras. Nehemiah, as a civil servant, might have been a role model for Flavius Josephus (Grojnowski 2015: 352–365). This interpretation, however, remains hypothetical.

According to a part of the textual tradition of the Targum of Malachi, Ezra is hidden behind the term Malachi, 'my messenger',[51] a tradition to which Jerome also refers in the Prologue to his Latin translation (the Vulgate) of the Twelve Prophets. Jerome does not mention this idea in his commentary on Malachi, so for him it seems just to have been a tradition. The idea is found also in the Talmud (Megillah 15a), where it is put aside immediately.[52]

Justin Martyr is the first datable Christian author (around AD 150) to refer to Ezra. He reproaches the Jews for having left aside – probably from somewhere in Ezra 6:20–21 – Ezra's explanation of the Passover as referring to (identical with?) the Saviour who would be humiliated on the cross. If the Jews had trusted in God, Jerusalem would not have been desolated (*Dialogue with Trypho* 72.1). Lactantius (*The Divine Institutes* 4.18; AD 311) repeats Ezra's quote, but without reproaching the Jews for having excised it.[53]

Irenaeus (140 – after 190; *Against Heresies* 3.21.2) relates the story of the LXX written in parallel sessions by seventy translators with an identical result and remarks that this was not so strange, as Ezra also had, after the exile, again written down the biblical

---

51 In fact, Malachi was a proper name (it occurred already in the seventh century BC; Gogel 1998: 25, 401), albeit one with a very appropriate meaning.

52 Therefore, it is not correct to present this hypothesis as broadly accepted in Antiquity (*pace* Steinmann 2010: 110).

53 NB: the reproach is against the Jews, not Ezra (*pace* Becking 2018: 17).

texts – referring clearly to 4 Ezra 14:44, but without mentioning the Apocrypha.[54]

In *Adversus Helvidium de Mariae virginitate perpetua* (PL 23.199C), Jerome mentions the possibility that Ezra had added expressions such as 'to this day' in Genesis 35:4[55] and Deuteronomy 34:6. Ezra is also mentioned by other early Christian writers (Schneemelcher 1966: 609; Kraft 1979: 125–127; Bergren 1998: 346–348), but this overview cannot be exhaustive, and it must be said that they generally are not very informative, as has already been made clear by the few examples mentioned above.

Probably the Quran refers to Ezra in Sura 9:30 (AD 632). According to this interpretation Ezra is put on the same level by the Jews as Jesus is put by the Christians.

Respect for Ezra in the Babylonian Talmud is parallel to Ezra's importance in Judaism: it is tantamount to that of Moses, had Moses not come earlier (Sanhedrin 21b), but in any case, thanks to Ezra, the Torah has been brought back to Israel's attention (Sukkah 20a). Moreover, Ezra is understood as having started writing Ezra-Neh. and Chronicles, while Nehemiah is stated as having completed it for the part Ezra did not live to see (Baba Batra 15a; see 3a. 'Components and redaction'). This, however, is seen differently in Sanhedrin 93b, where Nehemiah is presented as the only author (cf. 3b, 'One book or two?'). The reason why his name was not given to the book was, according to this text, that he had himself committed misconduct by boasting of his deeds (cf. Neh. 13:14). Another passage of Sanhedrin (38a) identifies Nehemiah with Zerubbabel, situating him again much too early. In Megillah 16b and in the Midrash on Song of Songs 5:5, reference is made to Ezra, who is understood not to have returned with the first group to build the temple in order to first finish his studies with

---

54   Irenaeus is not the only one with this story: see Steinmann 2010: 115 n. 329.

55   In the LXX, which was generous with adding this kind of chronological remark. In AD 383, the date of this text, Jerome had not yet arrived at the insight of the *Hebraica veritas*.

Baruch, Jeremiah's secretary.[56] In itself it is a laudable aspiration, but a chronological problem hinders the story: Baruch died in Egypt at the beginning of the sixth century, the first return was in 537, and Ezra was born around 500. Chronology and – related to it – identifications are recurring points of concern in the writings of Antiquity.

g. Literary terms
Some typical literary terms occur in the commentary with a certain frequency. They are explained in this paragraph.

i. Chiastic and concentric structures
While the chiasm is a reflection without a centre (ABB'A'), the concentric structure is a reflection with a centre (ABXB'A').

ii. Hendiadys
The hendiadys expresses an idea by giving two aspects of it in coordination instead of in one single construction (Lorein 2021a: 24).

iii. Key words
Key words are words occurring so often that they seem to carry the structure; for example, in the first chapters of Ezra, 'ālâ ('to go up', but also, in another form of the same verb, 'to make to go up', i.e. 'to sacrifice'; Aramaic səlaq), bānâ ('to build'), 'am ('people'), and connected by wordplays (around the same sound, without etymological or theological connection), such as 'im ('with') and ṭa'am ('order').

5. Theology

a. Blood and faith
It cannot be denied that God called Abraham to start a new phase in history with Abraham's offspring. At the same time, this had a

---

56 Or to avoid a possible conflict with Jeshua – Jewish exegesis has always been strong in offering parallel possibilities – but then the same chronological problem applies.

larger goal than just a question of family. All the peoples of the
earth should be blessed through Israel (Gen. 12:3b), there was
openness for foreigners who wanted to join the people of Israel
(e.g. Ford 2017: 177–183) and finally Abraham is called the father
of all believers (Rom. 4:11). Ezra-Neh. stays in this line: 'the holy
seed' does exist (Ezra 9:2) and it cannot be mixed with people with
some Jewish cultural features. It can, however, be enlarged with
descendants of Gentiles who had converted wholeheartedly. A
religious reasoning is always used, not a genealogical reasoning, as
already in Exodus 34:16 and Deuteronomy 7:4; 20:18. To marry a
believer of foreign origin was acceptable; placing oneself outside the
community of faith and into the pagan culture was not acceptable
for the Bible writer, even though the Jews were asked to commit
themselves to that society (Jer. 29; Lorein 2018: 261–264). This can
be compared to the New Testament theme of 'the world' (*ho kosmos*):
we must keep a distance from the sinful world (Rom. 12:2; Jas 1:27;
4:4; 1 John 2:15), but we must at the same time commit ourselves
to it (Matt. 5:14; Phil. 2:15), just as Jesus did (John 3:16–17; 6:33, 51;
12:47; 1 John 4:9, 14).

In any case, no contradiction is to be sought between matrimonial
purity in Ezra-Neh. and missionary awareness in Ruth and Jonah.
Openness existed also in Ezra-Neh. (see Ezra 6:21; Neh. 10:29;
Zehnder 2005: 433: 'the interdiction is in fact limited to those cases
in which the spouse is not willing to separate himself from the
"impurity of the peoples of the lands", and, on the contrary, it must
be feared that heathen elements would rub off on the Jewish spouse
and/or children'[57]). The importance of an original marriage with
a Jewish woman was protected in Malachi 2:16 (against a relationship with an unbeliever). When the Jewish women in Malachi 2
are demoted in favour of the heathen women of Ezra 10, Malachi
defends marriage and Ezra denounces the relationship with heathen

---

57 My translation; the German reads: 'Das Verbot [ist] wohl auf die Fälle
    beschränkt, in Denen der Ehepartner nicht bereit ist, sich von der
    "Unreinheit der Völker der Länder" zu trennen, und im Gegenteil
    befürchtet werden muss, dass heidnische Elemente auf den jüdischen
    Ehepartner und/oder die Kinder abfärben.'

women (van der Woude 1982b: 114–126; Lorein 2010b: 343–346). Ezra, Nehemiah and Malachi are all opposed to marriages (or secondary relationships) directed only at a better economic and political position.

Of course, in times when inter-convictional dialogues are so important, the remark that the theology of Ezra-Neh. is not about racial limitations but about religious impositions will not make acceptance much easier. Our attitude, amid all societal pressure, should be friendly, cooperative (the order of Ezra 9:12b is not addressed to us; we may find the same idea in Deut. 23:6, but Jer. 29:7 is nearer to our modern-day circumstances), communicative, accepting the other as co-sinner, with all the good things that God has given in his common grace, but maintaining at the same time our own identity and the willingness to communicate the exclusive character (God has not revealed to us any other way of salvation in Scripture, which we believe to be reliable) as redeeming good news, with people who (by God's grace) are open to it.

b. Joy and disappointment
The joy of being able to return from exile must have been enormous. The most important theme of the exodus (Lorein 2023b: 68) can be found here too, with the return as second exodus and as a new phase in salvation history (Bänziger 2023: 1178–1182, 1185–1186). It is the joy of going to the Promised Land and restoring there what had been interrupted (see also 5c, 'Continuity and innovation').

At the same time, we find in Ezra-Neh. a sense of limitation (Ezra 9:8; Neh. 9:36) and of continuous struggle (Ezra 4; 9 – 10; Neh. 4 – 6; 13). For those with a firm dose of optimism after Nehemiah's useful realizations and the beautiful liturgies, Ezra-Neh. ends with Nehemiah 13, where it is all too clear that in terrestrial life acquisitions are never definitive.

The combination of joy and disappointment is palpable in the simultaneous shouting and weeping described in Ezra 3:10–13 (cf. Bänziger 2014: 243–248).

c. Continuity and innovation
Continuity with pre-exilic Israel is not a massive fossilization. There is always at the same time an element of innovation. The

relationship with the past is valued, the principles are kept, but the process of interpretation of what God had already said continues (see Ezra 1:7; 2:1–69; 6:3, 7, 16–22; 7:6, 19; 9 – 10; Neh. 7:5–72). This combination of continuity and innovation is a difficult way to go in times when God no longer speaks directly or through prophets or miracles,[58] but this makes Ezra-Neh. especially parallel with our own days, when we must also develop our faith through prayer and instruction about what God has revealed, applying the principles we find in that way to recent societal developments (without just running after them).

d. Church and State, the church and other faiths

Reading Ezra-Neh. can be especially useful for all of us who live in a mixed society, in which we want to participate but where at the same time we need to keep a critical distance from the authorities, who permit us to function as churches or even support us, but who also easily change their minds. We see that the Jews were always trying to work together with the authorities, accepting their support (which was never complete: personal contributions were always necessary – Ezra 1:4; 7:16) and grateful for the offered opportunities, but also adapting when circumstances changed, in order to keep their religious community running, faithful to what they believed. A retreat from the world – with its mixed Persian and Judean political institutions and with its mixed believing and doubting Judeans – into the caves of the Judean desert is not an option promoted in Ezra-Neh.

Towards other faith groups it must be clear that we need to keep our identity and cannot introduce paganism into our organization. That makes their cooperation within the church as such impossible: our faith community as such would be threatened, if not immediately then at least by the next generation. At the same time we must

---

58   Cf. Deines 2013: 303: 'Ezra's authority and power … is based on his expertise in the law but no longer on an intimate knowledge of God or a revelation given to him by God.' See however Firth 2022: 12, 16–18, who states that already Joshua had to interpret Moses' prescriptions. Miracles still happen, but do not direct the church.

understand that, while our testimony could be lost if we do not define ourselves sufficiently, it could also be lost if we cut ourselves off. Finally withdrawing into a community of like-minded people can lead to fossilization in such a way that, while formally a link still exists with the faith community of olden times, intrinsically this link has ceased to exist. Ezra is eager to innovate in new situations, always standing on the basis of continuity.

In this way we try to achieve what is good for ourselves and our neighbours, in an uncomfortable relationship with the authorities (Smith-Christopher 2002: 191–193), without living totally different lives in our different contexts, just as Nehemiah was a man of prayer as well as of action, for the temple as well as for the city (Blenkinsopp 1989: 31).

If our efforts for the benefit of our neighbours are unappreciated, and even if direct persecution is imminent, we may know that God is able to make good come out of evil, even when we do not know on what timescale (Ulrich 2021: 31–32).

e. Then and now

More than once, Ezra and Nehemiah are presented as examples for today's church as, respectively, the pious Bible teacher and the manager who without any problem take action against mere pagans. Can we transpose the actions of Ezra and Nehemiah so easily to our church in our day? Not as such – this must be clear – but of course God's principles in their days can still be applied in the context of our day, on the condition that we understand the permanent theological *principles* about God and humankind behind the actions in Ezra-Neh., and that we understand our own days (not forgetting to take into account that we are living in New Testament days! – Mathewson 2002: 83, 101; Lorein 2008: 148–150).

f. God and his people[59]

God is sovereign (Ezra 1:1, 5; 7:27; Neh. 2:12; 7:5), merciful (Ezra 9:9; Neh. 9:31; 13:22b) and just (Ezra 9:15; Neh. 9:33), great and awesome

---

59 This last paragraph is a mix of Kidner's insights (1979: 20–27) and my own.

(Neh. 4:14; 9:32), the creator and sustainer of heaven and earth
and all its creatures (Neh. 9:6), active in history (Neh. 9:7–30) and
faithful to his promises (Ezra 1:1).

In reaction to this, the faithful understood that they were *the
servants of the God of heaven and earth* (Ezra 5:11), even though not
numerous (Ezra 9:15). Spirituality and activity go together (Neh.
4:9, 14), but we can discern a double service: specifically religious
and in daily life.

It is God's *teaching* (Ezra 3:2; 7:6; Neh. 5:7–8; 9 – 10) that defines
how doctrine and life (not limited to the temple) should develop in
relation to God and to other persons, and God has given us his good
Spirit (Neh. 9:20). This has taken form in a written text, available
(whether or not with translation – Neh. 8:8–9) for every member
of the community (Steinmann 2010: 93–98). This generalization of
responsibilities does not exclude the existence of more specialized
leaders (Lorein 2008: 150–154).

At the very beginning of Ezra-Neh. we find a reference to a
prophecy of Jeremiah (Ezra 1:1). In Ezra 3:11 we hear the vocabu-
lary of the Psalms. Nehemiah 9 especially is filled with references
to Scripture. The need to study Scripture is well understood (Ezra
7:10; 10:3; Neh. 8:1–8; 9:3). This study needs to go together with
application and teaching (Ezra 7:6, 10).

Only one form of religion has God's support: the religion centred
around *worship* in the temple at Jerusalem, a preview of Christ's
redeeming sacrificial death on the cross. Even though the temple
could not be rebuilt immediately, the altar was set up at the first
opportunity (Ezra 3:2). Worship not only honours God but also
encourages human beings.

Music plays an important role in worship and comes in an
organized form (Ezra 2:41; 3:10–11; Neh. 11:17; 12:8–9, 27–42).

Prayer is woven thoroughly into the fabric of Ezra-Neh. It
takes a variety of forms, from a momentary flash (Neh. 2:4) to an
eloquent address (Neh. 9). Rather special is the prayer 'as part of the
redaction', so to speak (Neh. 5:19; 13:14, 22b, 31b). Prayer is based
on what God has said and done before (Neh. 9:6–37) and expresses
a strong sense of solidarity (Ezra 9:6, 15; Neh. 1:6).

God works through sinful people, through Persian kings and officials
(Ezra 1:1; Neh. 2:9), and also through ordinary Jews (Ezra 7:27;

9:6–7; Neh. 1:6–7; 2:20a; 9:2, 33–37), with their natural skills (Ezra 1:1–4; Neh. 3:10, 23) and their individuality (the lists of names), who should document well what they are doing (Ezra 7:17; 10:18–44). *God's sovereignty and human responsibility* go hand in hand (Neh. 2:20a; 4:9, 15). This implies that believers should develop their piety as well as their abilities (Whybray 2002: 127). Leaders – that is, all those who want to bear their responsibilities – should be reliable in the long run, pray (Ezra 9; Neh. 1:4–11a; 4:5–9; 9), inform others in such a way that they volunteer to participate (Ezra 10; Neh. 2:16–18; 4:14, 20; 5:9), not impose God's written instruction but explain it, be an example (Neh. 5:14–18), feel connected (Ezra 9:6; Neh. 2:17) and stay goal-oriented in difficult circumstances.

g. Some specific terms
Below is an overview of some specific theological terms for which one might expect an explanation in this introduction but which receive some elucidation at the appropriate places in the commentary.

i. Abomination
See Ezra 9:1.

ii. Faithlessness
See on Ezra 9:2.

iii. Jerusalem
See on Ezra 1:3.

iv. Law
When Moses is mentioned, the 'Law' refers to the Pentateuch, but the term can also be used in the more general sense of 'instruction'. See on Ezra 3:2; 6:18; 9 – 10 (*Meaning*); Nehemiah 8:8, 14; 7:73b – 10:39. See also 2n, 'Ezra's Law'.

v. Steadfast love
Or 'loyalty': see on Ezra 3:11.

vi. Written
The expression 'written [in Scripture]' is used in Ezra 3:2, 4; 6:18; Nehemiah 8:14 15; 10:34, 36; 13:1. See on Ezra 6:18; Nehemiah 8:14–15. See also Bänziger 2014: 100–101.

ANALYSIS

EZRA

1. BUILDING THE TEMPLE (1:1 – 6:22)
A. Introduction (1:1–4)
    i. The Lord moves Cyrus – Cyrus moves the Jews (1:1–4)
B. Launch: return, altar, foundation, worship (1:5 – 3:13)
    i. Preparation for the return (1:5–11)
    ii. The list of returnees (2:1–70)
    iii. The construction of the altar (3:1–6)
    iv. The foundation of the temple (3:7–13)
C. Core: building the temple (4:1 – 6:15)
    i. Cessation of the building activities of the Jews (4:1–24)
    ii. The building of the temple (5:1 – 6:15)
D. Worship services (6:16–22)
    i. Service of dedication (6:16–18)
    ii. Passover (6:19–22)

2. BUILDING THE COMMUNITY (7:1 – 10:44)

   A. Introduction (7:1–28)
      i. King Artaxerxes sends Ezra to Jerusalem (7:1–10)
      ii. Artaxerxes' letter (7:11–26)
      iii. Ezra's conclusion (7:27–28)
   B. Launch: return, worship, information (8:1–36)
      i. The list of returnees (8:1–14)
      ii. Preparation for the return (8:15–30)
      iii. Journey and arrival (8:31–36)
   C. Core: building the community, purification (9:1 – 10:44)
      i. Ezra's reaction to interfaith marriages (9:1–15)
      ii. The treatment of the problem of interfaith marriages
        (10:1–44)

NEHEMIAH

3. BUILDING THE WALLS (1:1 – 7:3)

   A. Introduction (1:1–11)
      i. Nehemiah's reaction to sad news from Jerusalem
        (1:1–11)
   B. Launch: return, information (2:1–20)
      i. Nehemiah commissioned to rebuild Jerusalem (2:1–20)
   C. Core: building the walls (3:1 – 7:3)
      i. Brief report of the building activity (3:1–32)
      ii. The Samarians try to hinder the building activity
        (4:1–23)
      iii. The problem of the poor and Nehemiah's
        commitment (5:1–19)
      iv. Attacks on Nehemiah (6:1–14)
      v. Final remarks (6:15 – 7:3)

4. BUILDING THE COMMUNITY (7:4 – 12:47)

   A. Introduction (7:4–5)
      i. A large city with few inhabitants (7:4–5)
   B. Launch: return, information (7:6–73a)
      i. Documentation: the list of returnees (7:6–73a)
   C. Core: building the community, commitment to the Law
      (7:73b – 10:39)

EZRA
COMMENTARY

1. BUILDING THE TEMPLE (1:1 – 6:22)

A. Introduction (1:1–4)

This section introduces the first part of Ezra-Neh., describing contextual factors which eventually led to the rebuilding of the temple. This is made possible by Cyrus permitting men and means to go to Jerusalem. Section and unit fall together.

i. The Lord moves Cyrus – Cyrus moves the Jews (1:1–4)
Context
What is mentioned in these verses has been made possible by the accession of King Cyrus. See Introduction 2e, 'Persian kings'.

Comment
1a. Not long after the start of the Persian Empire *the word of the LORD by the mouth of Jeremiah*, which had already been available for a long time, comes in a new phase, that of its fulfilment. The Holy Spirit *stirred up the spirit of Cyrus*, the only way the human spirit can be touched. The word 'to stir up' is also used in Jeremiah 50:9; 51:1;

however, there it is not about a return to Jerusalem, but about an enemy for the Babylonian Empire (which can be applied to Cyrus). In Jeremiah 29:10 a period of seventy years is announced, after which God will bring the Jews back to their country. This period seems to start with the first departure in 605, when Judah becomes a vassal state. The number 'seventy' indicates a long period (normally not within the lifespan of one person), which nevertheless will end. Even if these numbers should not be read mathematically, the period from 605 to 538 is not far from it. If we think of the actual return in 537 (which here is only announced), it is still more precise. We also find a reference to this period in Daniel 9:2.[1] In Jeremiah 27:22 the return of the utensils (see Ezra 1:7–11) is prophesied. Although we cannot refer to a specific verse in Jeremiah, the ideas are found in this book, so that the author is correct in mentioning *the word of the* LORD *by the mouth of Jeremiah.*

It is not known whether Cyrus was aware of the prophecies of Isaiah and Jeremiah. Herodotus (9.42) seems to imply that Persian kings did have some interest in prophecies known among foreign people, and of course Cyrus could reckon on Jewish officials who were able to relate the Scriptures to their daily work.

1b. Cyrus made a *proclamation* (lit. 'voice'), that is, through a herald. Although it is written that this happened *throughout all his kingdom*, we may say that in practice this was limited to Jewish communities (who did not live so far from one another; see Snell 1997: 111). The use of the word *kingdom* implies that the writer considered Cyrus' kingship legitimate (Hölzel 1972: 190). This oral communication is later confirmed *in writing* (cf. Esth. 9:32 and already [701 BC] 2 Kgs 19:9–14 for the habit of written confirmation).

2. Although it has been doubted (Becking 2018: 25) whether the expression *king of Persia* was ever used for Cyrus, it must be kept in mind that only a few texts of Cyrus have been preserved, and that for predecessors as well as for successors this description was used

---

1 Jer. 25:11–12 is speaking about another period of seventy years, starting at the destruction of Jerusalem, and apparently not yet ended in the days of Zechariah (Zech. 1:12; 7:5).

(Kent 1953: 116).[2] *The God of heaven* in the Persian period represents the official description of Israel's God (see the Elephantine letters [late fifth century], Tobit 10:11–12 [180 BC] and Judith 5:8; 11:17 [150 BC]; nevertheless, it is also already used in Gen. 24:7). The Hebrew word order is literally 'all the kingdoms of the earth gave to me the LORD the God of heaven', impossible in English, but even in Hebrew quite special; in this way two points are emphasized: the extension of Cyrus' territory and the Giver of this dominion. In this way Cyrus recognizes the God of Israel as the Supreme God, in other words, as a synonym for Marduk (Briant 2002: 46); Jews would agree with the first part, but not with the second. God has visited (in this case favourably) Cyrus and so *has charged* him with the construction of the temple (although he himself will not touch one single brick). The specification *which is in Judah* is useful in an official text.

What is said here does not exclude that Cyrus might have had other reasons for being kind to the Jews,[3] perhaps considering the strategical location of Judah.[4]

3. When we read *of all his people* (lit. 'from the totality of his people'), we do not need to think of the Northern Kingdom. At this time, they had been almost completely dispersed and mixed with the populations of the regions where they had been exiled. On the other hand, people from the North had fled to the South before the fall of Samaria and in that sense people from the North were indeed involved with the return.

In *may ... God be with him* we find the usual words for blessing. Cyrus continues with two other wishes: *let him go up ... and rebuild*. These two verbs, 'to go up' and 'to build', will be used time and again in the text of Ezra-Neh.

When we read here that the people should go up to *Jerusalem*, we must think not only in a geographical sense (a well-defined city,

---

2 Old Persian 'xšāyaθiya Pārsa(iy)'.

3 See also Introduction 2e, 'Persian kings'.

4 This implies also that the expression *all the kingdoms of the earth* should not be taken mathematically, but rather as 'a fullness of kingdoms of the earth', as is more often the case with the Hebrew *kol* (cf. Lorein 2021a: 21).

albeit in ruins), but also of the symbolic, spiritual value of Jerusalem: it is the space near the temple (but larger than it!) in which you can serve the Lord. We can live our lives before God in a larger space than just the temple (Häusl 2013: 105–106).

The identification of God as the God *who is in Jerusalem* can also be found in the Elephantine papyri (fifth century BC).

4. The construction of this verse is a bit strange. Most English translations keep the word order and change the verb to a passive form; NIV reshuffles the sentence. The word translated as *survivor* is related to the word 'remnant', those who in difficult times had remained faithful to God (as in Hag. 1:12). The word for *sojourns* indicates that these people lived there as foreigners, even after so many years.[5] Probably *the men of his place* consist of all the neighbours of the travelling Jews, but some commentators think that only Jewish neighbours who will stay in Babylonia should help their fellow Jews who will go to Judah. The idea that construction of the temple is sustained by non-Jews is quite general: see Exodus 12:35–36.

The verse ends with the freewill offering (singular, with article: see AV). Probably this offering was also performed by pagan neighbours, as Cyrus could not know that not all Jews would want to return (Noordtzij 1939: 45). The 'freewill offering' should therefore not be considered as the technical term within the biblical system of offerings.

To summarize verses 3–4: Cyrus wishes that God might be with the Judeans, that they might go up to Jerusalem, that they might build and that people who do not go might give money.

Meaning
God is at the beginning of the story, chronologically and existentially. He takes the initiative, and sometimes even informs us beforehand. It is good when humans understand and confess that – not only the author (in v. 1), but also Cyrus (in v. 2), besides all his display of power. Nowadays we also try to understand God's Word and are

---

5   At the same time they lived there with the mission to 'seek the welfare of the city' (Jer. 29:7; cf. Rom. 12:17b)!

influenced by political circumstances, but – if everything is going well – we may see God's action behind both these factors. God is the Initiator, but he involves people, with all their natural skills.

Even when the government is sustaining the church, freewill offerings (v. 4) will remain necessary.

Cyrus' wish for them to go up will be easily realized; his wish for them to build takes more time, as will be seen in the coming chapters. As far as the first wish is concerned: God wants to be with each of us.

B. Launch: return, altar, foundation, worship (1:5 – 3:13)

While the previous section comprised the introduction, this section launches the main subject of the first part of Ezra-Neh.: (re)building the temple. Within this launch worship services are held (3:3b–5, 10–13). An important part of this section is taken up with the list of Ezra 2.

i. Preparation for the return (1:5–11)
Context
On the assumption that it was technically impossible to give heed to Cyrus' permission immediately, we situate the return in the spring of 537.[6] In order to avoid the desert, one would travel first to the North along the Euphrates, passing at the latitude of Aleppo to the Orontes Valley, and then back to the South. This will have taken some months (cf. 7:8–9a). The purpose was clearly the reconstruction of the temple (cf. 1:2–3) and this is launched by installing the altar in autumn 537 and by repairing the foundations in spring 536.[7]

---

6 This is a reconstruction; the text does not give fixed dates. This implies that Steinmann 2008 might be right when he situates it some years later (but his argument based on sabbatical years is not decisive).

7 This is about the same period during which Daniel received his last vision (Dan. 10 – 12).

Comment

5–6. When we read here of the family heads of Judah and
Benjamin (i.e. the Southern Kingdom; cf. 1:3) together with Levites,
this group need not have been very large. That God has stirred the
spirit was also found in 1:1. That this happened in order to go up
and to build the house of the LORD was also found in 1:3 (in both
cases not in exactly the same words). We meet in verse 6 the same
question as in 1:4 about who *aided* (lit. 'strengthened their hands';
thus AV). Did the gifts come from Jewish or Babylonian neighbours?
Only Cyrus' first wish is not fully repeated here, but when we read
that God stirred up people's spirits, we can easily suppose that God
was with them.

7. In 605, King Nebuchadnezzar[8] had brought the worship
utensils from the temple in Jerusalem to Babylon, in the first place
to his palace (2 Chr. 36:7), then finally to the treasury of his gods
(Dan. 1:1–2). The return of the utensils was foretold by Jeremiah
(Jer. 27:22) and is important for continuity between the worship of
past and present (cf. repetition of this fact in Ezra 5:14–15 and 6:5).[9]

8. *Mithredath* was Cyrus' financial manager in Babylon (Briant
2002: 66–67). The Persian Empire was equipped with a detailed
bookkeeping system (Williamson 1991: 54–55). Mithredath is a
typical Persian name meaning 'given by Mithras'; Mithras was the
Indo-Iranian god of light, supporter of the good (cf. the English
name Theodore). This high-ranking officer is working together
with the highest representative of the Jews. Although most translations present *Sheshbazzar* as being a *prince*, he is not mentioned in
1 Chronicles 3. The word used in Hebrew (*nāśî'*, lit. 'the elevated one')
need not designate a royal prince and can also be translated as 'the
leader' (thus NET). According to 5:14, he was appointed governor by

---

8 Nebuchadnezzar (*Nabû-kudurri-uṣur*, 'Nabu, protect the heir'; Berger
   1975: 224–225) reigned from 605 to 562. The form 'Nebuchadnezzar'
   occurs in 2 Kgs, 1 and 2 Chr., Ezra, Neh., Esth., Dan., Jer. and Ezek.
   and originated by dissimilation, possibly in Aramaic (Millard 1997:
   972).
9 In 7:19 and 8:25–27, 33–34 new utensils for worship are mentioned.
   This reminds us that there is place for renewal within continuity.

the Persian king, at least until the repair of the temple foundations (5:16), but after that he is no longer mentioned (Uffenheimer 1996: 223 thinks he died in 521). It seems attractive to identify him with Zerubbabel (for whom cf. 2:2),[10] for in that case he would have been a royal prince and the relationship between the two men would not be problematic; some arguments, however, plead against this.

(1) No reason exists why one person would have *two* Akkadian names: 'Zerubbabel' as well as 'Sheshbazzar' are Akkadian.[11]

(2) The way in which Sheshbazzar is mentioned in Ezra 5:14, 16 implies some distance towards him, either in time or in space, while Zerubbabel was, according to 5:2, present at the scene (Kidner 1979: 139; vom Orde 1997: 43).

(3) In 1 Esdras 6:18 (which admittedly cannot be seen as a beacon of trustworthiness – see Introduction 4f, 'The afterlife of Ezra-Neh. in Antiquity') Zorobabel and Sanabassar are mentioned together as two different persons. This argument, of course, is valid only if Sanabassar and Sheshbazzar designate the same person. It leads us, however, to another hypothesis. This name Sanabassar, used in 1 Esdras, is close to the name Shenazzar, who indeed was a royal *prince* (1 Chr. 3:18), of the generation before Zerubbabel's. Both forms, Sheshbazzar and Shenazzar, might be derived from the Akkadian *Sin-ab-uṣur* ('O Moon-god, protect the father'), later changed to *Šamš-ab-uṣur* ('O Sun-god, protect the father') when the moon-god became less important (Avishur and Heltzer 2009: 101–102).

If Sheshbazzar can be identified with Shenazzar, he would have been Zerubbabel's uncle, which would make it logical that when arriving in Judah he was higher in rank than Zerubbabel, and that he would also delegate tasks to his nephew; in the more probable

---

10 Flavius Josephus says only (*Ant.* 11.13) that King Cyrus sent his 'treasurer Mithridates and Zorobabel the leader of the Jews' (my translation) – not carefully formulated, but not tantamount to an identification of Sheshbazzar with Zerubbabel.

11 Vom Orde 1997: 43. It should not be doubted that Zerubbabel is an Akkadian name: it occurs with some frequency in Akkadian texts of the sixth century.

case that Sheshbazzar was not a royal prince (and that we do not
know why he had his higher rank), it would still be logical that he
delegated tasks to Zerubbabel, who was inferior in rank indeed,
but yet of royal blood and therefore much respected by the Jewish
people (Steinmann 2008: 519). Sheshbazzar's task is specified in
Ezra 5:14–15.

9. Apparently one cutting tool (cf. Vulg. and AV) had been lost.
Most English translations have *censers*, as 1 Esdras 2:9 has, but for
this translation no etymological basis exists. The Hebrew word is
a hapax as far as biblical Hebrew is concerned, but does occur in
Mishnaic Hebrew as 'knives'.

10. The *410 bowls* lack a further description in ESV; NET has the
same adjunct here as with the *1,000 vessels (other)*, although in Hebrew
these are different words; AV has 'of a second sort', which also is
a possible translation, but not the most fitting one. In the Persian
context we could think of 'different, individually decorated', an
attribute much appreciated by the Persians (Bleibtrau 2001: 200).

11. The total of *5,400* is clearly not the sum of the details mentioned
in verses 9–10. Numbers (not necessarily written in full letters, but
at least partly in numerals of different kinds) are especially liable
to transcriptional errors and cannot be restored, at least not with
certainty. Furthermore, bookkeeping documents in the Ancient
Near East in general (Kidner 1979: 35) and in Persia in particular
(Williamson 1991: 56–57) were not complete or faultless.

While Sheshbazzar *did … bring up* all these utensils, the people
were brought up; the same verb is used twice, once in the active form
and – closely connected – once in the passive form, indicating that
God was at work here.

Meaning
While Cyrus has created an opportunity, the Judeans still have to
respond to it, and they need some time to do so. That is not a
problem as long as the project goes in the right direction, heading
towards Jerusalem. So we too must be oriented to right principles
and take our time over Bible study, but practical work must also be
done. Bricks and cement are important for God's kingdom, but of
course so also are more intellectual kinds of work. We do not live
our Christian lives only within the church, but also in the city, as

long as we do our work fully conscious of God's presence on earth
(in Ezra's days symbolized by the temple).

Also at this point some parallels with the exodus can be observed
(Jer. 16:14–15; 23:7–8; Bänziger 2014: 126–129). In the first place we
have seen the use of the verb 'go up' (cf. Ezra 1:3). The Judeans leave
for Judah, as at the time of the exodus, with money (partly) coming
from Gentiles (cf. Exod. 3:22; 11:2; 12:35). It must be remarked that
the role of the pagan king (Pharaoh and Cyrus) is quite different in
the two places. We should not place the authorities automatically on
the side of the bad. In the second millennium BC the objective was
to worship in the desert (Exod. 3:18; 5:1–2); now the reconstruction
of the temple is intended, but as a nearer parallel to the worship
in the desert it can be observed that the altar is already installed
(Ezra 3:1–7) before the reconstruction of the temple can be started.
The temple mentioned in Ephesians 2:21–22 is itself formed also
of Gentiles.

ii. The list of returnees (2:1–70)

Context

While it is clear that the redactor has found this list in Nehemiah's
files (and has left it there as a second witness: see Neh. 7), it fits
here in the narrative.[12] Although one cannot exclude that the list
contains more than only the persons who returned with the first
group – dynamic lists did exist – verse 1 follows Ezra 1:11, which
mentions the group travelling with Sheshbazzar, and it is difficult
to imagine that many people followed them individually.

---

12 Is it archaeologically impossible that the whole group of this list
    (about 50,000 people; see vv. 64–65) travelled together (as Becking
    2018: 39 suggests)? At the beginning of the First World War many
    more people were on the move (De Schaepdrijver 2013: 112–113); in
    1948 more Jews travelled from Iraq to Israel (Ben-Gurion 1974: 133);
    in the night of 10–11 September 1989 tens of thousands passed the
    frontier between Eastern Germany and Hungary (Die
    Bundesregierung, 'Ungarn öffnet seine Grenze', <https://www.
    bundesregierung.de/breg-de/themen/deutsche-einheit/
    ungarn-oeffnet-seine-grenze-337804>).

Within the relationship of continuity and renewal the accent
in this chapter is on the first term, as being able to prove the link
with a family (vv. 3–20) or with a situation (vv. 21–35) from before
the exile is of utmost importance. Continuity is needed in times of
lack of clarity, unrest and a new start. This continuity takes form
in individuals, mentioned by name. This is the only thing we can
explain (we do not know anything else about most of them); we must
keep in mind that the etymology of Semitic names was normally
perspicuous. By explaining the etymology of the names,[13] we come
as near as we can to these individuals. As far as the numbers are
concerned, we have to note again that numbers specifically are
poorly transmitted through the manuscripts (see on 1:11). Nevertheless, the differences are not so important that they would not
give an indication. Probably only the males of at least twelve years
old are counted, without including people with the status of slaves
who accompanied them. These persons are nevertheless mentioned
in verse 65.

The fact that a list is provided marks the importance of the
return.

Comment

1–2. The list is about people of *the province* of Judah. All came
back to the South. The Northern Kingdom of Israel had lost its
independent existence since 722 (cf. Neh. 4). The city of Jerusalem –
well situated in the South – is considered as a separate entity. People
seem to be related mostly to different villages; that will turn out to
be a problem (cf. Neh. 11:1–2).

The Hebrew of this text shows a form of intensive play on
words.[14] Does it indicate the importance of this first verse?

Nebuchadnezzar (see on 1:7) *had carried captive* the Jews in different
phases: (1) some princes and nobles as hostages (among whom was
Daniel: Dan. 1:3) after Judah became a vassal state in 605/4 (2 Kgs
24:1b); (2) a group from the Judean countryside in 598 (Jer. 52:28;

---

13 Mostly based on *HALOT* and Tavernier 2007; and for the place names
    on Negev 1970; *EAEH*; Lemaire 1994: 19–21; and Zevit 2009.

14 Hebr. *wə'ēlleh … hā'ōlîm … ha-gôlâ … heglâ.*

Yamauchi 2002: 362); (3) a group after the rebellion of Jerusalem
(which made Judah a province instead of a vassal state) in 597 (2 Kgs
24:10–17); (4) a group so important that the country was considered
to be empty[15] after a second rebellion and definitive demolition of
Jerusalem in 587 (2 Kgs 25:1–21; Jer. 37:5–11, 21b; 39:1–10; 52:3–27;
Wiseman 1985: 36–37; Steinmann 2011: 135–138, 164–167, 170); and
(5) lastly a group after the murder of Gedaliah in 582 (Jer. 52:30;
van der Veen 2003: 238).

  Zerubbabel was a royal prince, grandson of Judah's last king in
function (1 Chr. 3:17–19; for the importance of Jeconiah/Jehoiachin
for the deportees, see Ezek. 1:2[16]). According to Ezra 3:2; 5:2;
Nehemiah 12:1; Haggai 1:1; 2:23 he was the son of Shealtiel, but
according to 1 Chronicles 3:19 the son of Pedaiah.[17] Later on he
became the governor of the province of Judah. Although the king of
Persia appointed governors at his discretion, he probably showed a
preference for persons who would also be respected by the locals for
historical reasons, just as Nebuchadnezzar did (Lemaire 1996: 53–54;
van der Veen 2007: 61–62). Apparently, this was only for a short
time: Sheshbazzar was governor at the moment of the return (see
on 1:8) and already shortly after the beginning of the building works
Zerubbabel seems to have disappeared (5:9; died through illness?
cf. Avishur and Heltzer 2009: 114–117). Is it possible that through his
Davidic origins, his name (Akkadian Zēr Bābili, 'seed/descendant
of Babel', parallel with the Hebrew name Zemah[18] ['branch'] in
Zech. 3:8; 6:12) and his sudden death he became a middle figure
between the historical David and the eschatological Messiah (Hag.
2:23;[19] Zech. 3:8; 6:12)? His importance is stressed also by the use of

---

15 Scripture never says that the land was 'empty', but that it was
    decapitated and ruined, not only through the exile, but also by other
    losses of war: Lorein 2018: 249.

16 See further Uffenheimer 1996: 222.

17 Perhaps Pedaiah was his natural father and Shealtiel his juridical father
    (Avishur and Heltzer 2009: 103).

18 A real name, as we can read in the Arad inscription (701 BC; Lemaire
    1996: 50–51).

19 Hag. 2:21 does not speak to, but about Zerubbabel/the Branch.

'my servant' (cf. Abraham in Gen. 26:24; Moses in e.g. Num. 12:7; David in e.g. 2 Sam. 3:18; the prophecies of Isa. 22:20; 37:35; 41:8–9; 42:1; 44:1, 2, 21; 45:4; 49:3; 52:13; 53:11: only to these persons does God apply this expression) and the use of 'signet ring' (Hag. 2:23), which in relation with Jeremiah 22:24 indicates a restoration.

The change of the vowel in the name of *Jeshua* (from 'o' to 'e'; cf. Joshua the successor of Moses, and Jesus; meaning: 'the LORD saves') has taken place in this period, but has not yet been applied in Haggai 1:1; indeed, although Haggai 1:1 and Ezra 2:2 are speaking about the same person, the redaction of Ezra-Neh. is at least one century later. *Jeshua* was the son of Jehozadak (Hag. 1:1), the last high priest before the exile (1 Chr. 6:14–15[20]).

In Nehemiah 7:7 the number of twelve leaders is completed by mentioning Nahamani; his name was possibly overlooked by the copyists of this chapter because it resembled so much the name of *Nehemiah* (not the same as the protagonist of the book of Nehemiah, nor the same one as in Neh. 3:16; meaning: 'the LORD consoles').

Seraiah means 'the LORD is ruler' (in Neh. 7:7 Azariah, 'the LORD has helped'); the meaning of *Reelaiah* is unknown (in Neh. 7:7 Raamiah, 'the LORD has thundered').

Mordecai (Akkadian, 'belonging to Marduk') cannot be Esther's uncle.

Bilshan: Akkadian, 'their lord'; *Mispar*: 'number'; *Bigvai*: Persian 'better by the god'; *Rehum*: 'to whom (God) has been merciful' (in Neh. 7:7 Nehum, writing error or '[God is] compassionate'); *Baanah* ('descendent of [the goddess] Anath').

3–19. In these verses we find laypeople described in relation to their descent. Steinmann (2010: 170) suggests that the people mentioned here were people deported by Nebuchadnezzar from Jerusalem, as this place is not mentioned in the next category.

Parosh: 'flea' (animal names were quite frequent; the flea indicates that the bearer ought to be a constant plague to his enemies; Goitein 1970: 517); *Shephatiah*: 'the LORD has judged'; *Arah*: 'wild

---

20   In the edition of the Hebrew text (as also in some versions, but it is wrong to say that the system of the Hebrew edition is older, or even original; Lorein 2014: 138): 1 Chr. 5:40–41.

ox'; *Pahath-moab*: '(under the jurisdiction of the) governor of Moab', with his sons *Jeshua* ('the LORD has saved') and *Joab* ('the LORD is [my] father'); *Elam*: '(coming from) Elam'; *Zattu*: Iranian, 'better born'; *Zaccai*: 'pure'; *Bani*: '(God) has built' (Neh. 7:15 has Binnui, 'the built one'); *Bebai*: 'pupil of the eye'; *Azgad*: 'Gad is strong'; *Adonikam*: 'my Lord has arisen'; *Bigvai*: Persian 'better by the god'; *Adin*: 'delightful'; *Ater* ('left-handed') with his only son *Hezekiah* ('the LORD is strong'); *Bezai*: 'in the shad(ow of God)'. Although the name *Jorah* seems quite different from Hariph (thus Neh. 7:24), the two names have almost the same meaning, respectively 'autumn rain' and 'autumn'. *Hashum*: 'broad nose'.

20–35. In these verses we find laypeople in relation to the places where the family came from: God has promised not only offspring, but also a territory. The places are mostly situated around Jerusalem; it must be noticed that places such as Hebron are not mentioned. This area was occupied by the Edomites, who found a new territory in the poorly defended southern area of Judah, either because as loyal vassals of Babylon they were permitted to extend their territory (Lipiński 2006: 418 refers to Obad. 10–14), or because they were chased from their territory by Nabonidus in 552 (Levin 2007: 245).

Although the name *Gibbar* can be explained as a man's name ('strong man'), we should start the list of place names here with verse 20 when we consider the parallel in Nehemiah 7:25. *Gibbar* would then be Gibeon (5½ miles north of Jerusalem, Tell el-Jib; cf. Josh. 9; 10:1–14; 2 Chr. 1:3; 1 Kgs 3:5), temporarily renamed to honour Gobryas.[21]

Bethlehem (5½ miles south of Jerusalem, on the ancient road to Hebron, Beersheba and Egypt; cf. Gen. 35:19; 48:7; Ruth; 1 Sam. 16:4; Luke 2:4; place where Jerome worked – Lorein 2014: 125–128) and *Netophah* (3 miles south of Bethlehem, modern Khirbeth Beit Falluh; cf. Neh. 12:28) are here mentioned separately, but together in Nehemiah 7:26 because of their proximity to each other.

Anathoth (3 miles north-east of Jerusalem, Ras el-Kharubbeh; cf. Jer. 1:1); *Azmaveth* (2 miles north of Anathoth).

---

21 Thus Zevit 2009: 130; cf. Pehel in Transjordan renamed after Pella, birthplace of Alexander the Great.

Kiriath-arim: MS error for Kiriath-jearim (thus in Neh. 7:29), on the border of Judah and Benjamin, 8 miles west of Jerusalem on the road to Tel Aviv, near Abu-Ghosh; *Chephirah* (territory of Benjamin,[22] 8¾ miles north-west of Jerusalem, in the same direction); and *Beeroth* (territory of Benjamin, 5 miles north-west of Jerusalem, Khirbet al-Bi'ar) are mentioned together because they are situated not too far from one another.

Ramah (territory of Benjamin, 5½ miles north of Jerusalem, ar-Rām; cf. Jer. 31:15 and Matt. 2:18)[23] and *Geba* (territory of Benjamin, 6 miles north of Jerusalem) are mentioned together because they are situated close to each other.

Michmas (territory of Benjamin, 7½ miles north-east of Jerusalem; cf. 1 Sam. 13:23; 14:4–5).

Bethel (near to the border with the North [cf. 1 Kgs 12:27–29; 2 Kgs 17:28], 10½ miles north of Jerusalem, Beitin; cf. Neh. 11:31) and *Ai* (2 miles east of Bethel, et-Tell – with the same meaning: 'ruins'; other possibility: 2½ miles south-east of Bethel, Khirbet ḥayyān, which has the sound of its name as an argument; cf. Gen. 12:8; 13:3; Josh. 7:2–5; 8:3–29; Neh. 11:31) are mentioned together because they are situated near to each other.

Nebo: perhaps Mount Scopus, just north of Jerusalem. In the same way as Gibbar (v. 20), *Magbish* can be considered as a temporary renaming of the city of Mizpah (7½ miles north of Jerusalem, Tell en-Nazbeh; not mentioned in Nehemiah's list) to honour Megabyzos.[24]

Apparently, *Elam* must not be confused with another Elam, but as the situation of this one is unknown, nothing more can be said. It is not about the region between Babylonia and Persia (Gen. 14:1; Jer. 49:34–39; Ezek. 32:24–25; Ezra 4:8–9).

Harim (unknown).

---

22 But it must be asked whether the original tribal territories still had any importance (Zevit 2009: 127).

23 Not to be confused with Ramah, the city of Samuel (1 Sam. 1:1, 19; 25:1).

24 Thus Zevit 2009: 130. This would situate the redaction date (not the date of the list) after 522.

Lod (10 miles south-east of Tel Aviv; cf. Neh. 11:35; Acts 9:32–35; burial place of St George, martyred during Diocletian's persecutions – AD 303 – and patron saint of England), *Hadid* (3 miles east of Lod, now al-Hadita) and *Ono* (5½ miles north-west of Lod, modern Kafr Ana; Neh. 6:2; 11:35) are mentioned together because they are situated not too far from one another. *Ono* is quite eccentric: see on Nehemiah 6:2. These places probably did not belong to the territory of Judah (cf. 1 Maccabees 11:34, about 145 BC; Lemaire 2015: 85–86); according to Knoppers 2009: 82*, it is possible that some Judean communities lived outside Judah (cf. Neh. 11:34–35). Is there a direct relationship between where they belonged and where they went to?

Jericho (territory of Benjamin, 9¾ miles north-west of the place where the river Jordan ends in the Dead Sea). By far the largest group is related to *Senaah*, 7½ miles north of Jericho, poor ground with a dispersed population (Zevit 2009: 128).

36–39. From verse 36 to verse 58 we find a list of priests and other temple personnel who do not have any problem with their status.

Priests are descendants of Levi by Aaron and therefore are allowed to administer sacrifices. We do not have the impression that this is only a very small selection of all the *priests*, so we must accept that no direct relation existed between the four families mentioned here and the twenty-four classes mentioned in 1 Chronicles 24; perhaps only these four families returned and were then split into six in order to get twenty-four classes again (Beckwith 1996: 82). *The sons of Jedaiah* ('the LORD has known [me]') are especially related to *Jeshua*, the high priest (cf. v. 2). *Immer*: 'lamb'; *Pashhur*: Egyptian, 'portion of (the god) Horus'; *Harim*: 'dedicated'. When we calculate the sum of these numbers, we arrive at 4,289 priests; this is about one-tenth (a tithe) of the total number of people mentioned in Ezra 2:64.

40–42. In contrast to the priests only a small number of *Levites* came along (the same problem will be met in 8:15). *Levites* are descendants of Levi too, but have less important functions in the temple service (cf. Num. 3:2–10). Are *the sons of Jeshua* (the third person with this name after v. 2) and *Kadmiel* ('God is before me') two different branches of the *sons of Hodaviah* ('praise the LORD'), or do we have three branches of the same level, or are the *sons of Hodaviah* the only branch of Kadmiel's branch? *Singers* are Levites who have been appointed by David for singing in the temple (cf.

1 Chr. 6:31). *Asaph*: '(God has) gathered' (cf. 1 Chr. 15:17). *Gate-keepers* are Levites who took care of the material management (cf. 1 Chr. 9:23–29). *Shallum*: 'compensated, satisfied'; *Ater*: 'left-handed'; *Talmon*: 'bright'; *Akkub*: 'protected'; *Hatita*: 'with perforated foot'; *Shobai*: 'the LORD has come close'.

43–54. *Temple servants* (lit. 'the given ones'; AV has left the Hebrew untranslated) are probably descendants of prisoners of war who had been 'given' to temple service (cf. Num. 31:30, 46–47; Ezra 8:20), but who are now completely integrated in the people of God, as becomes clear in the total of verse 64 and in their vows in Nehemiah 10:29–30 (ET 28–29). This group and the next one are taken together in verse 58 and are mentioned in groups that on average were quite small. *Ziha*: Egyptian, '(the god) Horus has spoken'; *Hasupha*: 'quick'; *Tabbaoth*: 'signet ring'; *Keros*: 'crooked'; *Siaha*: '(God has) helped'; *Padon*: '(God has) spared'; *Lebanah*: 'white'; *Hagabah*: 'locust'; *Akkub*: 'protected'; *Hagab*: 'locust'. *Shamlai* is read[25] in the Codex Leningradensis as it is written in the versions and in Nehemiah 7:48, that is, as Shalmai, 'being compensated, satisfied'; *Hanan*: '(God has been) gracious'; *Giddel*: '(God) has made great'; *Gahar*: 'born in a year with little rain'; *Reaiah*: 'the LORD has seen'; *Rezin*: 'favoured'; *Nekoda*: 'speckled'; *Gazzam*: 'caterpillar'; *Uzza*: 'force'; *Paseah*: 'hobbler'; *Besai*: 'puss' (Lipiński 2007: 195–196); *Asnah*: Egyptian, 'belonging to (the goddess) Neit'. The origins of *Meunim* and *Nephisim* are unknown, but the forms seem to be plural; are we speaking about groups instead of persons? *Bakbuk*: 'bottle' (according to Goitein 1970: 518 a nickname for a man with a protruding belly or with a manner of talking reminiscent of the bubbling sound of water poured out from a bottle); *Hakupha*; 'humpbacked'; *Harhur*: 'raven'; *Bazluth*: 'onion'; if *Mehida* is a copyist's error – but the same occurs in Nehemiah 7:54 – for Mehira (the letters 'd' and 'r' resembled each other): 'bought' (De Fraine

---

25   This means that the consonants ('Ketiv') are not changed, but that the desired reading is indicated in the margin ('Qere'). The Codex Leningradensis (kept in St Petersburg) is the oldest complete manuscript (AD 1008) of the original text and is used as the basis for its main edition (Biblia Hebraica Quinta).

1961: 30); *Harsha*: 'silent (deaf/dumb)'; *Barkos*: Idumean, 'devoted
to (the god) Qos' (Lipiński 2016: 146); *Sisera*: Phoenician name,
meaning unknown; *Temah*: meaning unknown; *Neziah*: 'faithful';
Hatipha: 'abducted'.

These verses (as well as vv. 55–57) are arranged in a special
way in the manuscripts, that is, in the form of two columns. This
arrangement highlights the names, making clear that they support
the community.

55–58. *The sons of Solomon's servants* are perhaps descendants of
Solomon's prisoners of war (Williamson 1985: 36) with some special
duties, not in immediate relationship to the temple. *Sotai*: 'runner';
Hassophereth: '(female) writer'; *Peruda*: 'unique' (Steinmann 2010: 187);
Jaalah: 'help'; *Darkon*: 'way-giver'; *Giddel*: '(God) has made great';
Shephatiah: 'the LORD has judged'; *Hattil*: 'babbler'; *Pochereth-hazze-
baim*: '(female) gazelle catcher'; *Ami* is written in Nehemiah 7:59 as
Amon, 'faithful'.

59–60. The people mentioned in these verses wanted to be
registered and to express in this way their solidarity with the pre-
exilic society. For those who were not priests, they were probably
proselytes: it was always possible for people from outside Israel to
join the people of Israel (cf. Exod. 20:6).

Because of lack of proven relation with the land, they are mentioned by the Babylonian places where they *came up from*: *Tel-melah,
Tel-harsha, Cherub, Addan, and Immer*. Unfortunately, none of them
can be situated with certainty, but we may presume (Yamauchi 1988:
616) that we are speaking about the Nippur area, between Babel and
Uruk (Ezek. 1:1) in Southern Mesopotamia.

Besides their origin in Babylonia, their descent is mentioned too
(apparently not sufficiently documented, however). *Delaiah*: 'the
LORD has drawn'; *Tobiah*: 'the LORD is good'; *Nekoda*: 'speckled'.

61–63. There are also priests without the necessary *registration*,
probably an official document (we find the same word in Esth. 3:14).
Habaiah (or Hobaiah, as in NIV and NET): 'the LORD has hidden';
Hakkoz: 'trimmer' (if we take Ezra 8:33 and Neh. 3:4, 21 together,
the problem of this family seems to have been solved). The fact
that *Barzillai* ('ironsmith'; Lipiński 2006: 181) had been connected
with the family on the mother's side because of the famous friend
of David (2 Sam. 19:31–38) must have complicated the research in

the registers. They are not *excluded* in a definitive way, but they are
suspended from their office, because a decision could not be taken.
We do not have here the normal word for *governor*, but a word of
Persian origin, meaning 'reverend'. At this moment, Sheshbazzar
was the *governor* (cf. 1:8). He wanted the *Urim and Thummim* to be
consulted by a priest. We do not know how these functioned,[26] but
the high priest had them stored in his breastplate (Exod. 28:30)
and they were able to produce light and perspective about the will
of God. They did not function any longer after the days of David,
but that does not prevent the governor from looking forward to
their functioning (cf. for the Qumran Community in their early
days 11QT LVIII, 18–21). We find the same waiting for a prophet
in 1 Maccabees 4:46; 14:41.

64–65. When we see the number of *the whole assembly*, we observe
again (cf. 1:11) that it is not the sum of the numbers already
mentioned.

The *male and female singers* were probably luxury personnel,
professional singers for feasts and funerals.

66–69. No animals are mentioned that would move rather
slowly (small stock, cattle). All together the people who went from
Babylon to Judah do not seem to have been poor.[27] They were even
able to contribute to the construction of the temple (in v. 69 briefly
the work). The list of gifts is not the same as in Nehemiah 7 – even
the categories are different. If we realize again the problem with
the transmission of numbers (see on 1:11; 2:64–65), it is impossible to harmonize the two lists. We find two translations for the
Hebrew *darkemônîm: darics* (ESV) and 'drachmas' (older versions of
NIV). The problem with darics is that they were created in 512 (as
a coin of 128 grains / 0.27 troy oz gold; Briant 2002: 409). The
problem with drachmas is that they were silver coins. The best

---

26   Van Dam 1997a: 330 speaks only about how God is able to
     communicate in general his guidance in the Old Testament, but not
     specifically through Urim and Thummim.

27   Altmann (2015: 110) says the Jewish migrants had known peace and
     economic growth in Babylonia. They were even richer after two
     generations: see Ezra 8:26 (Grosheide 1963: 237).

solution seems to be to suppose that at the time of the redaction the value was expressed in darics. It is impossible to give the exact value of ancient prices: our economy is different, our needs are different, the relation between gold, silver and local coins is different. But to give a very rough impression, the gold value for the *darics* would nowadays be (calculation according to Mitchell 1991: 431, with bullion prices and exchange rates 2018) £15,500,000 (€18,000,000); the silver value for the *minas* would be £930,000 (€1,000,000). Recently about twice this gold value was necessary to build a new museum in Bruges, but again comparing is difficult: a museum is not really a temple and salary costs account for half of the amount.

The price of the garments is not mentioned; it would not be important in any case: what matters is the expression of continuity (Altmann 2016: 225).

70. With this verse we come back to verse 1, the verse before the lists. In spite of the commitment of the people and in spite of the importance of Jerusalem, people actually start to live in the villages.[28]

Meaning

However unattractive for many persons a list may be, it is a list of real people, representative of all real people who have played a role in the history of the Bible and the church. Of course, it is only a selection (as the whole of Ezra-Neh. and more generally every part of biblical history is a selection), but it makes us feel the importance of individuals and helps us to appreciate the commitment of every single person living today in our own church. In order to limit the total dimensions of the Bible, usually only certain high points and main lines are mentioned (cf. John 21:25), but we should never forget the importance of real individuals who, under God's faithfulness, provide continuity through the generations. And if the name of Bakbuk is mentioned in Scripture, our name could have been there as well (if only we had lived in a different time).

---

28 For the problem of Jerusalem being empty, see further below (and Zech. 8:4–5).

When we read verses 64–69, we see that these people were not poor without any other option than to try their luck in Judah. On the contrary: they seem to have been quite prosperous. Are we ready to commit ourselves, to receive our calling, with all the prosperity we have (whether it be absolute or relative)?

These generous thoughts do not hide the problems. For one category, the priests, it is annoying that they have lost their documents: without them, they cannot exercise their office. The governor is aware of this, but does not want to take the risk of defiling the priesthood. He hopes that Urim and Thummim will come back. His hope was vain, but it is nevertheless a model for us. It is good to observe that while the governor suspends them by way of precaution, he does not strike off their names in a definitive way.

We find another problem in the last verse: the people have shown their commitment, but by leaving aside the city of Jerusalem, they create a problem: the ideal has not been reached.

iii. The construction of the altar (3:1–6)

Context

After the list of Ezra 2, we return to the point where we left the narrative in Ezra 1:11. In this chapter everything is ready after the return from exile at the start of the seventh month, our month October, of the year 537. This month is a month of holy feasts, with New Year's Day, the Day of Atonement and the Feast of Booths.

Comment

1. On New Year's Day (4 October 537), the *children of Israel* (not in the sense of 'people from the Northern Kingdom' but in the sense of 'believers') had found their own place outside Jerusalem, but for this occasion *the people gathered … to Jerusalem*. Although the expression *as one man* expresses the unanimity of the people, it does not guarantee that really everyone, those who had returned from the exile as well as those who had always lived in the land, had come together.

2. In this religious context, the name of *Jeshua* as the priest is mentioned first. For the names and persons of *Jeshua* and *Zerubbabel*, see on 2:2. They will be mentioned again in 3:8.

A start was soon made on executing Cyrus' order concerning the building of the temple, by reconstructing the altar *to offer burnt offerings on it*. The Hebrew uses here an expression with three words akin to the verb used so frequently in these opening chapters (*'ālâ*; basic meaning: 'to go up'; see 1:3, 5, 11; 2:1, 59; for the combination used in this verse, cf. Exod. 40:29; Deut. 27:6; Josh. 8:31; 22:23; Ezek. 43:18).

All this is done according to what *is written in the Law* [*tôrâ*, 'instruction'] *of Moses*. The words *the man of God* characterize Moses as a prophet (Steinmann 2010: 207). So reference is clearly made to revelation of past times (see Introduction 2n, 'Ezra's Law', and 5g, 'Some specific terms', for further information).

3. We read here that the altar was set *in its place*, that is, on its foundations (cf. AV 'upon his bases'), as was also the intention for the temple according to 2:68. Of course, it is easier to use some remaining pieces of the former structure, but the most important issue is the continuity that is expressed in this way.

The construction of the second half of this verse is not clear. ESV translates in a causal way (*for fear was on them*). The disadvantage of this translation is that it gives the impression that the Jews promptly built the altar with the hope that by giving something to God they could avert the risk. Another translation is presented in NIV ('Despite their fear') and NET ('even though they were in terror'); the fear remains the same (and indeed, believers too can have fear), but in spite of their fear, they still build.[29] This text seems to be a

---

29 As the text is unclear, other interpretations can be offered: (1) *They set the altar in its place, for fear* (of the LORD) *was on them* on the part of *the peoples of the lands* (Zillessen 1904: 144 refers to Exod. 15:16; 23:27; Neh. 6:16; his conjecture, however, is not necessary for this interpretation); (2) *They set the altar in its place, for* there was a (pagan) altar *on them* (the foundations) of *the peoples of the lands* (thanks to Professor Baron Julien Klener for the suggestion; see also Van Hoonacker 1891: 637), leaving undecided the question whether the word *b'ymh* has a Semitic (cf. *bāmâ*) or a Greek origin (cf. *bēma*; Greek influence in the Ancient Near East started early: Raaflaub 2004: 205–212). LXX confirms the text (causal: 'for') but translates in such a literal way that it gives the impression it

first indication of troubles with surrounding peoples (*peoples of the lands*, i.e. non-Jews).

When *they offered … burnt offerings morning and evening*, they just offered the standard offerings that were offered at 9 am and 3 pm (for further considerations about the time of the evening offering, see on 9:4). These consisted of the males of the herd (bulls), of the flock (sheep or goats), or of birds (turtle-doves or pigeons), without parts for the worshippers or the priests (cf. Lev. 1).

4. The *Feast of Booths*, when the people would live in temporary accommodation in remembrance of the period in the Sinai desert, is scheduled from the fifteenth to the twenty-second day of the seventh month (Lev. 23:34–36, 43; Num. 29:12); here it can be expressed as 19–26 October 537 (cf. Introduction 2b, 'Julian dates').

For each day of the Feast of Booths specific offerings were prescribed (Num. 29:13–38), *according to the rule* of the matter on its day.

5. The first day of the month was also a festive day (Num. 28:11–15). The Israelite calendar was based on (among other factors) the first appearance of the new moon, in a cycle of about twenty-nine and a half days. Other *appointed feasts* are the Day of Atonement (Yom Kippur; Lev. 16; 23:27–32), the Passover (Pascha; Lev. 23:5–8), the Feast of Firstfruits (Lev. 23:9–14) and the Feast of Weeks (Pentecost; Lev. 23:15–21).

6. From this moment on, the offerings are executed, *but* (or 'However', as NET has it: although the Hebrew has literally 'and not', this combination can best be translated as *but*) that does not mean that the temple was already rebuilt. Nevertheless, the launch had taken place.

The reference to *the first day of the seventh month* repeats what has been said at the start of this paragraph, and the mention that *the*

(note 29 *cont.*) did not understand it. Vulg. offers an interpretation 'while the peoples around deterred them'; 1 Esdras 5:50: 'because all the peoples on the earth were in hostility with them and prevailed over them' (my translation; even though 1 Esdras as a whole cannot be trusted as a historical source – see Introduction 4f, 'The afterlife of Ezra-Neh. in Antiquity' – it can be used for text-critical issues where the text is parallel).

foundation of the temple … *was not yet laid* announces the new paragraph (for the idea of *the foundation of the temple* see also vv. 10–12, where this idea occurs three times).

Meaning

How important it is that believers are able to come together *as one man* (v. 1). They gather at Jerusalem, apparently expecting something. In the New Testament we can refer to Acts 2:1. Jerusalem is a space where believers can serve the Lord. This space is larger than the temple, and the holy and the profane come here together (cf. 1:3). In our days we can say that doctrine and principles are important, but they take form in every day's work.

This coming together does not deny the importance of the individual, which has been highlighted in Ezra 2, and even in this paragraph some individuals do take their responsibility: Jeshua and Zerubbabel (for both, see on 2:2). But again: these individually named persons worked together with their *kinsmen* (v. 2).

They did not come together to start something completely new. On the contrary, they are oriented to the Law written by Moses (v. 2) and are building (physically) on what was available: *They set the altar in its place*, that is, on its foundations, which were still there. We should do the same: orienting ourselves on the Scriptures and continuing with what God has already done in the church. This does not imply that all problems had gone: it is clear that fear is dominating them. Nevertheless, they make daily offerings, from which the smoke rises upwards, just as they themselves had gone up to Jerusalem from Babylon.[30] Besides the prescribed offerings, *freewill offerings* are mentioned. Even in situations of State support, our generosity will always remain necessary.

In verse 6 we see that the Jews had started on all the activities that were already possible, even though the temple had not yet been rebuilt. In our day, let us not delay doing what we can already do, under the pretext that we do not have perfect circumstances.

----

30 This turn of phrase reflects the presence of Hebrew *'ālâ* 'to go up' in the text.

iv. The foundation of the temple (3:7–13)

Context

After the installation of the altar, preparations were made for the building of the temple. Ezra 3:8 indicates that they started in the second month of their second year in Jerusalem, on 29 April 536 if we suppose that the first day of the month is meant (Yamauchi 1988: 595). This was the same month as that of the building of the first temple (see 1 Kgs 6:1; 2 Chr. 3:2); this might be taken symbolically, but probably it was the right season for building activities in any case.

Comment

7. As verse 7 is about the building of the temple, this verse must be taken together with verses 8–13 (as in NIV and NET) and not with verses 1–6 (as in the Masoretic tradition[31] and ESV). There is no need to start the translation of this verse with *So*. The *masons and the carpenters* were not foreigners, but probably belonged to the Jerusalem elite (Carter 1999: 287–288). While a *mason* refers indeed to a stonemason, a *carpenter* indicates a person with broader skills than just those needed for working with wood (also stone and metal). Both categories of artisans were plainly paid in cash. The *Sidonians* and *Tyrians*, however, were paid in kind, not because the Phoenicians did not know coined money, but perhaps because in international trade this was more useful (cf. Ezek. 27:17; Altmann 2016: 226–227). They came from Sidon, 22 miles south of Beirut, and Tyre, 22 miles south of Sidon, both in present-day Lebanon. In those days Sidon was the more important of the two cities and was best known for building excellent boats (Herodotus 7.96; made of wood, of course). They had also collaborated on the first temple (1 Kgs 5:21–26 [ET 5:7–12]) and then as here their input is not seen as problematic (for possible problems with Tyrians, see Neh. 13:16–17; Altmann 2015: 116). The land of Israel lacked sufficient wood suitable for building. *Cedar trees* can be sawn into high-quality planks. The wood (not necessarily in complete trees; cf. NIV) seems to have gone from *Lebanon* near to Sidon and Tyre by the shortest way to the sea, then over the sea (because coastal navigation was easier than overland transport) to Joppa (cf. Acts 9:36;

---

31 From the first-generation editors of the Hebrew text, tenth century AD.

10:5), the harbour nearest to Jerusalem, and then again overland. What is described here is prophesied in Isaiah 60:13.

8. The *house of God* is mentioned proleptically: the building has still to start in 536, *in the second month*. In this practical context, the name of *Zerubbabel*, being a political leader, is mentioned first. For the names and persons of *Zerubbabel* and *Jeshua*, see on 2:2. The work was done, however, under Sheshbazzar's responsibility (cf. 5:16). Below Zerubbabel and Jeshua, *Levites* are appointed as supervisors (cf. Min 2004: 114–115). They have to be at least *twenty years old*, the age also earlier decreed by David (1 Chr. 23:24–27; we find other minimum ages in Num. 4:3, 23, 30; 8:24, but perhaps not always for exactly the same groups or tasks).

9. In this verse we meet another person with the name *Jeshua* (for the meaning of this name, see on 2:2). If we have to read 'stood'[32] (AV) as an independent verb, this seems to indicate a voluntary commitment. If we read this verb in combination with the preposition 'over', the translation *supervised* seems to be the best solution. *Kadmiel* means 'God is before me'. He belongs to the *sons of Judah*, but what does this mean: that he was a Judean, or that he was not a Levite? Or is the text wrong and should we read (cf. 2:40) 'the sons of Hodaviah' (thus NIV)?

10. This verse presents the transition from the technical activity of the temple foundation to the worship that rounds off this section (1:5 – 3:13). If we try to relate the two halves of this verse to each other, we get 'When the builders had laid the foundation … they caused the priests to stand … When we see *the builders* as Zerubbabel and Jeshua, it is clear that they had the authority to do so. Literally the priests were 'dressed'; this is not to say that they were not naked, but to stress that they were there in their official uniforms (AV: 'in their apparel'; NET: 'ceremonially attired'). *Trumpets* (or better 'clarions'; thus NET) are typical priestly wind instruments, 18 inches long, a little bit thicker than a flute, with a mouthpiece and an extremity as a trumpet, but without valves, used on joyful occasions. *Cymbals* belong to the category of percussion instruments, also a typical temple instrument, having two equal metal disks (Keel 1972:

---

32   The Hebrew has the sg. at the start of the sentence (GKC §145o).

318; Josephus, *Ant.* 3.291). We cannot refer to a text with David's *directions* (however, see 1 Chr. 6:31; 15:16; 16:4–6), but that docs not mean that they were just a literary invention; it is clear that not everything has been recorded in Scripture.

11. The two halves of the choir responded to each other in antiphonal singing. The two verbs (ESV *praising and giving thanks*) are not mere synonyms. The first verb (also used in v. 10) stresses the joyful honouring, the second the content of the honour. The basis for praising the LORD is the same as when the ark was brought to Jerusalem (1 Chr. 16:34) and to the first temple (2 Chr. 5:13) (Bänziger 2014: 244): God is good and his *steadfast love*, his loyalty, his commitment, goes farther than the obvious; it goes the second mile (or even the third). This *steadfast love* nevertheless hopes to meet a similar willingness on the part of the other. It was only a beginning, this *foundation of the house of the LORD*, but people were grateful that they could participate in it. We might think that Psalm 136 was sung, but the ideas occur often (e.g. Pss 100:5; 107:1; 118:1–2).

12. 'And many of the old priests and Levites and family heads who had seen the first temple wept with a loud voice at the foundation of it [i.e. of the temple before their eyes]; and many raised[33] their voices with shouting for joy' (my translation).

The syntax of the word *old* is understood differently in the English versions, but NIV seems closest to normal Hebrew grammar: 'many of the older priests and Levites and family heads' (adjective with the nouns, not an apposition). For *the priests and Levites*, see on 2:36–39, 40–42. The term 'family heads' is also found in 1:5. The pluperfect *had seen* is required by English grammar; the Hebrew form just indicates a past tense. The *first house* is the first temple, destroyed in 587 – see on 2:2 – while these lines are situated in 536. This implies that these people must have been quite old[34] and

---

33 The Hebrew infinitive just indicates a succession (Waltke and O'Connor 1990: §36.3.2).

34 Even in 520 (Hag. 2:3) some people were apparently still alive who had seen the first temple. In Antiquity, as soon as the age of infant diseases had been passed, the same age could be reached among well-to-do classes as in our own day. While certainly not much medication

probably no longer in service (cf. Num. 8:24–26).[35] It is not clear why this emotion would have occurred only among people with some responsibility and not among the other people. Was it perhaps because they were more aware of everything that had happened and that had gone wrong? Of course, at this stage a comparison between the two buildings was impossible, so a presumed inferiority of the new building cannot have been the reason for the weeping. On the other hand, it would have been clear that even when the temple was rebuilt (not yet the case at this stage), not all problems would be solved.[36]

13. If it only concerned some older dignitaries, it is strange to see this confusion between joy and weeping; moreover, it is said explicitly in this verse that *the people* wept; in short: it would be better not to present verse 13 as a consequence of verse 12 (*so that*), but rather as another communication (thus NIV, NET).

A conclusion is formulated in the second half of the verse: In short, *the people shouted with a great shout, and the sound was heard far away.*

Meaning
Much has been realized in a short time: the return of the people to Jerusalem (1:5–11), the resettling of the people (3:1), the reconstruction of the altar (vv. 2–3), the reinstitution of the offerings (vv. 3–6), the coming of the material to Jerusalem (vv. 7–9) and the feast for the foundation of the temple (vv. 10–12), an extraordinary feast in addition to all the regular feasts that help us to commemorate God's mighty deeds (vv. 4–5). This extraordinary feast, however, is not perfect either. Shouts of joy go together with weeping, and it

---

existed, traffic accidents and pollution were less significant. Adad-Guppi, Nabonidus' mother, reached 102 years old (649–547), Sophocles ninety years (496–406), Plato eighty (427–347), Cicero's wife Terentia 103 years (98 BC – AD 6), Polycarp eighty-six (69–155), the 'father' of the synagogue of the Jewish community from Asia in Rome 110 years (epitaph; no date).

35 Should we use the term 'emeriti' for them?

36 Cf. Bänziger 2014: 247–248 for a different approach.

will always be so in our days on earth. Mixed feelings exist, partly dependent on one's own personal history (v. 12).

C. Core: building the temple (4:1 – 6:15)

While the previous section only launched the main subject of the first part of Ezra-Neh., the (re)building of the temple now really starts in this section, albeit not without a quite impressive overview of preceding problems. The story of the construction of the temple will be followed by the description of worship services, which we will consider as a new section, in order to highlight the parallelism with the fourth part of Ezra-Neh. (Neh. 7:4 – 12:47).

In this section the redactor uses a lot of documents, which he does not quote integrally, but only as far as they are useful for his story, according to the normal economy of biblical narrative (Käser 2023: 262–264). As some of these documents were available in Aramaic, the redactor switches to this language when he starts quoting such a document. Between two quotes he does not switch back to Hebrew. Indeed, this was not necessary: Aramaic was generally understood by his audience.

For the Aramaic language and the situation of the documents, see Introduction 2g, 'The documents', and 4a, 'Languages'.

i. Cessation of the building activities of the Jews (4:1–24)
Context
The moment the foundation is laid, differences of opinion become apparent (vv. 1–3), even leading to the complete interruption of the construction of the temple from 536 to 520 (vv. 4–5, 24). Description of this problem invites the redactor to speak also about problems of resistance of surrounding people to the reconstruction of the walls, one in 485 (cf. v. 6), one about 460 (cf. v. 7) and one in 448 (cf. v. 8). Why did he mention these problems here, and not at the chronologically appropriate places later on in Ezra-Neh.? Two possible reasons are either that he had information at his disposal from sources other than those he used normally in the later parts of Ezra-Neh. and for that reason he did not want to integrate it there, or that he was convinced that he needed the information here to make clear that cooperation with

the Samarians (for this group, see the Introduction 2l, 'Samarians/ Samaritans – Judeans/Jews') was really not an option (Williamson 1985: 65). Porten 2002: 36 refers to the non-chronological order of Darius' report of his victories in the Behistun inscription (column IV).

Although the structure of this chapter is strange to us as twenty-first-century readers, it must be clear that it was not so for the original readers, who knew their history and recognized the linguistic indications. In verse 24 the word *Then* (not the same word as at the opening of v. 23) and the reference to Darius indicate that the text resumes its earlier chronological sequence.

Comment

1. Construction of the temple is initiated by *the returned exiles* from *Judah and Benjamin*, the Southern Kingdom (see on 1:5): they were ready to begin the reconstruction of the temple.

2. For *Zerubbabel*, see on 2:2. For 'family heads', see on 1:5; 3:12. The Samarians say they *worship* God, or rather, are engaged in seeking (cf. other English versions) God (this does not necessarily mark a distance ['only trying'], as the word is used frequently: not only 6:21, but also, e.g., 2 Chr. 15:12; 17:4; 34:3; Isa. 65:10). Are they making this proposal to the Jews in order to obstruct the whole project? Not necessarily so. Indeed, they *have been sacrificing to him*, but according to 2 Kings 17:25–33 they started doing so in order to solve an issue with lions and continued to worship other gods too (syncretism; see *Context*). The Jewish resistance to the Samarians seems to be reflected in the basic Hebrew text (Codex Leningradensis), where we find a negation ('not') instead of *to him*: 'for we have not been sacrificing' (in Hebrew, the negation – 'not' – strongly resembles the form *to him*). The Masoretes, however, already wanted to read[37] *to him*, in unison with the ancient versions. The problem has left no trace in the English versions.

The Assyrian king *Esarhaddon*, son of Sennacherib (2 Kgs 19:37), reigned from 680 to 669 and in 674 relocated people from conquered

---

37   For this Codex, cf. n. 25.

regions in Mesopotamia and Syria into the Judean countryside, in order to be better prepared for a military campaign in Egypt (Schmökel 1957: 276; for the Egyptian campaign in general, cf. Drioton and Vandier 1989: 551; Veenhof 2001: 260, 270). This action followed an earlier relocation by Sargon II (2 Kgs 17:24; Younger 2004: 256, 259, 277–278). Perhaps Esarhaddon is also the king meant in 2 Kings 17:27. As far as the Southern Kingdom is concerned, since the start of the exile many immigrants had come from Moab and Edom (Ezek. 35:10–15). They had adopted not only the dwelling-place, but also in some measure the religion of the Jews (as many had not gone into exile but simply stayed in Judah). These immigrants did not of course want to give up their national and religious identity, which helps to explain their resistance to the rebuilding of the temple and the walls.

3. *Jeshua*: see on 2:2.

You have nothing to do with us is a good translation for the literal 'not for you and for us (is it) to build a house for our God'.

Although English versions translate as *we alone will build*, a better translation[38] would be 'we, the congregation, will build'. Indeed, the Jews considered the Samarians as not belonging to the community, as the Samarians had put themselves outside the community by identifying themselves in verse 2 as strangers and not as proselytes. 'The primary motivation behind the elders' refusal was religious' (Brown 2005a: 45). It is also a fact that *Cyrus the king of Persia* had given his decree only to the Jews (see 1:3).

4. The expression *the people of the land* can have a specific meaning, but must always be explained in its context. Looking at 3:3 and 4:1–2, it must mean the Samarians (Stiegler 1994: 127). These people were 'weakening the hands of the people of Judah and were disturbing them so that they could not build' (my translation), not once but continuously. To 'weaken the hands' is a metaphor for discouragement.

5. They hired *counsellors*, perhaps some local lower Persian clerks (De Fraine 1961: 39). The opposition lasts from the first attempt to

---

38   The translation 'alone' for the Hebrew *yaḥad* cannot be excluded: see Job 34:29.

rebuild the temple in 536 through Cambyses' reign (530–522) until the days of Darius (522–486). While Cyrus was very generous with his decree, he does not seem to have given any attention to the actual building of the temple.

6. Ezra 4 speaks not only about the reigns of Cyrus, Cambyses and Darius (previous verse), but jumps in this verse also to the reign of Xerxes, who reigned from 486 to 465 (see Introduction 2e, 'Persian kings'). Through the use of *And* (or 'As for') this change in period is made clear to readers. With *the beginning of his reign* the accession year (the non-numbered year before the first full year of a king; in this case December 486 – April 485) may be indicated (Williamson 1985: 60), which places this verse chronologically between the facts of Ezra 6 and those of Ezra 7.

The *accusation* (the word has the same etymology as 'Satan') cannot be about the building of the temple (because it was completed in 515), but must be about the building of the city walls, as also becomes clear in the next verses. The difference is not very big: in the work of Ezra-Neh. building the temple, building the walls and building the community are described as fully parallel.

7. In this verse we also make a jump, now introduced by *In the days of Artaxerxes*, who reigned from 465 to 424 (see Introduction 2e, 'Persian kings'). There is no specification of the date, although we may presume that it happened somewhere at the beginning of his reign, let us say about 460 (Brown 2005a: 37 says 465, but in this verse there is no reason to think of the accession year). *Bishlam* ('Bēl gives peace') is apparently the leader of the gang (Steiner 2007: 401), also composed of *Mithredath* (for the etymology of the name, see on 1:8; of course, here it is another person), *Tabeel* (Aramaic: 'God is good') and some unnamed *associates*.[39] Were they ordinary people (nevertheless able to write) who hoped for rich rewards (cf. Xenophon, *Cyropaedia* 8.2.10–12) by reporting things that might be

---

39 This word is a hapax in Classical Hebrew, but quite common in Aramaic, where the main meaning is 'colleague' (cf. NET). In that case Bishlam, Mithredath and Tabeel would be officials. For Persian officials, the relation with 'colleagues' is always very important (Porten 2003: 57; Lindenberger 2003: no. 30a, 34, 42).

harmful to the king? *The* text[40] of the *letter was written in Aramaic and translated* into Aramaic. When you write a letter in Aramaic, why should it then be still translated into Aramaic? The ESV keeps away from the problem by translating the term *in Aramaic* only once, the NIV by making the distinction between Aramaic script and Aramaic language, but it forgets the word *translated*. If we try to keep all the words as they are and where they are, we should interpret this sentence as 'The text of the letter was written in square script and translated from Hebrew into Aramaic'. Another option might be to transfer the second 'in Aramaic' to the next verse, as an introduction to the first Aramaic part of Ezra (just as in Dan. 2:4). By doing this, however, the question remains concerning the language from which the letter was *translated*. We learn nothing of the actual content of the letter,[41] nor of the result.

8. At this point the text changes to Aramaic (see introductory comments on 4:1 – 6:15). We may have expected that now the text of the letter would be quoted, but we observe again a transition to a new situation of opposition, the transition being much rougher than before (unless we transport 'then' from the next verse to this verse: see v. 9). We are still in the days of Artaxerxes I, but most probably later[42] than in the previous verse. The most probable reconstruction is to put it in a time shortly before 448, to see it as the cause of Nehemiah's mourning (in 446; Neh. 1:1–4) and to understand the change in the king's mind by referring to the Peace of Callias in 449, which brought the king generally into a more comfortable position and specifically into a more generous mood towards the Jews (Bengtson 1977: 212; Badian 1993: 32, 49; Briant 2002: 557–558, 579–580, 582, 974–975).

Rehum (for the etymology, see on 2:1–2) is *commander* of the chancellery (supervising the satrap's administration and responsible

---

40 Many English versions (among which ESV) telescope 'text' and 'letter' into one single term. That does not change the meaning, but the Hebrew text is completely understandable and should not be changed.

41 Unless Steiner's hypothesis is followed and the following verses are read as Bishlam's summaries of earlier letters (Steiner 2001).

42 Not in Steiner's hypothesis (see previous note), of course.

for communication in Samaria; Dušek 2007: 509). During this period
Judah has no governor for itself and the Persian king's interests are
administered from the Samaria office. *Shimshai* ('sunny') is *scribe*.
The combination of the functions of chancellor and state secretary
was quite common and they seem together to form the top of the
provincial administration (Meinhold 2001: 198). The proposition
that is translated *against* in ESV can also be translated as 'concerning'
(thus NET); the translation does not change the situation. The verse
ends with the indication *as follows*, which makes us think that in
verse 9 the actual content will be transmitted.

9. This verse gives the actual content of the letter announced in
the previous verse, but rather awkwardly repeats the introduction.
The Hebrew text of this verse has before *Rehum* (with which most
English versions start) the word 'Then' (thus AV). This word cannot
be explained here (cf. AV, which has to add 'wrote'). On the other
hand, the word would be very useful at the start of the previous
verse, which also has *Rehum* at the start; this resemblance may be
the origin of the copying error.

Persian officials are mentioned according to their function,
together with their 'colleagues',[43] but also people according to their
place of origin. No consensus exists about the boundary between
the two groupings. In ESV we start with (1) *judges*, (2) *governors*
(etymologically 'with leading position'; functionally 'inspectors';
Achenbach 2000: 142–143) and (3) *officials*; we continue in ESV with
(4) *Persians* (see below), (5) *men of Erech* (Uruk/Warka in Sumeria),
(6) *Babylonians* (from the city of Babel, not from the region) and (7)
men of Susa, who are *Elamites*.

The AV (just as the LXX) considers groups 1, 2 and 3 as geographical names also (Steiner 2006: 676–679): people from Din
(Din-šarri near Susa), Apharsat (Media) and Tripolis (North
Phoenicia). It furthermore presents an eighth group, as it
interprets[44] what ESV translates as *that is* as 'Dehavites' (the Elamite

43 Cf. v. 7, esp. n. 39.

44 AV bases itself on the consonants of the Hebrew text, while the
    other versions base themselves on what was read by the Masoretes
    (cf. n. 25).

city of Daeba?); a disadvantage of this interpretation is that again a whole region (instead of a city) would be mentioned. In NIV we find the combination of the third group ('administrators') with the following national groups ('administrators over the people from Persia' etc.). Some lesser used versions, probably influenced by an earlier NIV edition, combine this with the second group (NIV 1984: 'the judges and officials over the men from Tripolis' etc.). It offers a solution for the strange combination of offices and peoples but has no foundation in the text. NET considers the fourth group also as officials, namely as 'secretaries' (presumably by changing the order of the consonants in Aramaic). For this fourth group, 'men of Sippar (north of Babel)' has also been proposed; this option would have the advantage that this term would also represent inhabitants of a single city, but it demands a rearrangement of the consonants. An option that should be mentioned because of the conjunction between the first and the second group (but for which I do not find an example in major English versions) is 'judges and inspectors, Tripolitans, Persians, Warkites, Babylonians and Susians'.

Achenbach (2000: 136–143) explains all terms as functionaries except the inhabitants of Babel and Susa.

10. The group is still larger but is not specified further. *Osnappar* most probably is short for Ashurbanipal (Ash(urba)nipal > Asnipar [there are no Persian words with *l*] > Osnappar; Millard 1976: 11), who reigned over the Assyrian Empire from 668 to 630. In the second half of his reign he captured Babylon, made Elam an Assyrian province and suppressed rebellions in the west (Veenhof 2001: 271–274). All these people were brought to one or another city[45] in Samaria and the rest of Trans-Euphrates. Yamauchi situates this in 648 (Yamauchi 2002: 357). For the organization of the satrapy Trans-Euphrates (the term *province* has been added by ESV), see Introduction 2f, 'Organization of the Persian Empire'.

---

45 The Aramaic has the singular, but for practical reasons it cannot refer to just one city; hence the interpretation as a collective, with as translation *cities*. The interpretation in the main text keeps the singular, but thinks also of different cities in Samaria.

The Masoretes made this verse end with 'and as far as now is the case', 'well then'. This has been left out by ESV; we do find it in RSV ('and now'), but as the first term of the next sentence.

11. It seems that Rehum and his colleagues now quote from the *copy* which they could consult, so somewhere in the archives of the satrapy of Trans-Euphrates (and so the address is short; Porten 2003: 56–57). It is not clear whether the words *To Artaxerxes the king* help to define the letter (thus the Masoretic partition and AV) or are part of the quote (other translations).

The Masoretes made this verse also end with 'and now', 'well then'. ESV and RSV keep it in this verse, but have it as the first term of the next sentence; NET does the same, but transfers it completely to verse 12.

12. At last we find here the content of an accusation: *the Jews …* *are rebuilding* (a very frequent word in Ezra) *that rebellious and wicked city*. These Jews *came up*, a word regularly used for migration and the Aramaic counterpart of the frequent Hebrew *ʿālâ* (see on 3:2; Porten 2002: 37). Why is it mentioned that they *came up from you*, from before the king? It is difficult to surmise that they blamed the king for having sent these people. Was it an aggravation of the complaint, in the sense that they had not been thankful enough? *They are finishing the walls* [or at least: 'they are about to finish the walls'[46]] *and repairing the foundations* (when we think about the logical order for foundations and walls, here a resultative translation is necessary: 'they have already repaired[47] the foundations').

13. If *this city is rebuilt* completely, they will not pay customs (Altmann 2016: 232) and tax in kind (Kreissig 1973: 90) and they will not do their statutory labours any more (Briant 2002: 401). Taxes in the Persian Empire were heavy and were (for the most part) not meant for public services; gold and silver went straight to the king's treasure house (Schaper 2000: 147–148). By no longer doing anything for the king or his empire, 'the city will harm the kings'. Unfortunately, we have here only the most probable translation. In

---

46 Following what the Masoretes wanted to read (cf. n. 25; Bauer and Leander 1927: 167m).

47 Pael of *y-ḥ-ṭ* (Vogt 1971: 75).

the first place, there is a grammatical problem: as Aramaic uses the same verbal form for the third-person singular feminine and the second-person singular masculine, grammatically the king could be addressed ('you will harm the kings'; in that way AV). It seems improbable, however, that the officials would blame the king for harming the kings (but cf. v. 12, where such a reproach is also an option). The passive form *will be impaired* is not justifiable, but goes together with a lexical problem, namely the interpretation of the word that is translated as *revenue* in ESV. With this choice, a passive translation becomes attractive, even though grammatically inconsistent. The word can, however, also be translated as 'for sure', or 'in the end'. This does not have consequences for the story. It is clear that in the end the kings will certainly lose revenue. Nevertheless, the technical problem remains.

14. The ESV maintains the verbal form of the Masoretic text and translates *because we eat* [lit. 'ate'!] *the salt*. Other translations opt for a small adaptation of the Aramaic form (because the past tense is a bit awkward) and read 'because the salt of the palace is our salt' (Muraoka 2020: 71). The officials understand well the basis for their loyalty (cf. 'that we are loyal' in NET): they depend on the palace for their salary. The English word 'salary' comes from the Latin *salarium* ('salt portion' > 'money to buy salt' > 'salary').

Where the Aramaic mentions that 'we have sent', as a standard it can be supplemented with the object 'messengers' (or 'this message', as NIV does).

15. The intention of the letter is 'that one should investigate (rendered as a passive: *search may be made*; other option: 'that the king should investigate' [cf. NET], but given that we should not expect the king to do this work personally, the actual difference is not that important) in the book of memories/records of your forefathers'. The Persian archives were quite extensive (cf. Stronk 2007: 38) and probably also contained documents of the Babylonian Empire (Dandamayev 2006: 373).

It is repeated that Jerusalem was *rebellious* (cf. v. 12) and that *sedition was stirred up in it*. The terms are synonymous; the second one stresses the treacherous breaking of the peace (a euphemism for obedience to the conqueror). Jerusalem's purported attitude is seen as the reason for her fall (but see 2 Chr. 36:16–17).

16. The writers of the letter stress again that they are informing the king about the eventual consequences of what is happening (cf. v. 13). If they are claiming that the whole satrapy (not *province*; see Introduction 2f, 'Organization of the Persian Empire') Trans-Euphrates will not belong to the king any more, they are clearly exaggerating. In this case 'part' is interpreted as 'any part': 'not any part of Trans-Euphrates will be yours (any more)'. It is also possible, however, to interpret 'part' as 'some part': 'some part of Trans-Euphrates will not be yours (any more)' (thus NET). That they are writing concerning Trans-Euphrates as a whole has already been said in verses 10–11.

17. In this verse we arrive at the king's formal answer (and so the address is long; Porten 2003: 56–57). For the addressees, see the senders of verse 8. The answer itself, however, is more concise (as is normal when emperors answer letters of subjects: cf. Trajan's answer to Pliny in AD 111); nevertheless, one detail is mentioned here that was not in verse 8: the addressees live in Samaria, as well as in the rest of Trans-Euphrates. After the address, the king sends his *greeting*, literally 'Peace' (thus AV). This word has turned out to be important in the discussion about the authenticity of the Aramaic letters in Ezra. According to some recent scholarship this short form is the rendering of a Greek formula and points to an origin in Hellenistic times. This conclusion, however, is not compulsory: *greeting* occurs also in the fifth century BC, probably as a summary for a longer greeting (Williamson 2008: 57, 60–61), and a rich variation already existed in the Persian period. See Introduction 2g, 'The documents'.

In the Masoretic text this verse too (see on v. 10) ends with 'and now'. Again, this should be transferred to the next verse.

18. The *letter* [same word as in the Hebrew of v. 7] *has been ... read* for the king paragraph by paragraph, not restricted to a summary (as an equivalent of our 'I have read your letter with great interest'), possibly with a translation (thus NIV and NET), as it is not sure that the king himself knew Aramaic, although it was the lingua franca of his empire (see introductory comments on ch. 4).

19. An order had been given by the king and his servants had done some research and they found out that the accusation that Jerusalem always was a rebellious city was correct. For the words *rebellion* and *sedition*, see on verse 15; these words may be considered together (hendiadys;[48] 'armed rebellion'; Muraoka 2020: 72).

20. David and Solomon indeed reigned, as direct kings or as suzerains, over a large part of what later was to become Trans-Euphrates (cf. Williamson 1985: 64; Malamat 2001: 197; Kitchen 2003: 617). Those who believe in the historical trustworthiness of the biblical report about David and Solomon will find a confirmation in the answer of the king of Persia; those who do not, will not. For the taxes and duties, see verse 13.

21. Although an order is given *that these men be made to cease*, it is not accompanied by an order to demolish what has already been constructed. The king keeps all his options open to come to another decision later[49] (cf. Neh. 2:5–6).[50]

22. Between the two halves of this verse an Aramaic word has been used that etymologically means 'why' (cf. ESV), but which in this period of the Aramaic language meant 'so that not' (cf. NET) (Bauer and Leander 1927: 363–364w; Vogt 1971: 98). The king seems to come back to the reproach that he would harm the kings (see on v. 13): now he tells the officials that they should not harm the king.

23. For the addressees, see on verse 8. They *made them cease*, and did so *by force and power* (lit. 'with hand and power'; a hendiadys [see Introduction 4g, 'Literary terms'] meaning 'armed force', as NET has it).

And cease they did; probably they even went further, with some destruction (cf. Neh. 1:3).

24. The word *Then* does not make verse 24 follow on from verse 23, but ends the digression and so we return to the situation of the year 536.[51] The actual year of the restart is mentioned: *the second year of*

---

48 See Introduction 4g, 'Literary terms'.

49 A law of Medes and Persians could not be changed without reason, but it was not unchangeable in the literal sense of the word. Moreover, this is not a law, but a king's rescript.

50 Perhaps it was also during this period that the king permitted Ezra to go to Jerusalem.

51 Another indication of this transition might be the repetition of the words *reign of Darius king of Persia*, called 'resumptive repetition' by Brown 2005b: 186. See also Ezra 8:15.

the reign of Darius. As soon as the return mechanism is recognized, it is clear that Darius I is intended, also mentioned in verse 5 just before the digression. The redactor did not think of Artaxerxes' successor Darius II (reigned 424–405; contra Becking 2018: 75–76). As Darius I reigned from 522 to 486, the building work on the temple was interrupted from 536 to 520. The verb *ceased* occurs in this verse for the third and fourth times in this unit (cf. vv. 21, 23). The first occurrence in this verse mentions the actual stopping (hence ESV *stopped*); the second occurrence in this verse underlines the continuation of the cessation. In this way the subject of the whole item is confirmed.

Meaning
While in the previous section (Ezra 1 – 3) attention was given to what had been realized in continuity with the past, this section is characterized by confrontation and conflict. It was not an easy, straightforward way, just as in the days of the exodus.

The Jews who returned from the exile were of the opinion that they needed to keep a very sharp distinction from their neighbours (possibly impressed by Jer. 24) even when these neighbours claimed to confess the same faith. The former exiles judged that it was not the same confession, as becomes clear from what the 'Samarians' themselves said in verse 2. This is not the same thing as being naively happy at the start, as Goswell (2011: 197) sees it. Some deconstructivist Bible readers[52] will tell us that the Jews were narrow-minded separatists and the Samarians actually broad-minded people. Although it may not be our intention to be narrow-minded people to our fellow citizens in society, the Bible is clear about the necessity to draw boundaries at certain points. It takes wisdom to know at which moment cooperation in society must have priority and in which cases this is no longer possible, and limits must be drawn, avoiding the Scylla of being too aggressive towards society and the Charybdis of being too accepting and adaptive. Pitfalls await on both sides; it is possible to be too accommodating while staying in a breakaway church or to be too severe in a national church.

---

52 E.g. Hensel 2017.

We have in this unit almost a catalogue of different means of opposition. It should not lead us to make trouble for other people,[53] but prepare us for when other people make use of these means against us. Opposition starts with discouragement and intimidation (vv. 4–5). Later come accusations (vv. 6–16). It is good to analyse the elements of the accusations (Fyall 2010: 77–78): the authors present themselves as quite important (v. 9) and fully respecting civil authorities (vv. 10, 11, 14), they generalize what applies only to a specific group (v. 12a), present the same argument in different words (v. 13b) and exaggerate (v. 16).

Resistance will continue (vv. 6–23). With this digression we are reminded to consider history and not to limit our perspective to our actual problems. At the same time, it spotlights the importance of what will be realized in Ezra 5 – 6. The two go together: 'a wide door for effective work has opened to me, and there are many adversaries' (2 Cor. 16:9).

ii. The building of the temple (5:1 – 6:15)
Context
At the beginning of Darius' reign (522) there was no building activity. Under favourable political circumstances (from 521 on, with the king well established and peace restored; cf. Zech. 1:11) but unfavourable economic circumstances (poor harvests), Haggai ('born on a festive day') reacted in the second half of the year 520 to the attitude behind the situation of the temple: no construction activities, and where there is no construction, the weather does its destructive work. Haggai's activity was rather short. Did he die soon after 520? That is possible, but not necessary. Zechariah was active from October 520. We read here that he was also instrumental in the construction of the temple (cf. Zech. 1:16), but that was not the main point of his message (rather, continuation and extension of God's covenant with Israel). Zechariah had a long career, which lasted from 520 to 475.

Building activity starts soon after the end of Haggai's activity,

---

on 18 December 520 (Hag. 2:18), and ends 12 March 515 (Ezra 6:15); Tattenai's inspection (5:3–4) can be situated in 517.

Haggai and Zechariah are mentioned in Ezra 5:1 and 6:14 and mark thus the unity of this unit (Bänziger 2014: 223). We are still in the Aramaic part of the book of Ezra.

Comment

1. Literally this verse states somewhat redundantly 'Then Haggai the prophet [standard description for Haggai] and Zechariah the son [see further] of Iddo [standard description for Zechariah], the prophets, acted as prophets[54] [rather than 'prophesied']', which is reduced in most versions. In Aramaic the same word is used for *son* and further descendants; with the information of Zechariah 1:1, NIV is justified in using 'descendant', but this word should have the definite article (*'the* descendant of Iddo'). Its mention suggests the importance of Iddo, but we do not know why.

At the end of the verse we read *over them*. Most probably this is connected with *the name* through the idea 'which was proclaimed' (cf. Jer. 15:16). Ultimately, the difference from most translations (who connect it with *God*) is not so important, as *the name* represents the essence of the person concerned.

2. *Zerubbabel* and *Jeshua*, the political and religious leaders (see on 2:2), worked together and *began*[55] *to rebuild the house of God that is in Jerusalem*; the clause *in Jerusalem* must be connected with *the house*, as English translations generally do. The verb *arose* must not be taken too literally: they decided to launch the action of rebuilding the temple (Muraoka 2020: 72).

3. *Tattenai* (probably the shortened form of an Akkadian name meaning 'protect the one you have given') was from 520 to 502 a

---

54   The verb has a third-person singular form (instead of the plural expected because of 'the prophets'), probably because it stands at the front of the sentence.

55   Pael of *š-r-ḥ* (Vogt 1971: 174). Becking 2018: 77 doubts the translation *began*, but this is also the best translation in 1QapGen XII, 13, 15.

kind of satrap in Trans-Euphrates.[56] *Shethar-bozenai* ('saved by the god of the stars')[57] is a civil servant (see on v. 6). As is normally the case in the Persian Empire, the *associates* are mentioned too.

Tattenai decided to come to Jerusalem to inspect the building works, possibly because Darius liked to have a central overview (Lemaire 1996: 56, referring to Herodotus 3.89). He poses the question about the building to them[58] in a neutral way. The building is already at such a stage that the word *finish* can be used, although it is not clear what is being finished; it must have something to do with wood, so we might think of 'equipment, furniture', although it cannot be excluded that only the wood for the finishing of the walls and the roof is meant. Tattenai's question is repeated in 5:9 and answered in 6:14.

4. Most manuscripts have in the first half of this verse 'we spoke to them'. One manuscript and some versions have 'they spoke to them', which fits the context much better, obviously. The mistake could have been triggered by 5:9, which rightly has *we spoke*.

Of course, the report must contain the names of the people who were responsible for the work (Muraoka 2020: 73; cf. v. 10).

5. While in a Persian context the eyes and the ears of the king indicate his spies, 'the eyes of the LORD run to and fro throughout the whole earth, to give strong support to those whose heart is blameless towards him' (2 Chr. 16:9; cf. Ps. 94:9).

Tattenai is rather neutral in his conclusion; things must simply be looked up in the archives. The building activity is not stopped, which is much more positive for the Judeans than the situation with the rebuilding of Jerusalem in 536 (as described in 4:4–5). Tattenai's letter is presented in verses 7–17; it will be answered in 6:6–12.

---

56 Tattenai's precise status is as complicated as the status of his territory; cf. Meinhold 2001: 194–195; Dandamayev 2006: 376–377; see also Introduction 2f, 'Organization of the Persian Empire'.

57 If the Aramaic transcription is right; some scholars think of an original 'Shatibarzan', which is a frequently used Persian name.

58 The form for *to build* and that for *to them* are old-fashioned forms (although recurring with some frequency for *to them*), one from the redactor, one in the mouth of Tattenai.

6. For *Tattenai*, see on verse 3. *Shethar-bozenai* (see on v. 3) and his *associates*[59] are called 'inspectors' (Williamson 2008: 53; not 'the Apharsachites' as AV has it, although the vocalization in Aramaic points in that direction).

7. With *all peace*, the wish is expressed that the king might have peace everywhere in his empire (Becking 2018: 81).

8. The use of the term *province* confirms again the importance of *Judah* already at this moment (and not only after the arrival of Nehemiah).[60] The stones with which the temple is being built have a specific quality, but it is not clear which one: ESV translates *huge stones*, but probably these are 'wrought stones' – in other words, no expense was spared (Williamson 1991: 47–49). And indeed, the builders are complimented here: *This work goes on diligently.*

9. In the report to the king the original question of 5:3 is repeated.

10. The first *their* refers to *the names of their leaders* (cf. v. 4); the second *their* to the labourers with whom Tattenai had spoken (Muraoka 2020: 73).

11–12. Verse 11b is again (cf. 2:55, 58; 4:20) a reference to Solomon, this time without mentioning his name. The first temple was finished in 959 BC and so had been standing there for a long time (Muraoka 2020: 74).

After having called their God *the God of heaven and earth*, the Judeans have to explain why his temple had been destroyed: *because our fathers had angered the God of heaven*. It is a reason (*because*) and not just an indication of time (as NET sees it: 'after'). It is to the Jews' credit that they are open about this reason.

Although it is superfluous to mention that *Nebuchadnezzar* is a *Chaldean*, this might be helpful at a political level, as it will promote the Persians' favourable attitude towards the Jews. For the facts, see 2 Chronicles 36:15–21.

13. Now reference is made to the year 538, the first year a Persian was king of Babylon; for the facts, see 1:1–4. In an Akkadian text,

---

59 See n. 39 for the importance of collegiality for the Persians.

60 For an overview of the political structure, see Introduction 2f, 'Organization of the Persian Empire'.

Cyrus calls himself 'king of Babylon'[61] (Cyrus Cylinder, l.20) in a whole series of historical pretensions.

14. For the transfer from Jerusalem to Babylon, see 2 Chronicles 36:18; for the transfer from Babylon to Jerusalem, see Ezra 1:7–11. Although *Sheshbazzar* was the governor during the time described here, he was no longer active at the time of the writing of this letter (see 1:8, 11; 3:8). That is why he is introduced here as an unknown person (Williamson 1991: 46–47), *one whose name was Sheshbazzar* (cf. 1:8). The Aramaic expression behind this[62] does not occur after the Achaemenid period and so is important for ascertaining the date of our text (Williamson 2008: 56).

15. In this verse three orders are given: *Take these vessels, go and put* … This could be summarized as 'bring these vessels back', but it is better to maintain the formal elements of the Aramaic in translation whenever possible in the target language, as they express the importance of the order. The temple should be *rebuilt on its site*, that is, on its original foundations.

16. Although *Sheshbazzar* could not achieve very much, he is mentioned here as the governor in charge at the date of King Cyrus' decree (see 1:8). For the expression *house of God … in Jerusalem*, see on 5:2.

17. With the previous verse, the report about what the Jews have said ends. Now the inspectors ask for what *seems good to the king*, the king's *pleasure*.

Apparently, the Jews had the order written on their behalf at their disposal (see 1:2–4), but not the original decree (see 6:3). As far as they understand, this decree can be found *in the royal archives … in Babylon* (this assumption will turn out to be wrong: see 6:2). The *king* was kindly asked to *send* Tattenai his decision (thus NIV; ESV: *his pleasure*).

6:1. Although the same words are used and in that way the translation *made a decree* is correct, we find in this verse simply a practical

---

61   My translation; the Akkadian reads 'LUGAL TIN-TIR[KI]' (Schaudig 2019: 19).

62   Lit. 'Sheshbazzar his name'. See for an overview Introduction 2g, 'The documents'.

order issued by the king and not a law that will be valid for ages. Then *search was made* (literally 'they searched'[63] – thus NIV – but as the subject is not expressed, the translation with a passive form is a good solution) *in the house of the archives where the documents were stored*, as we read in ESV. A more precise translation would be: 'in the house of the documents/writings where the treasures were deposited', as the combination of documents and precious objects – not totally unjustifiable – seems to have been quite normal in the Persian Empire.

2. The document was not *found* at Babylon (where Cyrus had been until sometime during spring 538), but at Ecbatana (where he had spent the summer that year; Yamauchi 1990: 158).[64] The average temperature at Ecbatana being somewhat lower, it was more appropriate as a summer capital (Tuplin 1998: 68, 71–73); it does not play any other role in the Bible. The word translated in ESV as *capital* normally indicates the citadel of a city. Although the citadel seems the normal place for the most important government buildings, this has not yet been confirmed archeologically (possibly due to limited archaeological activity). The *scroll*[65] that *was found*[66] contains a memorandum (*a record*), quoted in verses 3–5.

3. Although the headlines agree with Cyrus' order found in 1:2–4, this document is not an identical copy. The text here is the Aramaic archive version, with date (*In the first year of Cyrus the king*, i.e. 538 BC: see *Context* for 1:1–4) and subject (*Concerning the house of God at Jerusalem*) at the front; the text in 1:2–4 is the order aimed at a Hebrew audience. Kitchen (2003: 76, 78, 519–520) describes how different authentic versions occurred in the Persian Empire, sometimes even

63 The Ezra scroll from Qumran (4Q117 fr. 3 3) has the singular form, with the same impersonal meaning: 'one searched'.
64 For the different capitals of the Persian Empire, see Introduction 2e, 'Persian kings'.
65 The text being in Aramaic, a scroll (and not a clay tablet) is an obvious material (Grosheide 1963: 172).
66 The verb has a third-person singular masculine form (instead of the feminine expected because of 'the scroll', which is feminine in Aramaic), probably because it stands at the front of the sentence.

on the same monument. In this case the decree must have been considered as more consequential than the order, as otherwise the Jews could simply have shown the order. The temple is described as *the house of God* [or: the god] *at Jerusalem*, in Aramaic a neutral term, as normally can be expected in a State decree. In this archival version introduction and closing words were not needed.

As King Cyrus had decreed that *its foundations be retained* (not 'laid', as NIV has: see Vogt 1971: 117; Williamson 1985: 71), it was necessary to mention the permitted height, but superfluous to mention the permitted length and breadth. The Masoretic text, however, does mention a breadth of *sixty cubits* (about 30 yards), which is not concordant with the breadth of the old temple mentioned in 1 Kings 6:2 (only twenty cubits, about 10 yards), although it should be, as the king as well as the Jews aimed at continuity. On the other hand, the height mentioned is quite impressive. All this together suggests a copyist's error (easy to make when numbers are concerned), which must have been early, as the ancient text witnesses (LXX, the Ezra scroll at Qumran [4Q117], Josephus, *Ant.* 11.99 and Vulg.) have the same dimensions.[67]

4. Most translations think of *three layers of great stones and one layer of timber.* It is, however, difficult to understand how to visualize these layers. For that reason, it is better to translate with 'course' (thus NIV): a kind of three-row brick wall, with inside panelling in new wood – that is, no recycled timber, and wood was expensive in the Ancient Near East. In any case, this text does not speak about the foundations (thus TLB). When we hear about wood, we are reminded of the reproach of Haggai 1:8[68] and in this way also of the fact that there was not only external resistance to building the temple, but also internal.

5. This part of the decree confirms what has been said in 5:14. This verse is one of the few verses of Ezra mentioned in a Qumran manuscript (4Q117); instead of the singular (*Nebuchadnezzar ...*

---

67 See Bänziger 2014: 251–254 for another approach.
68 In most translations also Hag. 1:4, but that verse might be translated as: 'As far as you are concerned, is it for you the time to live respected in your houses, while this House is in ruins?'

brought to Babylon), that manuscript has the plural ('they brought it to Babylon'); in both cases the king was responsible and the soldiers did the work.

6. Having quoted King Cyrus' decree in 6:3–5, King Darius starts his accompanying letter in this verse.

Tattenai, the satrap, and *Shethar-bozenai* and his *associates*, the inspectors (see on 5:6), must *keep away* from the temple, not in the geographical sense, but in the juridical sense (Steinmann 2010: 258): they are not allowed to hinder the building enterprise. The Aramaic has 'their associates' (thus NET), but this is based on the fact that vocatives are supposed to be in the third person (Koopmans 1957: 33); this is not the case in English and so *your associates* is a correct translation.

7. With *the governor of the Jews*, Zerubbabel is meant. The principle of continuity is mentioned again: the temple will be rebuilt *on its site*.

8. This verse contains an interesting parallel with 4:21 (maintained in NIV; in ESV reduced to *without delay*). While in that verse it is asked to 'give an order to stop these men', we read here that 'the price must be paid to these men in order that they do not stop' (building, presumably; or spending, but that does not make any difference at the level of content). This price must be paid 'with due diligence'. The source is the same as for the tax mentioned in 4:13: 'customs'.

9–10. Indeed, the Aramaic can be translated by 'young bulls, rams, or sheep' (thus RSV; cf. AV), but it is also possible to interpret it as 'individuals belonging to the class of' (hence simply *bulls, rams, or sheep*; see Joüon and Muraoka 2006: §129j). For the use of wheat, wine and oil for grain and drink offerings, see Exodus 29:40; Leviticus 23:13; Numbers 15:4–10. For the use of salt for grain offerings, see Leviticus 2:13. Apparently, Jews had been consulted for the redaction of the decree, just as the Egyptian physician Udjahorresnet (see on Neh. 13:31b) had done for the formulation of King Cambyses' titles in Egypt (Naoforo Vaticano l.13; Posener 1936: 170).

The Persian authorities subsidised all kinds of religions, not only their own (Persian) ones but also Elamite, Babylonian and Egyptian. Delivery was done on a *day by day* basis. This just-in-time subsidy was also applied to other religions (Williamson 1991: 50–54). This arrangement is more generous than the one offered by King Cyrus. The Persian king saw an advantage in offering these grants to the

Jews: they would continue to *pray for the life of the king and his sons* (or 'his children', as the plural form can be considered as the plural of 'son' and 'daughter' together; NET 'his family' is too large). The exact meaning of what is translated by *without fail* is not clear: should there be no problem in the sense of 'without interruption' (cf. NET: 'without any neglect'), or in the sense of 'without protest' (thus Vulg.)?[69]

We should not be surprised by the detailed character of the arrangement: as noted above, probably Jews were involved in its redaction. The arrangement for the dissident Jewish temple at Elephantine in Egypt also mentioned the details of 'meal offerings' and incense.[70]

11. Pulling a beam out of someone's house has a double result: the house falls down and you have an instrument to impale the owner, lying on his back, with the sharp point of the beam in the stomach (cf. Esth. 2:23; Jeremias 1916: 559). Hence ESV *impaled*.[71] This was the normal way to carry out the death penalty (unless it was lengthened by torture: Brosius 1996: 116). Afterwards the beam was raised up, with the body on it. This is not the same as 'hanged' (thus AV).[72] Indeed, ruined houses were used as toilets (*dunghill*; Grosheide 1963: 180–181).

12. While according to 4:22 King Artaxerxes would be concerned for damage to the kings, King Darius is, according to this verse, concerned for damage to the temple in Jerusalem (English translations do not use the same word for 'damage' in these two verses; on the other hand, AV uses the word 'destroy' twice in this verse, as a translation of two different verbs in Aramaic).

13. *Tattenai* and *Shethar-bozenai* (see on 5:3) were waiting for the king's answer, without bad intentions (see on 5:5); once they received

---

69 The difference in translation is due not to polysemy (different translations of the same word), but to homonymy (two different words with the same sound): *šālû* 'insolence' and *šālû* 'negligence'.

70 Lindenberger 2003: no. 35 l. 9.

71 The Egyptian sign for impalement in *Papyrus Leopold II* (end second millennium) is clear: 𓂀𓏏.

72 Indeed, 1 Esdras 6:32 has 'that he would be hanged on it' (my translation).

his answer, they 'acted accordingly' (thus NET) *with all diligence* and
without any further problems.

   14. For *Haggai* and *Zechariah*, see *Context*. The combination of
'building' (the structural work) and 'finishing' (the finishing touches)
was also found in 5:11 and the two verbs should be distinguished
here as well. For God's *decree* and the *decree* of the kings two variants
of the same word are used, probably in order to avoid placing the
different actors on the same level.[73] The original building order had
been given by King *Cyrus* in 538 (1:2–4), while King *Darius* had just
now, in 520, confirmed it (6:6–12). The mention of King *Artaxerxes*,
who would reign from 465 to 424, makes it clear that only after
his time would it really be possible to say that the building was
finished. It was he who enabled Ezra to improve the functioning
of the temple (7:21–26) and Nehemiah to rebuild the city (Neh.
2:5–8), two projects already touched on in 4:7–23, the second one
only negatively (cf. Porten 2002: 40; Goswell 2010: 193, 196).

   15. The building activities were *finished* on 12 March 515, about
seventy years after the destruction of Jerusalem in 587,[74] although
this fact does not trigger any comment at this point in the text (see,
however, 1:1). This second temple looks much like the first temple,
but the Most Holy Place stays empty, as the ark disappeared with
the earlier destruction of Jerusalem. The temple remained in this
form until Herod's renovations beginning in 19 BC.

Meaning
When we read that *the prophets were ... supporting* the politicians
(5:2), we can think of the need in today's society for Christians to
create, in the media or in private conversation, public support for
changes in society (or to restrain them), by expressing themselves

---

73 Not only the vocalization, but also the junction between preposition
    and noun is involved; cf. Estelle 2006: 69–70.
74 The strange construction in AV and NET is caused by use of the most
    frequent translation of the Aramaic *dî*; the semantic field of this word
    is, however, so large (cf. Kumon 2016: 70) that it is better not to
    translate it here, interpreting it as 'more precisely' or the like
    (Grosheide 1963: 185).

and showing the way. Of course, we must be very careful when we speak, because you can never take back what once was uttered.

The visit by the authorities (5:3) must not be seen as opposition, but could have taken place because the satrap was in the region anyway and wanted to see what was happening. The reaction is quite friendly: the work is not stopped (as in 4:21), but the archives would be consulted. The Jews see this decision of the authorities, with the prophets in the background, as God's protecting presence (5:5). We find this combination again at the end of the unit, in 6:14: (1) *the prophesying of Haggai the prophet and Zechariah the son of Iddo* (2) *by decree of the God of Israel* and (3) *by decree of Cyrus and Darius and Artaxerxes king of Persia.* These three factors do not exclude one another; they go together, just as according to Romans 13:4 state action can concur with divine action.[75] At the same time, this verse answers the question of 5:3b.

When we read the letter in 5:7–17, we find the opinion of the Jews themselves in 5:11–16. Ezra 5:12 shows how honest their analysis of the facts and of themselves was. A correct evaluation of a situation is always necessary to go on. It is no use always emphasizing the mistakes of the past, but they should not be denied either. Together with this honesty and self-knowledge goes a balanced assessment of Nebuchadnezzar: he has indeed destroyed the temple, but he was also God's instrument (Jer. 25:9; cf. Jer. 27:6; 43:10, which go even further when God calls him 'my servant'; cf. Dan. 4). In the end, Nebuchadnezzar's action has been repaired by another king of Babylon, this time from the Persian dynasty, but also one with a complicated assessment in the Bible: Cyrus (Ezra 5:13). And so history continues, always with active (though changing) kings, sometimes (rarely) with prophets, always with God who is unchanging.

When we read in Ezra about problems with external factors, we must bear in mind that Haggai shows us that the internal resistance to rebuilding the temple was at least as important.

---

75 Cf. Porten 2002: 40: 'This, indeed, is the underlying assumption of the book. Events are propelled by dual causation, divine and royal.'

The decree found back at Ecbatana prescribes (6:3) rebuilding, but by keeping the foundations; in theological terms, there is continuity and innovation.

Ezra 6:4–8 shows us that the Bible does not impose the separation of Church and State: here we have a State which pays (6:4, 8), does not intervene (6:6) and only asks for prayer (6:10; cf. Jer. 29:7 and 1 Tim. 2:1–3). As long as it is possible to cooperate with the authorities, Christians should do so – and prayer always remains possible.

At the end of the whole section, in 6:14, we find some actors together who were not actually active at the moment the work was finished (12 March 515): Haggai and Zechariah had respectively been active from 29 August to 18 December 520 and from 15 February 519 to 7 December 518, while Artaxerxes would be active only much later (465–424). This verse seems to imply that we should not forget people who have served at another time, but nevertheless have played their role.

D. Worship services (6:16–22)

In this last section we find two worship services (this being a recurring element: see the end of the fourth part, Neh. 7:4 – 12:47), closing the book's first part (1:1 – 6:22): the temple is built. The description of the service of dedication is closely connected with the previous verses, as well as the documents quoted in Aramaic, and continues in that language. With the description of Passover, the language turns to Hebrew again.

Joy is mentioned in the first and last verses and thus marks the unity of this section.

i. Service of dedication (6:16–18)
Context
No date is mentioned for the service of dedication but it must have taken place between the end of building (12 March 515) and the Passover (21 April 515).

Comment
16. For this service of dedication the religious term *Israel* is used.

17. It seems that an enormous number of animals (see on v. 9) are sacrificed, but this quantity is almost nothing when compared with the dedication of the first temple (1 Kgs 8:63). The *12 male goats* are offered 'to atone for the sins of' (Muraoka 2020: 76) *all Israel*, that is, *the* twelve *tribes of Israel*. The ten northern tribes continued to be represented because people from the Northern Kingdom who did not appreciate its religious politics had fled to Jerusalem. In that way the group that starts here again at Jerusalem can rightly be called *all Israel*; it represents also a certain breadth, not strictly limited to those who had been in exile themselves. Porten (2002: 40–41) calculates that although the numbers are lower, the same ratio of herds and flocks is maintained as in Numbers 7:87–88 and 1 Kings 8:63–66.

18. The priests were classified into 24 *divisions*, each of which always served one week in the temple. We do not find the elaborated system in the Pentateuch; it occurs for the first time in 1 Chronicles 24:4–19, where we read (v. 19) that it was based on a 'procedure established for them by Aaron' (we might think of Num. 18:2–7, 21–23). Not only did the priests have *divisions*, but according to 1 Chronicles 24:31 the Levites had a similar system (the Aramaic does not use the same word, although ESV uses *divisions* here in 6:18 for both systems; AV uses 'courses', NIV 'groups' for the Levites). So it is rightly written that this happened 'according to the prescript of the book of Moses'.[76] Reference to *the book of Moses* suggests – and in a stronger way than in 3:2 – a longer-existing writing and not a synchronic creation of Persian law (see further Introduction 2n, 'Ezra's Law').

Meaning
As the two units go closely together, reference is made to the *Meaning* at the end of the next unit.

---

76 This should not be branded as 'deceitfully claiming authority', but as 'generalizing'. It is obvious that the risk exists that an author might go too far with this and ascribe to the Pentateuch what was never its intention; this happens e.g. in apocryphal literature. For an overview of the problem from a critical standpoint, see Najman 2003: 111–117.

ii. Passover (6:19–22)

Context

The Passover (v. 19) took place on 21 April 515; the Feast of Unleavened Bread from 22 to 28 April 515. With this unit, the redactor returns to Hebrew.

Comment

19. Should we read here a limitation to the *returned exiles*, or would people whose families had always stayed in the land have been welcome too? Bänziger (2014: 156) mentions the possibility that especially in this context of Passover the end of the exile (to be compared with the stay in Egypt) was mentioned.

20. Although some doubt exists over the reading of this verse, the most obvious choice (also keeping into account the Masoretic accentuation)[77] is to keep *the priests and the Levites* together. It is difficult to say how they *had purified themselves*, because we find no description of the content of a normal, recurring purification. The next question is: who *slaughtered*, and for whom? Originally every man slaughtered the lamb for his own family (Exod. 12:3–6, 21); later on, in the time of the kings of Judah, this task was passed to the Levites, especially when not everyone was clean (2 Chr. 30:17; 35:6; see also the remark in this verse that as far as the priests and the Levites were concerned, *all of them were clean*: perhaps this was not the case for every believer). This implies that *the Levites* (because it was their normal duty and they are the last mentioned) did the work for the people of the exile, for their brothers the priests, and for 'them', in Hebrew as well as in English a rather strange word for 'themselves' (Bänziger 2014: 154).[78]

21. This verse specifies the group for whom Passover was served: *the people of Israel* (here again the religious term) *who had returned from exile* (without further specification because those who had returned had already made a specific choice) and also some of those who had stayed in the land, namely those who had also made a specific choice

---

77 See n. 31.

78 It must be kept in mind that, although not all Levites were priests, all priests were Levites.

by separating themselves (cf. 9:1; Neh. 9:2; 13:3) *from the uncleanness of the peoples* [Hebr. *gôyē*, plural, which makes us think of idols of the Gentiles] *of the land*, or, more positively *who had joined them … to worship* [or 'to commit themselves to'; lit. 'to seek', thus AV] *the* LORD.

22. The *Feast of Unleavened Bread* (see Exod. 12:15; 23:15; Lev. 23:6–8; Num. 28:17–25; Deut. 16:1–8) always immediately followed the Passover. The king of Persia is called here the *king of Assyria* in order to emphasize the enormous change that has occurred (cf. Neh. 9:32): once the king of Assyria had oppressed Israel (cf. 2 Chr. 30:6) and displaced the persons who now had resisted to rebuild the temple; now *Assyria* had been reduced to the double-satrapy of Trans-Euphrates and Mesopotamia and its new (Persian) king had *aided* (same word as in 1:6) the building of the temple at Jerusalem. This support is gratefully accepted; that does not exclude, however, that the Jews find their joy in God who has guided history in such a way that rulers have turned from enemies into supporters (cf. Prov. 21:1), and who has turned joy mixed with sadness (3:12–13) into perfect joy (Porten 2002: 41).

Meaning
In this last section there is much joy, with a 'big barbecue' (vv. 16–17) and unleavened bread (v. 22). There is a time for work, but also a time for enjoyment (even for people who enjoy their work): both are good in God's eyes.

Once again, we find continuity, but also some innovation: for different reasons a simple copy of the dedication of the first temple was neither possible nor deemed necessary.

The Passover had a large group of participants: not only Israel (already a large term), but all who committed themselves to the LORD, the God of Israel. An openness exists, in spite of what we might have thought while reading 4:3. Ezra is restrictive only towards unbelievers, towards those who (in 4:2) had spoken rather detachedly about 'your God'. Kidner (1979: 60) concluded: 'only the self-excluded were unwelcome. The convert found an open door, as Rahab and Ruth had done.' Indeed, this openness is not new, although it is more open than in, for example, Exodus 12:48, where circumcision is required, while here commitment is required, based on an individual decision (cf. Neh. 10:28–29). The Hebrew word indicating this commitment in verse 21 (lit. 'to seek', translated by *to worship* in ESV) is parallel in content with the Greek word in Matthew 6:33: 'seek first the kingdom of God and his righteousness'. Of course, this openness does not make things much easier in our day, where openness with rules is not considered open enough, but where a complete pluralism is requested.

2. BUILDING THE COMMUNITY (7:1 – 10:44)

A. Introduction (7:1–28)

This section introduces the second part of Ezra-Neh. The second part speaks about reconstruction of the community, positively through the introduction of the Law and negatively through the purification of the community.

This section starts with Ezra's journey to Jerusalem (7:1–10), mentions his task on behalf of the king (7:11–26) and ends with Ezra's reaction (7:27–28). This last unit stems from Ezra's memoirs (or 'personal accounts', as Klement 2011: 62 prefers).

In this section too, Aramaic is used. It is limited to the quotation of the letter in 7:12–26. As only one document is quoted in Aramaic, the text returns immediately again to Hebrew after the quote.

i. King Artaxerxes sends Ezra to Jerusalem (7:1–10)
Context

We make a jump of fifty-seven years (a period in which Esther in Susa saves the Jewish people and in which Ezra 4:6–7 must be situated) from the temple building to the appearance of Ezra (see Introduction 2h, 'Ezra'). The reason for and goal of his action can be concluded only from what he actually did in Jerusalem. Possibly a relation existed with a threat that had arisen in Egypt, which might have made it necessary for the king to undertake positive action towards Judah, in order to have more loyal Jews on the Egyptian border (Bringmann 2005: 43).

This unit presents the idea of King Artaxerxes sending Ezra to Jerusalem in the year 458 BC, as well as the person of Ezra.

Ezra stayed in Babel, one of the empire's capitals and an important city for the Jews (Daniel always stayed in the region of Babel from the moment he went into exile, so from 604 to 530).

Artaxerxes, already mentioned in the preview of Ezra 4:7–23, was the fifth king of the Persian Empire, reigning from 465 to 424 (see Introduction 2e, 'Persian kings').

For the transfer of this episode to one or two generations later – as proposed by some exegetes – see Introduction 2j, 'Relationship between Ezra and Nehemiah'. Other commentators want to transfer this episode to the Hellenistic period. Nothing invites us to do that either. On the other hand, parallels in Persian times do exist (Altmann 2016: 217–218).

Comment

1a. The words *after this* indicate that the new part must be situated chronologically after the previous part, but there may be a big jump (cf. Gen. 22:1). For the period passed over and *Artaxerxes*, see the above *Context*.

1b–5. Ezra apparently is a priest. In this genealogy only high priests are mentioned. That is the reason why his first ancestors, who were ordinary priests, are not mentioned. The first half of our text mentions seven high priests. *Seraiah*: 'the LORD is ruler' (cf. 2 Kgs 25:18–21; Jer. 52:24); *Azariah* (IV): 'the LORD has helped' (mentioned on a bulla, a small piece of clay with a seal impression on it); *Hilkiah*: 'the LORD is my share' (2 Kgs 22:8–12; 2 Chr. 34:9,

14–22; 35:8); *Shallum*: 'compensated, satisfied'; *Zadok*: '(God is) righteousness'; *Ahitub*: 'my brother is goodness'; *Amariah* (III): 'the LORD has spoken' (2 Chr. 19;11); *Azariah* (II, the second one in this list'); *Meraioth*: 'friendliness'; *Zerahiah*: 'the LORD has shed light'; *Uzzi*: 'my strength'; *Bukki*: 'bottle'; *Abishua*: 'my Father is salvation'; *Phinehas*: 'Nubian' (Num. 25:11–13); *Eleazar*: 'God helps'. This list is incomplete, as the list of 1 Chronicles 6:3–15 (Hebrew text edition 5:29–41; the list is partially repeated in 1 Chr. 6:50–53 [Hebr. 6:35–38]) clearly shows: everyone is skipped between Azariah (II) and Meraioth (in Ezra's order, which goes from later to earlier). That longer list, however, is incomplete too, because we find some other names of high priests in the biblical texts. The selection of Ezra (and of the Chronicler) is strange: it is not based on the general importance of the high priests. Probably the selection is accidental, caused by the difficulty to see and to understand the role of the different Azariahs and Amariahs.[2] Literarily, two high priests seem to have been highlighted: Aaron, mentioned in the last place, the first high priest; and Azariah, placed in the middle, the first high priest actually active in the temple. This suggests that Ezra, mentioned in the first place, will also assume a preponderant role, not as a high priest, but at the start of a new period in the history of God's people by his study of the Law and by the guidance he gives to the Jews in this new situation.

6. Ezra *went up* to Jerusalem: this is the usual verb for a journey to the temple.

Ezra has become a priest through birth, within a familial tradition; he has become a *scribe* through studying what God revealed in the past. Ezra combines both qualities, which makes him especially fit to proceed in continuity and renewal. Ezra was also a civil servant (cf. 7:14) and the title *scribe skilled* might indicate a high-ranking official, with a large expertise and authority to seal documents (Heltzer and Avishur 2002: 221); in that case, *in the Law of Moses*

---

1   Azariah III is mentioned in 2 Chr. 31:10.

2   As this is a commentary on Ezra-Neh. and not a history of the high priests, we stop here as far as historical notes are concerned.

might indicate his department of specialization. Ezra's commitment is seconded by the king's favour, which in turn is based on God's favour ('and the king gave him – as the hand of the LORD his God was on him – all that he requested').

7–9. Ezra is not going alone, but actually we see a second return from the exile (cf. 1:3; 7:13). We must keep in mind that not everyone was able (or willing) to join the first group. Numbers are not mentioned here. The laity is mentioned as *the people of Israel*; *priests* are descendants of Aaron and are allowed to administer the sacrifices; *Levites* are descendants of Levi too, but have less important functions in the temple service (cf. Num. 3:2–10); *singers* are Levites who were appointed by David for the service of song in the temple (cf. 1 Chr. 6:31); *gatekeepers* are Levites who took care of the material management of the temple (cf. 1 Chr. 9:23–29);[3] for *the temple servants* see the comment on 2:43–54.

On *the first day of the first month* (v. 9) of *the seventh year of Artaxerxes* (v. 7), that is, 8 April 458, people gathered in Babylon to start the journey. This is elaborated in Ezra 8. The actual date of departure is somewhat later (see 8:31), which is the reason why it is written *he began to go up* (v. 9; lit. 'the foundation of the going up from Babylon'). They arrive in Jerusalem on 4 August 458. This is quite a long time, but understandably so when we keep in mind that it is not a delegation but a real migration, with families and goods, and possibly new participants who joined at different places during the journey. They did not follow the shortest way through the desert, but travelled for 900 miles through easier regions along the Euphrates and the Orontes; this makes an average of 9 miles per day (Yamauchi 1988: 650).

The expression *for the good hand of his God was on him* is for a large part a repetition of verse 6.

10. Ezra is committed to studying Scripture, acting accordingly and teaching it. Through this combination of study and action, 'study was saved from unreality, conduct from uncertainty, and teaching from insincerity and shallowness', as Kidner (1979: 62;

---

3   Singers and gatekeepers were probably few in number, as they are not
    mentioned in Ezra 8.

cf. Ulrich 2021: 79) remarks. *Israel* is used here in the sense of 'the believing community'.

Meaning
See the *Meaning* at the end of Ezra 7.

ii. Artaxerxes' letter (7:11–26)
Context
This unit presents Artaxerxes' letter which explains Ezra's status. The letter itself, verses 12–26, is presented in its original language, that is, Aramaic.

Comment
11. This verse starts the description of what the king did for Ezra. Documents with an international function were written in Aramaic in the Persian Empire and the book of Ezra does not feel the need to make a translation, as many members of the Jewish audience were able to understand Aramaic. The king's letter has some Jewish particularities, but this is not strange if we realize that the group concerned normally is involved in the preparation of these kind of texts (even in our day, legislation about the pharmaceutical industry is prepared with the help of the pharmaceutical industry). For the combination *priest* and *scribe*, see on verse 6.

12–13. We find the title *king of kings* not only in Old Persian texts, but also for Assyrian and Babylonian kings (Ezek. 26:7; Dan. 2:37). The title *the scribe of the Law of the God of heaven* indicates that Ezra held an official position in the Persian Empire. *God of heaven* is the normal name for the God of Israel in an international context (cf. 1:2). This introduction ends with 'completed, etcetera'. AV puts this word with a supposed 'peace' ('perfect peace', without manuscript evidence). The best solution is to see it as a closing term of the introduction: 'etcetera'. The very last word of verse 12 was in earlier days also considered to conclude the introduction and so it was placed at the end of verse 12. Later on, the right interpretation was found (*And now*), but that did not always bring a change in verse division (in NIV it did; see Grosheide 1963: 205 for the two problems). Theoretically, the *decree* applies to the whole of the Persian Empire; in practice, only Babylonia is concerned.

14. Ezra has been *sent*[4] *by the king and his seven counsellors.* These counsellors represented the seven Persian noble families who had free access to the king (cf. Esth. 1:10, 14). The Iranian religion also knew seven holy ghosts.

Ezra received not only permission to return with a group of exiles, but also the mission on behalf of the king and the State Council to develop a juridical system based on God's Law, perhaps with the function of 'travelling commissioner' (Steiner 2001: 629; cf. Knoppers 2009: 79*) for *Judah and Jerusalem*.[5] Ezra had God's Law at his disposal and the king knew this. The Law existed already; Ezra did not need to write it (or to have it written). See Introduction 2n, 'Ezra's Law' for the theory of the *Reichsautorisation*.

15. The king gives not only his permission (and commission), but also his funding (cf. vv. 20–22).

16. The status of the *province of Babylonia* was situated somewhere between a satrapy and a province. Because the Persians respected existing situations, uniform structures did not exist in their empire and terms could have different meanings in different regions (Tuplin 1987: 111–112, 121–122; Högemann 1992: 127–128, 269). Government funding goes together with the gifts of the believers.

17. With the translation *money* instead of 'silver' we avoid the question what had to be done with the gold. Probably Artaxerxes wanted a sacrifice in his favour to be offered after the arrival in Jerusalem. The *diligence* requires a correct administration.

---

4 No doubt exists about the subject of the sentence even though Ezra is not mentioned in full; so it is not necessary to change the text (*pace* Muraoka 2020: 77; cf. Muraoka 2012: §47b1).

5 Muraoka 2020: 77 suggests that Ezra would have been commissioner for (Aramaic *'al*) Judah and that Jerusalem indicates the direction in which (*lə*) he had to go, but the use of the coordinator *wə* pleads against that interpretation (Lettinga and von Siebenthal 2016: §82B/729). The Greek parallel in 1 Esdras 8:12 is related to the English word 'bishop', which gives a good impression of his task: 'overseer', but also 'defender' (see Steiner 2001: 626–627; Lorein 2021c).

18. Apparently the combination of the king's order (it is the king who is writing!), the preference of the Jews (*Whatever seems good to you and your brothers*) and *the will of your God* is possible.

19. These *vessels* must be new: this proves that besides the importance of continuity (cf. 1:7–11), room for renewal exists.

20–21. For the money that is needed, subsidies from *the king's treasury* will be available. The general source is specified in the next verse. Not *all the treasurers* of a satrapy were in one single place. Probably every province's capital had its own treasury, of course under the authority of the satrapy's treasury (Tuplin 1987: 116–117, 128; Williamson 1991: 59).

22. Some maximum amounts have been determined: *100 talents of silver* (calculation according to Bivar 1985: 612; see also the comments at 2:66–69; with bullion prices 2019, at least £1,100,000 or €1,250,000), *100 cors of wheat* (45,000 to 100,000 lb, i.e. 20 to 45 tons; probably the lower value[6]), *100 baths of wine* and *100 baths of oil* (both 450 to 1,000 gal., probably the lower value). Apparently, the king was not afraid that Ezra would exaggerate with the *salt*: a prescript was unnecessary. Indeed, the sacrifices did not need much salt. For the different ingredients, see on 6:9–10. Since the days of Darius (cf. 6:10) the insight had arisen that it was easier to transport money than to transport the animals and all things needed (Williamson 1991: 52).

23. For this form of self-interest, see on 6:10.

24. With *you*, the treasurers (v. 21) are meant. The first two groups (*the priests* and *the Levites*) are taken together as being the highest classes of the temple personnel (Muraoka 2020: 77).

All *servants of this house of God* (according to Williamson 1998: 155 a recapitulation of the categories mentioned earlier in this verse: *the priests* and *the Levites, the singers, the doorkeepers* and *the temple servants*) are exempted from customs, tax in kind and statutory labours (see

---

6   The basis of the measures is a homer (estimations from 450 to 1,000 lb), which must be related to what a donkey (Hebr. *ḥᵃmôr*) is able to carry. A donkey cannot carry 1,000 lb; even 450 lb is quite a lot (cf. Lipiński 1994: 66–67). Usually the Persian king made promises for one year, which also fits better with the lower value (Williamson 1991: 53–54; Briant 2002: 491).

on 4:13), just as King Darius had done some thirty years earlier for the temple servants at Aulai (in Asia Minor; Briant 2002: 491–492). **25.** In this verse Ezra is prominently addressed again (*you, Ezra*). *According to the wisdom … that is in* his *hand* (a quite literal translation; cf. NIV 'which you possess') he had to *appoint … judges*. The first word used here (ESV *magistrates*) is a typically Canaanite term and is explained by a typically Aramaic term for *judges*. The group aimed at comprised those living beyond the Euphrates as far as they knew the laws of Ezra's God, or at least should have known them. We must keep in mind that a judge not only tries to decide between two quarrelling citizens, but also guides society (see on v. 10 for the importance of teaching). In any case, this order is larger than the order in verse 14, for the realm (probably not an attempt to go back to the days of the kingdom of David and Solomon, but rather taking into account the actual geographical spread of the Jews), as well as for the authority (Knoppers 2009: 79*–82*).

26. We can read the two terms as referring to two different legislations: (1) *the law of your God* and (2) *the law of the king* (Williamson 1998: 162). Here again, however, the second term (*the law of the king*) might be understood as an explanation (Schaper 2000: 135–136) of the first term (*the law of your God*): the king ordains that God's law must be kept, because he considers it as being his own law. Ultimately, the two interpretations do not differ so much, because in any case two other interpretations must be refused: (1) the general Persian legislation is *not* nullified (it remains valid alongside the Mosaic law, in the same way as two legislations were valid in Egypt in King Darius' day; cf. Drioton and Vandier 1989: 602; Yamauchi 1990: 256–258; Briant 2002: 474; Kiel 2017: 329; Knoppers 2009: 80* rightly remarks that the Persian Empire was not a secular state and that for this reason in practice the difference between the two legal systems is not too important); and (2) the Pentateuch is *not* a result of this royal intervention (see v. 14).

The phrase *let judgement be … executed on him* leaves unexpressed who should take care of this. In any case, it must be done 'with due diligence' (the same word as in 6:8). Although English translations generally have *banishment* as the second punishment (and this translation starts with the Vulg., *exilium*), this word is not completely clear: (1) Stiegler (1994: 157) thinks of exclusion from

the congregation of an individual who had not shown the right
attitude towards God during the liturgy or in daily life (although
the text was written by the king, it might have been prepared by
Jewish advisors: see on v. 11); and (2) Persian etymology leads to the
meaning 'corporal punishment' (and this translation has the LXX
on its side, *paideia*, as in Heb. 12:5). Between *death* and *confiscation of
his goods* we expect a punishment of the person, but less strict than
death; this argument, however, does not help, as it can be applied to
both possible translations. In Antiquity, *imprisonment* was normally
used only as preventive custody (Snell 2001: 44).

Meaning
See the *Meaning* at the end of Ezra 7.

iii. Ezra's conclusion (7:27–28)
Context
Immediately after the quotation of a document from Ezra's files,
the redactor comes to a reaction of Ezra kept in the memoirs part of
his files. This reaction was written in Ezra's own language, that is,
Hebrew. It comments on the king's initiative, which was explained
in the previous unit and executed in the first unit of this section.

Comment
27. The phrase *God of our fathers* is used already in Deuteronomy
26:7 and again in intertestamental literature (Prayer of Azariah 3:26;
Song of the Three Young Men 3:52). For God's influence on people's
hearts, see Exodus 7:3 and Jeremiah 31:33 (Helberg 1990: 111).
28. The king's *counsellors* are probably the seven representatives
of the Persian nobility. At the end of the first half of the verse, *all
the king's mighty officers*[7] are mentioned. After having received permission, Ezra *took courage*, so that he *gathered leading men*, described
in more detail in 8:1–14.

---

7 These words form the last category (Polak 2006: 599) and *mighty* is an
   adjective (Clines 2009: 60).

Meaning

With this second part of Ezra-Neh., Ezra has arrived on the scene. Ezra combined several aspects in his person. Based on his birth Ezra had become a priest. The list of priests in verses 1–5 thus first underlines Ezra's importance at the threshold of a new period, deeply rooted in history, so that continuity and innovation again come together. In the second place, Ezra had taken the profession of a scribe, wanting wholeheartedly (the basis for everything that follows!) *to study* the Law of the LORD (cf. v. 6a), *to live* according to it and *to teach* it (see v. 10); of course, this must not be understood in a purely chronological way (as if we could first study for twenty years, then live for twenty years, and finally teach for twenty years), but in the sense that study must stay related to real life, that life must have a firm foundation, and that teaching must be rooted in study and in real life (Kidner 1979: 62) – and this idea applies to Sunday school and university. In the third instance, Ezra was an official. Ezra's engagement was followed by God's blessing (vv. 6b, 9b), which took form in the king's graciousness (v. 6b), a safe journey (v. 9), the permission to go to Jerusalem (v. 13, with its stress on voluntariness) and subsidies (v. 15). It must be remarked that these subsidies do not prevent believers from giving on top of them (v. 16). The order to practise good business administration (v. 17) applies to both categories of income mentioned in the previous verses (subsidies and donations).

Of course, other aspects also play a role in the king's decision. It was in the interests of the king to have a loyal population in Judah. In our day, spiritual principles and practical considerations can have their interplay too.

The theme of continuity and innovation appears again in verse 19. As the old vessels had already come to Jerusalem on the journey mentioned in 1:7–11, the vessels mentioned here (v. 19) must be new vessels. Old and new will play their part together in the temple of Jerusalem. The question remains to what extent we can apply this principle in our day; in other words, how can we know that in our situation a particular innovation is according to God's will? Indeed, not every innovation can automatically be approved; leaving the foundations is liberalism. But on the other hand, what we see already in the Old Testament prevents us from automatically disapproving of every change. We must stay with the tradition: accept thankfully what we have received from former generations, foster and elaborate it, and pass it on with conviction to the next generation. These two dangers, fossilization and liberalism, threaten every church not continuously drawing water from the well in dialogue with its context, and prevent it from continuing to grow on the foundation once laid.

B. Launch: return, worship, information (8:1–36)

While the previous section formed the introduction, this section elaborates on 7:7–9, launching the nucleus of the second part of Ezra-Neh.: the building of the community. This launch is accompanied by a worship service (8:35).

While the section starts with a list (vv. 1–14), it continues with Ezra's memoirs, completed by the lists of verses 26–27 and verse 35 (Klement 2011: 62). The interruption of Ezra's memoirs by the long list is marked by the words *I gathered* in 7:28; 8:15 (respectively the last verse prior to and the first verse following the list; Brown 2005b: 186).

i. The list of returnees (8:1–14)
Context
This list mentions the people who, having been gathered by Ezra (7:28), made the same journey as he did. It dates from before the arrival of the Levites (Williamson 1985: 108–109). See *Context* at 7:1–10 for the geographical and historical setting. For the importance (and the limits) of the list, see *Context* at 2:1–70. We do not know other details about these family heads (meeting the same names does not mean that we have to do with the same persons). Apart from the priestly and royal families, about 1,500 (probably adult) males are counted. Large families with small children probably stayed in Babylonia. We explain again the names of the main characters, in order to emphasize the importance of individuals and their names (who were in any case clear to the original readers).

Comment
1–3a. In the first place, two priestly families (cf. Exod. 6:23–25) and one royal family are mentioned, with *Gershom* ('a sojourner there'), *Daniel* ('God is my judge') and *Hattush* (Akkadian, 'his sceptre'?; according to 1 Chr. 3:22 a descendant of Shecaniah, which implies that the first words of v. 3 must be taken with v. 2; Fensham 1982: 110–111).[8]

3b–14. *Zechariah*: 'the LORD has remembered (me)'; *Eliehoenai*: 'on the LORD my eyes (are set)'; *Shecaniah* (probably from the descendants of *Zattu*, although this name is lacking in the Masoretic text and the Vulg.; the LXX, however, has it): 'the LORD dwells (here)'; *Ebed*: 'servant'; *Jeshaiah*:[9] 'the LORD is salvation'; *Zebadiah*: 'the LORD has given'; *Obadiah*: 'little servant of the LORD'; *Shelomith*[10] (probably from *the* descendants of *Bani*; same situation as with Zattu): 'Peace'; a second *Zechariah*; *Johanan*: 'the LORD has been gracious'; *Eliphelet*: 'my God is deliverance/rescue'; the correct spelling and the meaning of *Jeuel* are uncertain; *Shemaiah*: 'the LORD has heard'; the meaning of *Uthai* is unclear to us; Zabud ('gift') is read[11] in the Codex Leningradensis as it is written in the Vulgate, that is, as *Zaccur*: 'remembered' (in the Hebrew square script the two names, Zabud and Zaccur, can easily be confused; the name occurs broadly in the West-Semitic area, e.g. in the Zaccur stela from 785, but that person considered himself to be remembered by his own gods; Lipiński 1975: 16, 19–23).

Meaning
See the *Meaning* at the end of Ezra 8.

---

8   This is confirmed by 1 Esdras 8:29, although that text has quite some deviations.

9   It is the same name as that of the prophet from the eighth and seventh centuries, but in his case we write 'Isaiah'.

10 A feminine name; for the masculine we would expect an ending in *-oth*, which we indeed find in 1 Esdras 8:36. (For historical aspects, 1 Esdras cannot be trusted [cf. Introduction 4f, 'The afterlife of Ezra-Neh. in Antiquity]; it can, however, be trusted for details.)

11 Cf. n. 25 at 2:43–54.

ii. Preparation for the return (8:15–30)

Context

This unit presents the last preparations for the journey (vv. 15, 21–30) and tackles a problem (vv. 16–20). The appointment was made for the first day of the first month (7:8–9a; see further at the beginning of chapter 7).

Comment

15a. The train is set up at the channel *that runs to Ahava*. We know that other watercourses existed besides the Euphrates, normally running from west to east and so not immediately in the right direction for arriving at Jerusalem; nowhere, however, is it said that they followed the Ahava Channel, only that for the last preparations they gathered at that watercourse, probably indicating a certain point on the Euphrates, which they then would follow in the direction of Carchemish.

15b–17. At the moment when Ezra wanted to leave Babel for Jerusalem with the group he had gathered, he realized that an important category of persons was missing: the group did not count any Levite, and Levites were necessary as *ministers for the house of our God* (v. 17). (Indeed, according to Beckwith 1996: 192, Levites were not very numerous, as compared with the priests.) For that reason,[12] he formed an important delegation that had to go to a certain *Iddo* ('strength'), the *leading man* (probably himself a Levite – Grosheide 1963: 227–228) of the Jews at *Casiphia* ('silver place'? Becking 2018: 125). We are unsure where this *place* must be situated; it might be a 'holy place' (Lipiński 2001: §64.2; 2006: 91), and then some people think of Ctesiphon, on the Tigris, 50 miles north of Babylon (and 20 miles south-east of modern Baghdad), where seven centuries later a school for Levites existed – but that is of course an important chronological difference. Although the message is not quoted, Ezra tells the delegation exactly what they have to say to get a number of Levites into the company. Most

---

12   Indicated by the Hiphil cohortative form *wâ'ôṣi'â* of the Ketiv (see n. 25 at 2:43–54)? This reasoning might also be applied to 7:28; 8:17, 23, but not to 8:24, 25, 26, 28, 31.

English versions (and the Masoretic text) suggest that Iddo was one of *the temple servants* (see on 2:43–54), but from a sociological viewpoint this would be strange; for that reason ESV adds *and*, in this way creating a difference between the *brothers* and *the temple servants*.

The delegation consists of the following *leading men*: *Eliezer*: 'God is my help'; *Ariel*: 'God's lion'; *Shemaiah*: 'the LORD has heard'; *Elnathan*: 'God has given'; *Jarib*: '(God) will do justice'; a second *Elnathan*; *Nathan*: '(God) has given'; *Zechariah*: 'the LORD has remembered (me)'; *Meshullam*: 'given as a compensation, satisfaction'. They were assisted by *Joiarib* ('the LORD will do justice') and a third *Elnathan* as advisors.

18–19. As the genealogies are quite shortened here, NIV opts for the translation 'descendants'. *Jeshaiah* is the same name as the well-known prophet Isaiah, but – being a different person – has received a different transcription in English translations.

20. It is clear that the *temple servants* (see on 2:43) were too numerous to call them by their name.

21. Whereas in verse 15 a channel was mentioned *that runs to Ahava*, the same watercourse now is called 'the channel Ahava'.[13] A channel and city with the same name occurs more than once (Herodotus 1.179).

22. That the *hand of our God is for good on all who seek him* can also be apparent from the king's protection. So Ezra could have asked for a military escort without any problem (cf. Neh. 2:9): it would not have made God's blessing redundant. So not wanting to make a request gives the impression that Ezra had spoken too hastily to the king or had exaggerated a little in speaking with him. In any case, the principal road was generally well monitored, although from time to time something went wrong on the Persian Road (Briant 2002: 364–369). So Ezra's attitude might be described as 'not too clever, but not irresponsible' (cf. Williamson 1985: 118; for a more positive impression of Ezra's decision, see Ulrich 2021: 83).

---

13 For the construction in Hebrew, see Joüon and Muraoka 2006: §131h. Is the name of the watercourse the basis and is it Indo-European (cf. Latin *aqua*, German place names ending in -*ach*)?

When the Hebrew words behind *the power of his wrath* are not translated literally (as 'his power and his wrath' – thus AV), a translation such as 'his powerful anger' (cf. NIV's 'his great anger') is to be preferred (hendiadys; see Introduction 4g, 'Literary terms').

23. It is unclear whether the phrase *he listened to our entreaty* (cf. Gen. 25:21; 2 Sam. 21:14 [see NET note: 'God allowed himself to be supplicated through prayer'[14]]; 24:25; 1 Chr. 5:20; 2 Chr. 33:13) should be read as an expression of trust in the eventual result or as a redactional addition (Goswell 2010: 197).

24. Two groups of twelve people are mentioned here: on the one hand, *twelve of the leading priests*, and on the other hand, the Levites *Sherebiah* ['the LORD has heated', i.e. born on a hot day], *Hashabiah* ['the LORD has thought'] *and ten of their kinsmen with them* (cf. vv. 18–19); ESV's colon is at least misleading.[15] One should not leave everything to the priests, especially not when it involves the temple. Ezra trusts God completely, but as far as humans are concerned, even regarding priests and Levites, he is careful (Noordtzij 1939: 129).

25. In this period, it was not yet possible to 'count' the money: it had to be *weighed* (Balzaretti 2013: 306). Accountability is important (cf. 7:16).[16] *The offering* (more often translated as 'contribution') has no clear definition, could consist of all kinds of belongings, and was used in order to build and maintain God's dwelling-place (cf. Exod. 25:1–7) or to remunerate the priests and the Levites (Neh. 12:44).

26–27. Wealth at this time is more substantial than two generations earlier (2:69) and the gifts are impressive (as they often were in Persian times). The train counted a large number of people with *650 talents of silver* (at least £9,000,000 or €10,000,000; for all calculations, see the comments at 2:66–69; 7:22); *silver vessels worth* 100 *talents* (some

---

14 GKC §51c: 'to express actions which the subject allows to happen to himself', used regularly about God.

15 The Hebrew text is unclear; however, 1 Esdras 8:54 is clear and Vulg. goes in the same direction.

16 The article before *the king … had offered* functions as a relative pronoun (Joüon and Muraoka 2006: §145d).

textual problems occur here; ESV thinks they were worth *200* talents, but 1 Esdras simply has 'hundred talents': 100 talents – £1,400,000 or €1,500,000); *100 talents of gold* (at least £27,500,000 or €31,000,000); *20 bowls of gold worth 1,000 darics* (at least £320,000 or €360,000; cf. Bivar 1985: 616).

28. The people as well as *the vessels are holy* (lit. 'a holy thing'), which means 'consecrated to the LORD' (as the NIV has it) in a positive way. Almost by definition, a *freewill offering* is not a systematic sacrifice and so it can be understood in this verse in the common sense of the word.

29. The priests and their companions have to stay vigilant in order to care for the treasures. The *chambers* opened onto the Inner Court of the temple (cf. Neh. 13:7).

30. The delegates accepted their responsibility.

Meaning
See *Meaning* at the end of Ezra 8.

iii. Journey and arrival (8:31–36)
Context
Finally, the journey takes place and the Jews arrive in Jerusalem. This unit has the same geographical and historical setting as the whole of this section and of the previous section (see *Context* at 7:1–10).

Comment
31. For the *Ahava* Channel, see on verses 15, 21–23.[17] The Hebrew uses two different words for the two occurrences of *hand*, the first with a positive connotation, the second with a negative connotation. The phrase 'the enemy and the one lying in ambush' can be considered as a hendiadys: 'the enemy who lies in ambush', and must be considered as a wordplay.[18]

---

17   But a different construction in Hebrew: for this one see Joüon and Muraoka 2006: §129f 7°.
18   Hebr. *'ōyēv wǝ'ōrēv*; Becking 2018: 130.

32–33. Considering the warning of verse 29, what is the reason for waiting three days? Possibly it was a matter of purification after passing through foreign countries (van Leeuwen 1968: 138). And after all, the journey had also started with three days of rest (v. 15).

For the term *weighed*, see on verse 25. Probably *Meremoth* ('elevations') is the same person as the one mentioned in Nehemiah 3:4, 21. This means that the sons of Hakkoz were no longer considered to have a doubtful background as in Ezra 2:61. Possibly *Jozabad* ('the LORD has endowed') is the same person as the one named in 10:23; Nehemiah 11:16. *Noadiah* ('the LORD has kept his appointment') is obviously not the prophetess mentioned in Nehemiah 6:14.

34–35. After transportation, the accounting is done again (a Persian parallel from the year 503 is mentioned by Williamson 1991: 55–56) and the practice mentioned here is taken over as a piece of advice for accountability in Sirach 42:7. While the bullion was *weighed*, other items could be *counted*.

The adjunct *At that time* belongs, according to the Masoretic text,[19] to verse 34 (thus e.g. AV: 'all the weight was written at that time'); in English translations ESV seems to be in a minority position by putting it with verse 35.

The number *twelve bulls* and *male goats* refers again to the tribes of *Israel* (see on 6:17).

Although a change from *seventy-seven* to seventy-two would not be very drastic and would produce a symbolic number, divisible by twelve (as Williamson 1985: 114 remarks), it is better to stay with the Hebrew text and to see it as a reference to perfection.

36. The king's law (see the Introduction 2n, 'Ezra's Law') is transmitted to the *satraps* of Babylonia (in Babylon) and of Trans-Euphrates (in Damascus) and to the *governors* of the different provinces of Trans-Euphrates.

---

19   And according to 1 Esdras 8:62 and Vulg. The LXX can be read both ways and perhaps the divergence started there.

Meaning

This chapter has another list of names (see on Ezra 2). We must never forget that the Law (and the gospel) is about real people. God works through individuals. As far as possible in written history they are highlighted here, with their names. And ultimately, God revealed himself in the form of a human being (John 1:14).

This does not exclude the importance of leadership. Of course, Ezra has received his position from the king, but this does not free him from getting information (8:15), making strict arrangements (8:17, 24–29) and trusting God (8:18, 22, 31). This can be a difficult combination: it is not always clear when straightness is most important (cf. the stress on accountability) or when trust must reign. Combinations always exist: efforts and blessings, birth and study (think of Ezra), continuity and innovation, arrangements and trust. This itself is also a combination: it is a task and a comfort. We are asked to combine all these aspects, but at the same time we may know that this complexity has been there, and is apparently part of God's acting with us, from biblical times, at least from post-exilic times, without a legislative Moses, without a guiding Elijah, without a king David. And after all, Ezra does not ascribe his 'success' to his powerful leadership, but to *the good hand of our God* (8:18): thorough preparation does not exclude recognizing God's goodness.

C. Core: building the community, purification (9:1 – 10:44)

Just as in the first part (1:1 – 6:22) the building of the temple and the external problems joined with it formed its central point, the building of the community and the internal problems joined with it, described in this section (9:1 – 10:44), form the central point of the second part (7:1 – 10:44; Brown 2005a: 46). At the end of this section we find no worship service. Indeed, the description of Ezra's activity stops quite abruptly[20] (such a situation occurs also in Greek history writing: Eskenazi 2010: 229).

---

20 Cf. Brown 2005b: 192: 'The narrator seems to walk off stage with the last of the women and children, leaving the reader contemplating the significance of the final scene.'

Although Ezra 9:1 – 10:44 must be considered as one single
section, Ezra 9 presents Ezra in the first person and Ezra 10 presents
him in the third person. This change is a device that occurs with
some frequency (Williamson 1985: 145–148; Becking 2018: 153; also
in Greek history writing: Eskenazi 2010: 231), so that this section can
be considered in its totality as coming from Ezra's memoirs, the list
of 10:18–44 excepted (from the lists). Another difference between
the two chapters is that Ezra 9 uses a term referring to marriage,
while Ezra 10 uses a term pointing to a concubine. The difference
between the two situations, however, should not be exaggerated,
as no strict monogamy existed. Throntveit (1992: 49) sees a strong
structure:

A Report of the problem of intermarriage (9:1–2)
   B Ezra's public mourning (9:3–4)
      C Ezra's prayer (9:5–15)
         X Shecaniah's confession and request for action
           (10:1–4)
      C' Ezra's exhortation and the people's oath (10:5)
   B' Ezra's private mourning (10:6)
A' Resolution of the problem of intermarriage (10:7–44)

Ezra's prayer is also well constructed: general confession of
guilt (9:6–7), God's grace (vv. 8–9), specific confession of guilt
(vv. 10–12), assessment of what had to be done (vv. 13–14), closing
remark (God's rightfulness and human limitations; v. 15). What
is lacking – and this is quite special – is a request for forgiveness. The conclusion is stated in the form of a question in the
assessment (v. 14): would marital intermingling with heathen
nations not be impossible because God's punishments would
follow?

For the presumed dependence on Nehemiah 8 and an ensuing
rearrangement of this chapter, see Introduction 4c, 'Replacing
Nehemiah 8?'

The prayer seems to have been part of Ezra's files, having
made sufficient impression to be redacted immediately after it was
prayed, possibly with reduction to the line of argumentation and
redactional adaptations (by Ezra himself?), as is always the case

when spoken language is written down. We must, however, point to the impressive list of parallels with the prayer in Nehemiah 9:6–37 (see at that chapter).

Leaving aside the organization of the return, Ezra's main contribution in this part (7:1 – 10:44) is rather negative: the purification of the population. Introduction of the Law, requested by the king, was only announced in 7:25–26, but has not been worked out, possibly to the king's dissatisfaction (Blenkinsopp 1989: 34). Perhaps this can be paralleled with the problems mentioned at the end of the book of Nehemiah: there the Law has not met its fulfilment either.

i. Ezra's reaction to interfaith marriages (9:1–15)
Context
We find a firm date in Ezra 10:9, 19 December 458, four and a half months after the arrival in Jerusalem. This means that the passage must be situated in autumn 458. This must have followed within the delay mentioned in proclamation of 10:7, which must have followed with a delay of one day or so to Ezra's reaction to the news and Shecaniah's proposition (9:3–10:6), which must have followed immediately on the report of the officials to Ezra (9:1–2), which must have followed rather quickly after the communication with the governors mentioned in 8:36 (we do not have here the vague general *After these things*, but *After these things had been done*, i.e. the communication with the governors mentioned in 8:36; Grosheide 1963: 247). This implies that the time between Ezra's arrival and the situation described in these two chapters must have been spent on communication with the governors.

It is necessary to define the group which has caused the problem. They were neither the people who had just come back with Ezra (no children would have been born yet; see 10:3), nor the people who had always stayed in the land (see v. 4: *the returned exiles*). We must think of people who had returned earlier from exile and among them – although it is always possible that a general lack of Jewish women did occur – those who in view of economic interests had married daughters of non-Jewish trade partners. We must keep in mind that even these people had not themselves personally returned

from exile. The first return had taken place almost eighty years
before what we read here. Nevertheless, their descendants can still
be called *returned exiles*.

Comment

1–2. *After these things had been done*:[21] after they had completed the
communication with the governors mentioned in 8:36.
The *officials* may be district rulers (see Neh. 3:9; Williamson 1985:
130).

With *the people* and *Israel*, the laypeople are meant; after them *the
priests and the Levites* (including the specific functions within this
group: cf. 10:24) are mentioned.

The peoples of the lands are non-Jews who during the exile had
occupied the geographical space that had become available in Judah.
The Jews had not kept themselves away from *their abominations*,
which are the same as those of the *Canaanites* and the other nations
mentioned here. Most of these peoples did not exist any more as
such. Their mention is based on Exodus 34:11 (*Amorites, Canaanites,
Hittites, Perizzites, Jebusites*); Leviticus 18:3 (*Egyptians, Canaanites*);
Deuteronomy 7:1 (*Hittites, Amorites, Canaanites, Perizzites, Jebusites*);
23:3 (*Ammonites, Moabites*). The text in Ezra is not about these peoples
(and in that sense it is not racist;[22] Bänziger 2014: 66), but about
their *abominations* by which they have influenced the believers' community: idol worship and everything that goes with it, especially
child sacrifices, men behaving as women, unfair trade (Lev. 18:22;
20:13; Deut. 12:31; 22:5; 25:16; 27:15; 32:16–17). Where the text as
such cannot be applied any more, the principle remains valid: it is
about the religion of nearby pagan nations. Such a qualified application seems already to be the case in Joshua's day (Firth 2022:
10–13, 16–18).

---

21 In Hebrew the verb is in the active form, but without a subject: Joüon
     and Muraoka 2006: §124s.

22 That it is not racist but religious does not necessarily make things
     easier in a twenty-first-century society where different religions have
     to coexist and even – preferably – work together; see *Meaning* for
     10:1–44.

Verse 2 starts with a general particle that introduces a clause. This
particle is generally translated by *For*, but 'Indeed' (thus NET) is also
a valid translation. The phrase *the holy race has mixed itself* [23] *with the
peoples of the lands* sounds racist, as does the translation 'they mixed [24]
the holy seed [which occurs also in Isa. 6:13, although there without
the definite article: 'a holy seed'] with the peoples of the lands'. We
must consider this in the totality of its context and theology (see
Meaning at the end of ch. 10).

Seeing that *in this faithlessness* (a very strong term, always used for
people in relation to the covenant, not for outsiders; Throntveit
1992: 52), *the officials and chief men* (people with secular authority,
lower in rank than governors; Tuplin 1987: 126) [25] have *been foremost*
(lit. their 'hand was first', cf. AV), a quick reaction seems necessary:
if this bad example is followed generally, it will be difficult to then
suppress the practice.

3. Ezra *tore* his *garment* [cf. Gen. 37:34; 2 Sam. 1:11–12] *and* his
cloak [worn only by high-ranking people, so the translation 'robe'
[NET] is better] *and pulled hair from* his own [different from the
situation in Neh. 13:25!] *head and beard* (cf. Isa. 3:24; 22:12; Ezek.
27:31; Amos 8:10), as signs of mourning, *and sat appalled*: [26] he finds
the situation unbelievable, expressing a mixture of sorrow and
dissatisfaction.

---

23 'The race' considered as a collective term and so with a plural verb
(GKC §145b).

24 Also interpreted as a Hithpael, but with the sense that the subject is
specifically involved (GKC §54f); thus NIV.

25 In any case, *chief men* is not a happy translation, as everywhere else
in Ezra-Neh. *segānîm* is translated as 'officials'. Of course, this
translation could not be used twice in the same verse for different
words, but *śārîm* is represented by a large array of translations and so
should have been translated here by another word than *officials* (and
then use the same term in v. 1) – e.g. 'the leaders and the officials'
(NET; cf. NIV).

26 Why has the Polel form of the verb here a passive meaning? Zorell
1968: 860 does not solve the problem, but at least remarks that it is
'intrans.' LXX and Vulg. have active forms.

4. Gradually[27] *all who trembled*[28] *at the words* [to be found in e.g. Josh. 23:12] *of the God of Israel* (the proper term in this religious context) *gathered*, not because they were afraid of what was to come, but because they took the holy God and his Word seriously. For *faithlessness*, see on verses 1–2. Ezra *sat appalled* [same phrase as in the previous verse] *until the evening sacrifice*, which at first was offered 'between the evenings' (Exod. 29:39, 41; Num. 28:4, 8), interpreted as 'at evening twilight' (a few minutes more than half an hour: Dalman 1928: 623–624; quite short for everything needed to occur, but apparently a fitting time, according to Gen. 24:11, 63). Some interpret this expression as 'between midday (when the sun goes in the direction of the evening) and dark (when the evening has arrived)'; in New Testament times, the offering took place from 2.30 to 3.30 pm according to Josephus, *Jewish Antiquities* 14.65 and the Babylonian Talmud, Pesahim 58a (Houtman 1989: 163–164; Beckwith 1996: 1–2).

5. Apparently Ezra's appalled state has turned into 'humiliation' (the word is used with the sense of 'fasting' [thus ESV] only in post-biblical Hebrew). Ezra is praying *upon* his *knees*; other prayer positions mentioned are standing (1 Sam. 1:26), sitting (2 Sam. 7:18; 1 Chr. 17:16) and kneeling (Ps. 95:6, perhaps a specific kind of praying, but praying nevertheless).

6. Ezra's prayer must have been spoken aloud, otherwise the reaction in 10:1–2 cannot be understood; as far as the content is concerned, verses 8–9, 13–14 have, within the prayer, a highly homiletical character.

Ezra is desperate, feeling shame inside and that he has been brought into disgrace by the people (had he presented too rosy a picture to the king? – Williamson 1998: 162). We find the same combination of *ashamed and blush* in Isaiah 41:11; 45:16–17; Jeremiah 31:19. For that reason, he does not dare *to lift* his *face*: the *iniquities* of the Israelites have grown above Ezra's head (the Hebrew text does

---

27   Because of the imperfect *yēʾāsəphû* (Williamson 1985: 126).

28   The Hebrew word is at the origin of the Haredim, the ultra-orthodox segment of the Jews, who are afraid to violate even one of the 613 commandments of the Torah.

not have *our* or a plural) and their *guilt has mounted up to the heavens*; these two expressions should not be taken literally and so do not need further explanation. The word *guilt* recurs six times in these two chapters and so indicates that the concept is quite important (Duggan 2006: 173).

7–9. Everything is felt as having been *given* – negative things (according to v. 7: *into the hand of the kings of the lands, to the sword, to captivity, to plundering, and to utter shame*) and positive things (according to vv. 8–9: *a secure hold, reviving* (twice), *protection*; according to v. 13 *a remnant*). For the negative things, however, a single passive form is used, and even though a *passivum divinum* (passive form with God as agent) can be supposed, God is nevertheless not mentioned explicitly. This contrasts with the mention of positive things: the verb is used four times (although ESV has opted for variation) and God is always mentioned in the direct context (although only in v. 13 as a grammatical subject).

We can compare the confession of verse 7 with what we read in 1 Kings 17:7–23 (for other references, see on Neh. 13:18). With *the kings of the lands*, not only Assyrian and Babylonian kings are meant, but also Persian kings, as Ezra considers his situation as problematic (see *For we are slaves* in v. 9). Continuity exists between the Assyrian and Babylonian Empires (Vanderhooft 1999: 51; Dalley 2003) as well as between the Babylonian and Persian (Wiseman 1991: 250–251; Waters 2021). The *utter shame* might be caused by the taunting which is always the fate of conquered nations; we find 'open shame' also in Daniel 9:7; 'sword … captivity and plunder' in Daniel 11:33. In Hebrew, the similar sounds of the last three terms witness to a high literary quality.

A literary combination of sounds comes again in the first words of verse 8.

We sense a tension in verses 8 and 9 between the feelings of oppression (*slavery, slaves*)[29] and some relaxation at this very moment (*for a brief moment favour, remnant, secure hold, a little reviving, protection*).

---

29 The alternative interpretation of Becking 2018: 149 (God's servants) seems to have a problem with the construction of the *û* (Waltke and O'Connor 1990: §39.2.1d).

The *remnant* consists of those who had returned from exile and those who had stayed in the land and belonged to the same community. The fact that God has given a tent peg (AV 'a nail'; ESV translates as *a secure hold*) *within his holy place* means that the Israelites will again have (under God's care) a permanent basis in Jerusalem (cf. Isa. 22:23; 33:20; 54:2; Moffat 2013: 298). Brightening of the eyes normally occurs when one recovers from weakness after hunger (1 Sam. 14:27), illness (Ps. 38:10) or danger of death (Ps. 13:4 [ET 3]); see Deuteronomy 28:65 for the opposite ocular metaphor (failing eyes).

God ... has extended to us his steadfast love seems to be the right interpretation here (although some want to think of the king's beneficence).

The permission *to set up the house of our God* (the temple) had already been given in 538.

By *protection* ESV translates a word for a wall marking off vineyards (as in the Yorkshire Dales, I imagine, even though not for vineyards there; cf. Num. 22:24; Isa. 5:5). Not only the temple has been given, but also some extra room around it; the temple is the most important, but the surroundings also have their function.

With verse 9 reference is made to the returns under Zerubbabel and Ezra and the rebuilding of the temple and the walls, which links part 2 (7:1 – 10:44) with part 1 (1:1 – 6:22; Duggan 2006: 177).

10–12. After the more didactic part of verses 8–9, *And now* brings the reader back to the actual prayer. On the other hand, what is put between quotation marks in English translations is again directed to the audience. In fact, it is a summary of the teaching of men who had spoken on behalf of God (see the plural *your servants the prophets*, including Moses: see Deut. 18:15; 34:10) and indicates that Scripture was seen as an authoritative unity (Werline 1998: 46–47).

While *The land that you are entering*[30] reminds us of Deuteronomy 7:1, the order *do not give your daughters to their sons, neither take their daughters for your sons* is very near to Deuteronomy 7:3.

The *land* is not *impure* because of interfaith marriages; it is rather the other way around: because of the *abominations* (see on vv. 1–2)

---

30   Actually futurum instans (GKC §116p).

related to the religion of *the peoples of the lands*, marriages with them cannot be allowed. See Exodus 34:12–16, where their religion is discussed, and mixed marriages receive only a few words.

The phrase *never seek their peace* is also found in Deuteronomy 23:6, but seems to contradict Jeremiah 29:7, written during the exile from which Ezra had returned! What is the difference? Apparently, we must be committed to society as long as this creates no harm on the religious level, but not when it would bring idolatry with it (cf. Lorein 2018: 261–263 and *Meaning* at the end of ch. 10). The goal for the Israelites themselves is *that you may be strong and eat the good of the land and leave it for an inheritance to your children for ever.*

13. The second half (v. 13b) comprises two elements: 'You have withheld/spared less than our sins' (probably in the sense of *have punished us less than* [lit. 'below'] *our iniquities deserved*) and 'You have given a remnant' (for which see on vv. 7–9). Different solutions have been proposed to relate these two elements and to relate the second half of the verse to the first half. Most probably the two elements of the second half should just be read in parallel and seen as a form of astonishment following the first half (indeed the option taken by ESV): 'after (and together with) all that has come upon us … we realize indeed that you have spared us, below the measure of our sins … and have given us a remnant'.

14. After a long introduction comes the conclusion (formulated as a question): interfaith family relations cannot be continued because God would then send yet more severe punishment. (Grace cannot be a licence for a sinful life: see Rom. 6:1–2. Otherwise, God will be 'completely'[31] angry.) The expression *until you consumed us, so that there should be no remnant, nor any to escape* is recycled by the Qumran Community in their Treatise on the Two Spirits (1QS IV, 13–14). It is not applied to the writer's group, as Ezra does, but to the group of the spirit of darkness.

15. The prayer ends with two main ideas: God is just, we are guilty. God's justice is put in relation to being a remnant; this relationship is normally seen as causative in English translation (*for we are left a remnant*), but it is easier to understand when translated as

---

31 Waltke and O'Connor 1990: §35.3.3a.

'even though': God is just, even though only a remnant escaped; or, the other way around: even if we are so limited in number, that is according to God's righteousness (Zorell 1968: 353). Ezra considers himself to be a part of the group: he does not blame the group but confesses their collective guilt. This may be appropriate when one feels a genuine relationship with the group; without a genuine relationship with the group that has sinned, such a confession is pointless.

The text now attracts attention to the situation of *guilt* (van der Merwe 1990: 140; see on v. 6). By just observing that *none can stand before you because of this* (or that 'there is nothing to stand on before you as far as this is concerned')[32] the prayer ends in a minor key, without a prayer for forgiveness or grace, but only with the observation that the situation is hopeless before a righteous God. In specific situations of confession this can be necessary. Of course, this does not negate that God wants to be gracious towards those who fear him.

Meaning
See *Meaning* at the end of Ezra 10.

ii. The treatment of the problem of interfaith marriages (10:1–44)
Context
This unit follows immediately on from the previous one: with the problem having been pointed out and considered in Ezra 9, now the solution is presented and worked out.

As already mentioned in the introductory comments to this section (9:1 – 10:44), the book of Ezra ends quite suddenly with Ezra 10. Later we find Ezra again in Jerusalem (Neh. 8:2), apparently after a period of absence. It seems as if Ezra's intervention was less than successful and that this compelled him to leave. During Ezra's absence, work on the reconstruction of Jerusalem continued, but met with opposition (Ezra 4:8–23). It was this situation that was communicated to Nehemiah (Neh. 1:3).

---

32 See Waltke and O'Connor 1990: §36.2.3f for the different possibilities.

Comment
1. The *weeping* excepted, all the verbs in the first half of the verse
have forms that indicate intensity. Someone who weeps does not see
any way out and must be helped by other people. When one person
weeps, others will follow (it is contagious). In the second half of the
verse, not only *men*, but also *women and* even *children* (climax) *gathered
to* Ezra as an *assembly* (typical term for the religious congregation)
and 'the people wept tears intensively'. The mention of the wives'
presence highlights the importance of the gathering, as in Nehemiah 5:1; 8:2–3; 10:28–29; 12:43 (Williams 2002: 63).
2–3. Finally *Shecaniah* (a popular name – see 8:3, 5; Neh. 3:29; 6:18;
12:3; not always the same person) 'reacted' (most frequently translated
by 'answered' – thus AV; ESV here has *addressed*) and spoke the words
that opened the way to a solution. His words are quite solemn, with
(in Hebrew) three words with alliteration and three words with an
end rhyme: they have *broken faith* (same root as 'faithlessness' in 9:2)
and caused to dwell (not *married*!) *foreign* (mostly used in the sense of
'hostile': Konkel 1997: 109) *women*. The problem is clearly defined,
but at the same time, with a right attitude (*hope for Israel*, 'Israel' as the
right term for faithful Jews), the solution (an uneasy one!) is pointed
at: *a covenant with*[33] *our God to put away* [not 'divorce'!] *all these wives
and their children.* Does the fact that unusual terms for marrying and
divorcing are used (and this is confirmed by the words used in Greek,
in LXX as well as in 1 Esdras 8:89–90 [ET 92–93] and Josephus, *Ant.*
11.145) point to concubinage? Although this practice was normal in
Ancient Near Eastern eyes, it is difficult for us to understand that the
children have to leave with their mothers. Furthermore, that would
not contribute to a good Jewish education.
  Although many manuscripts present the reading *the counsel of* 'the
Lord' (or 'the LORD'; this combination is far from impossible: see
Ps. 33:11), 1 Esdras 8:90 (ET 93) and the parallel with *those who tremble
at the commandment of our God* (cf. 9:4) tends to understand *my lord* as
Ezra, here in his status as a Persian official. The *counsel* itself is only
cited, not quoted.

---

33 This is a correct translation (Grosheide 1963: 267; *pace* Becking 2018:
   155–156).

According to classical Hebrew grammar, Shecaniah puts this in an affirmative sentence: 'We shall make a covenant … and it will be done according to the Law.' These standard rules, however, are not always followed. Basing themselves on this observation, translations have *let us make* and *let it be done*.[34]

4. Just like Joshua when installing the people of Israel in the land of Canaan (Deut. 31:23; Josh. 1:6–9), and just like Solomon when building the temple (1 Chr. 22:13; 28:10), Ezra had to *be strong* in order to act[35] at the moment of reinstalling the people of Israel at the return from exile. This citation stresses the relationship between the building of the temple (part 1, 1:1 – 6:22) and the building of the community (part 2, 7:1 – 10:44).

5. Sometimes the leader cannot take the initiative, but when someone else has done so (Shecaniah in this case), the leader must take responsibility and take care that the people (here clearly together with the religious leaders) confirm it formally: strike while the iron is hot.

6. Apparently, Ezra did not have a detailed plan in mind (this proves that his prayer in Ezra 9 was no play-acting); indeed, he retires to the accommodation of Jehohanan (a frequent name, which makes identification difficult; he must be an important priest, but not the high priest [VanderKam 2004: 94]), near the temple (cf. the cloister in a collegiate church). According to the Hebrew text 'he went there' (the second half of the verse starts with the same word as the first half does, just as in LXX; AV 'he came thither'); most English translations base themselves on a textual modification, translated by *he spent the night* (Josephus, *Ant.* 11.147, however, says 'he spent all that day [!] on the spot'; my translation). By using the same words as Exodus 34:28 (cf. Deut. 9:18), the phrase *neither eating bread nor drinking water* indicates another covenant renewal. Fasting is meant to enable us to orient ourselves in all humility and openness to God in prayer, not in order to force him: it is not a mechanism. The Old Testament does not have general prescriptions for fasting, although generally a context of conversion and good works is presupposed (Jon. 3:7–8).

---

34 Lettinga and von Siebenthal 2016: §78A/714.1 and §77B/711.7.

35 Indirect volitive: Joüon and Muraoka 2006: §116f3.

For *faithlessness*, see on 9:1–2. For *the exiles*, see *Context* for 9:1–15.

7. The decision is well communicated through a *proclamation* (see on 1:1b) *to all the returned exiles* (see *Context* for 9:1–15).

8. The villages furthest removed from Jerusalem were still within 20 miles. This made it possible for anyone to arrive in Jerusalem, after some preparation, *within three days*, even during winter. *The officials* [see on 9:1] *and the elders* decided on penalties: all belongings would be devoted to God (in other words: confiscated for the benefit of the priests; Fensham 1982: 138) and the transgressors would be excommunicated. The penalties are so severe that those who took the decision must have been sure that Ezra's authority backed them (see on 7:26).

9. As Ezra 9 – 10 follows immediately on from Ezra 7 – 8, we are still in Artaxerxes' seventh year, which brings us to the date of 19 December 458 (see *Context* on 9:1–15), so during winter, warmer than Cambridge, but still only 10 °C (50 °F), and rainy (Scott 1952: 14–15).

10. They have been unfaithful (see on 9:1–2). The consequence[36] of having brought in (see on vv. 2–3) *foreign* [see on v. 2] *women* is that they *increased the guilt* [see on 9:6] *of Israel.*

11. The first imperative in this verse can be interpreted in different ways: (1) it could be *make confession* (mentioning one's sins before God; more probable in the context); (2) or it could be 'give praise to the LORD' (more probable when considering the exact Hebrew wording, which is different from the verb used for Ezra in v. 1; so ESV in Josh. 7:19); (3) *HALOT* 1696 suggests 'a doxology in court', by which 'the accused gives praise to Yahweh in recognition that in his acts and in his judgement he is just'. The third option seems to combine all elements: context and etymology; in any case, when we praise God, we should recognize our own sins and confess them.

The three imperatives in the verse are closely related: giving praise to God must go together with acting according to what pleases God; this general attitude must have consequences[37] – in this case to be separated from the foreign women.

36 Joüon and Muraoka 2006: §124l.
37 Joüon and Muraoka 2006: §116f3.

12–13. The faithful (*the assembly*) consent, but draw attention to a concrete problem: the decision can be taken in one single sentence, but the practical consequences cannot be worked out in the given setting (cold and rainy: see on v. 9).

14. By allowing those who had brought in foreign women[38] to go back to their places of residence[39] during the working out of the consequences, daily living is not disturbed more than necessary. Perhaps several teams worked at different places simultaneously so that the conclusions could be implemented as soon as possible. Working in teams is important in these circumstances: individuals can make a mistake too easily and the subject matter is too sensitive.

15–16. In most English translations *Jonathan* ('the LORD has given') and *Jahzeiah* ['may the LORD see'] *opposed*, though it is unclear what they opposed: did they want to have a more lenient procedure? Or a stricter one? *Meshullam* ['compensated, satisfied'] *and Shabbethai* ['born on a Sabbath'] *supported them*, that is (most probably), the two men just mentioned. They did not get a majority and – in this interpretation – at the end *the returned exiles did* as was proposed in verse 14. The Vulgate and 1 Esdras 9:14 suggest another way to interpret the Hebrew text: the four 'stood up', took their responsibility (thus AV: 'were employed about this matter'). The first word of verse 15 (Hebr. *'akh*, translated in ESV by *Only*) is not in favour of this interpretation, but it may be translated various ways.

Verse 16 presents another problem. Most translations do not follow the Hebrew text, but base themselves on 1 Esdras 9:16, offering *Ezra the priest selected men* (implying that Ezra was not a member of the commission). Staying with the Hebrew we read: 'Ezra the priest (and) the men who were family heads went away

---

38 The article before 'had brought in foreign women' serves as a relative pronoun (Joüon and Muraoka 2006: §145d).

39 The vocalization of *be'ārênû* cannot be explained by reducing it to the Masoretes (*pace* GKC §127i): all vocalizations are Masoretic. Of course, the *e* is quite common before ' and it might be used here for euphonic reasons (Joüon and Muraoka 2006: §140c). Other MSS have *b*ᵉ*ārênû*, in line with the normal grammatical rules (Baumgartner and Rudolph 1976: 49).

[AV 'Ezra [etc.] were separated'] to the house of their fathers, all of them with their names (well noted) and they were in session on the first day of the tenth month in order to study⁴⁰ the matter.'

17. The investigation takes place from 29 December 458 to 27 March 457, that is, seventy-five session days (but perhaps during winter more days dropped out than only Sabbaths and festive days), for 113 cases in which the woman is effectively sent away – that is, 113 cases in a population estimated at between at least 50,000 (Lemaire 2017: 185) and more probably 150,000 (Yamauchi 1988: 568). That this took such a long time (especially if parallel teams were at work: see on v. 14) implies that foreign women were not just evacuated, but were screened as to their religious attitude and concrete relationships. Of course, this remark is useless if the list of verses 18–44 is limited to those who indeed decided to expel the women (as Josephus, *Ant.* 11.151 puts it), and does not mention those cases where Jews with foreign women came to a different conclusion. Nevertheless, people are mentioned by name, individually.

18–22. The cases among *the priests* are categorized according to their family relations. In the first place, some sons of the high priest *Jeshua* (see on 2:1–2) are mentioned. In the second place, priests of other branches are mentioned, according to their ancestor: *Immer*, *Harim* and *Pashhur* (see on 2:36–39). They made a promise (lit. 'gave their hands'), owing (or, based on LXX, *their guilt offering was*) *a ram of the flock for their guilt*.

Maaseiah ('the works of the LORD'), *Eliezer* ('God is my help'), *Jarib* ('[God] will contend') and *Gedaliah* ('the LORD is great') were sons or nephews (or more distantly related: Grosheide 1963: 286) of the high priest (four cases).

Hanani ('[God] is gracious'), *Zebadiah* ('the LORD has given'), a second *Maaseiah*, *Elijah* ('the LORD is my God'), *Shemaiah* ('the LORD has heard'), *Jehiel* ('may God live'), *Uzziah* (the LORD is my strength'), *Elioenai* ('my eyes are on the LORD'), a third *Maaseiah*, *Ishmael* ('may God listen'), *Nethanel* ('God has given'), *Jozabad* ('the

---

40   Following the versions, as every translation does (most Hebrew manuscripts have 'to Darius', apparently a plain copyist's error [Marcus 2006: 44*; Baumgartner and Rudolph 1976: 49]).

LORD has endowed') and *Elasah* ('God has acted') are the other priests concerned (thirteen cases).

23–24. Among *the Levites* we find *Jozabad* ('the LORD has endowed'), *Shimei* ('the LORD has heard'), *Kelaiah* (meaning unknown; *Kelita* means 'dwarf'), *Pethahiah* ('the LORD has opened'), *Judah* ('praise'), *Eliezer* ('my God is help') in the general category; one singer (see on 7:7–9), *Eliashib* ('God will restore'); and three gatekeepers (see on 7:7–9), *Shallum* ('compensated, satisfied'), *Telem* ('brightness') and *Uri* ('my light') (altogether ten cases).

25. In verses 25–43 the laypeople (*Israel*) are categorized according to their forefathers, mentioned in 2:3–19 (or according to their city: see 2:29, 32). The name *Bani* occurs twice in the list (vv. 29, 34), but it would be strange if two families had the same name (Kidner 1979: 72, however, sees no problem in a second Bani family). Of course, personal names are prone to transmission errors, and this may be the case not only with *Bani*, but also with other names. The most probable hypothesis asks for the replacement of the second *Bani* by 'Bigvai' (cf. 2:14).

Descendants of *Parosh*: *Ramiah* ('the LORD is exalted'), *Izziah* ('the LORD besprinkles'), *Malchijah* ('the LORD is my king'), *Mijamin* ('from the right side'), *Eleazar* ('God is [my] help'), another *Malchijah* and *Benaiah* ('the LORD has built') (seven cases).

26. Descendants of *Elam*: *Mattaniah* ('gift of the LORD'), *Zechariah* ('the LORD has remembered'), *Jehiel* ('may God live'), *Abdi* ('servant of [God]'), *Jeremoth* ('height'), *Elijah* ('the LORD is my God') (six cases).

27. Descendants of *Zattu*: *Elioenai* ('my eyes are on the LORD'), *Eliashib* ('God will restore'), *Mattaniah* ('gift of the LORD'), *Jeremoth* (see on v. 26), *Zabad* ('[God] has endowed'), *Aziza* ('strong') (six cases).

28. Descendants of *Bebai*: *Jehohanan* ('the LORD has been gracious'), *Hananiah* ('the LORD has been gracious'), *Zabbai* (perhaps short for Zebadiah, 'the LORD has given'), *Athlai* ('the LORD is exalted) (four cases).

29. Descendants of *Bani*: *Meshullam* ('compensated, satisfied'), *Malluch* ('[God] is king'), *Adaiah* ('the LORD has adorned'), *Jashub* ('he will return'), *Sheal* ('ask'), *Jeremoth* (see on v. 26) (six cases).

30. Descendants of *Pahath-moab*: *Adna* ('pleasure'), *Chelal* ('perfection'), *Benaiah* ('the LORD has built'), *Maaseiah* ('the works of the LORD'), *Mattaniah* ('gift of the LORD), *Bezalel* ('in God's shadow'), *Binnui* ('built'), *Manasseh* ('[God] makes one forget') (eight cases).

31–32. Citizens of *Harim*: *Eliezer* ('my God is help'), *Isshijah* ('the LORD caused to forget'), *Malchijah* ('the LORD is my king'), *Shemaiah* ('the LORD has heard'), *Shimeon* (even if the original meaning was 'little hyena', people must have understood it as '[God] has listened'), *Benjamin* ('son of the right side'), *Malluch* ('[God] is king'), *Shemariah* ('the LORD has protected') (eight cases).

33. Descendants of *Hashum*: *Mattenai* ('gift of the LORD'), *Mattattah* ('gift [of God]'), *Zabad* ('[God] has given'), *Eliphelet* ('my God is deliverance'), *Jeremai* ('the LORD has exalted'), *Manasseh* ('[God] makes one forget'), *Shimei* ('the LORD has heard') (seven cases).

34–42. Descendants of *Bani* ('Bigvai'?): *Maadai* ('ornament of the LORD'), *Amram* ('[my] people is exalted'), *Uel* ('the will of God'), *Benaiah* ('the LORD has built'), *Bedeiah* ('protégé of the LORD'), *Cheluhi* ('the LORD is perfect'), *Vaniah* (Persian, 'victorious [by God]' – Hutter 2009: 89–90; the girl's name is the Russian female form of Jehohanan), *Meremoth* ('elevations'), *Eliashib* ('God will return'), *Mattaniah* ('gift of the LORD'), *Mattenai* ('gift of the LORD'), *Jaasu* ('may [God] act'), Bani (or, opted for in ESV and according to LXX, *sons of*; the number of descendants pleads for this interpretation, but not the Hebrew text), *Binnui* ('built') *Shimei* ('the LORD has heard'), *Shelemiah* ('the LORD has given satisfaction'), *Nathan* ('gift'), *Adaiah* ('the LORD has adorned'), *Machnadebai* (deformed for Akkadian 'possession of [the Babylonian god] Nabu/Nebo'? cf. LXX Machadnabou), *Shashai* ('splendour'; Hutter 2009: 88, 92), *Sharai* ('the LORD is master'?),[41] *Azarel* ('God has helped'), *Shelemiah* ('the LORD has given satisfaction'), *Shemariah* ('the LORD has protected'), *Shallum* ('compensated, satisfied'), *Amariah* ('the LORD has spoken'), *Joseph* ('may [God] add') (twenty-seven cases).

43. Citizens of *Nebo*: *Jeiel* ('God has healed'), *Mattithiah* ('gift of the LORD'), *Zabad* ('[God] has endowed'), *Zebina* ('bought [as a

41 But then it ought to be 'Sarai', unless Akkadian influence had worked out in Hebrew.

child]'), *Jaddai* ('the LORD has card for'), *Joel* ('the LORD is God'), *Benaiah* ('the LORD has built') (seven cases).

44. At the end of the list we find its 'title': *All these had married* [here we have the normal word for 'to marry'; see on vv. 2–3] *foreign women.* The second half of the verse can be translated by 'and among them (presumably the women?)[42] were women who (lit. 'and they'; obviously the women)[43] had put children (into the world)' (confirmed by Vulg. and LXX). A translation such as RSV 'they put them away with their children' is not based on the Hebrew text, but on the apocryphal 1 Esdras 9:36.

Meaning
After a safe journey, Ezra sees himself confronted with difficulties in the city of the temple: the problem of interfaith marriages, to be compared with the relationships with the Canaanite population upon arrival in the land after the exodus. Possibly he had hoped to arrive in an ideal situation, but apparently the risk of assimilation was as impending in Judah as it had been in the Diaspora, and perhaps even more so (Bedford 2002: 159).

When Ezra is informed about the problem, he does not immediately have a solution: the situation is clearly problematic, but how to handle it? Should he act with the authority given to him by the king? This is not the option that is taken in these verses. Indeed, no other option is left than to send away these women, but it must be done carefully, not with police action.

In Ezra's prayer (9:6–15) we should observe the relation between Ezra ('I') and his people ('we'). Ezra's connection with his ancestors stresses the importance of continuity (9:7). Ezra presents himself as belonging to the group; he does not blame that group, but only confesses collective guilt (9:10–15). The admission of their own failure is typical for Israel and is absent from other Ancient Near Eastern literature.

---

42 Often the form of third-person plural feminine is replaced by third-person plural masculine: GKC §135o.

43 Often the form of third-person plural feminine is replaced by third-person plural masculine: GKC §145p.

The support of King Artaxerxes (and earlier of Kings Cyrus and Darius) is appreciated and is indeed considered as grace from God, but the situation is not considered ideal. Ezra feels himself and his compatriots to be subject to slavery. As God has helped out in recent times, however, he is able to do so again. The attitude towards Persian authorities remains ambivalent and ours is the same: how should believers find the correct position in a secularized society? We know that God is acting, and we cannot be happy with everything that is happening in society: 'The elements of rejection and acceptance work together' (Firth 1997: 22; cf. 23–24 – albeit concerning the book of Esther), and our task in life is to learn how we should live.

It is typical for the period after the exile that this measure is initiated not by prophecy, but by reference to the Torah, the Instruction, or the Law as it is called in the New Testament (see Introduction 2n, 'Ezra's Law') and that the initiative for this is made by individual believers (10:3), approved by the community (10:12) and worked out by a commission (10:14). An important role is played by a class of officials (9:1; 10:8, 16–17).

In 10:12–13, a positive attitude goes together with pointing out the problems in all sincerity. This is a right attitude for the believer (in short: 'Yes, but', even though this expression is often declined in evangelical circles): 'Pious dishonesty is not something that God desires from us' (Grant 2001: 66).

A detailed list of the results is important (10:18–44). Even though these verses will probably never appear in a Bible-reading schedule, they remind us of the importance of keeping people in mind individually. Because most of the names were understandable for Ezra's contemporaries, their meaning has been mentioned in the *Comment*.[44]

When we realize that we are reading here about real people, we may wonder whether Ezra's measures were too severe. Of course, it is not the first time that the Bible warns against non-believers, but the systematic handling of them is exceptional. This shows that

44 Mostly based on Steinmann 2010: 178–188; *HALOT*; and Yamauchi 1988.

it is a serious matter, and it is not just about foreigners. Zehnder 2005: 433 remarks that openness exists when the women are ready to accept the Jewish religion. The books of Ruth and Jonah are witnesses to this. Neighbouring people are especially mentioned, because the possibility of enduring negative influence is the most substantial in their case, through their continuing contacts with the families where they came from (Grosheide 1963: 248). A relationship with a believer of non-Jewish origin was acceptable; placing oneself outside the believing community and within the surrounding cultural community was not.[45] This implies that no contradiction exists between Ezra's marriage-purity policy and the missiology of the books of Ruth and Jonah (and see also Zech. 2:15 [ET 11] for eschatological times), but a common appeal to conversion (Howard 1993: 46, 294, 306).

We might add that we are not speaking about starting a relationship with a Gentile woman, but about divorce, so clearly opposed by Ezra's contemporary Malachi. Some remarks may be made in this regard. In the first place, Malachi was not the first biblical writer who was opposed to divorce. We find the principle already stated in the Pentateuch. Even there, however, the exception of 'some indecency' is mentioned as grounds for divorce (Deut. 24:1–4), where we might easily think of foreign religious practices. In the second place, we must read Malachi 2:14–16 in its context, that is, as a plea for maintaining Jewish wives instead of secondary relations with non-Jewish women (van der Woude 1982b: 120–126; Snyman 2006: 29–30; Lorein 2010b: 343–346), and in that light Malachi is in line with Ezra.

---

45 To put things into perspective, it is notable that later Essene theology was much stricter about foreigners and excluded the possibility of their getting involved in the Jewish religion (Lorein 2021d: 257–261, 266–267). The fact that society is considered from a male viewpoint can on this occasion only be observed.

NEHEMIAH
COMMENTARY

3. BUILDING THE WALLS (1:1 – 7:3)

A. Introduction (1:1–11)

This section introduces the third part of Ezra-Neh. (Neh. 1:1 – 7:3), about the reconstruction of the walls. We consider it as a third part of a combined writing 'Ezra–Nehemiah'; on the other hand, it is clear that a new part starts (v. 1a).[1] The historical order structures the third part, but not always in one straight line, and it does not produce a tidy literary structure. Before the construction itself can take place, Nehemiah needs information, in the first place in Persia (this section) and then in Jerusalem (next section).

According to verse 1, this section is based on Nehemiah's memoirs. Nehemiah's reaction to the news about Jerusalem is sketched. The prayer (vv. 5–11) develops Israel's prayer tradition.

---

1 See Analysis.

i. Nehemiah's reaction to sad news from Jerusalem (1:1–11)
Context
For the general relationship between this chapter and the last
chapter of Ezra, see Introduction 2j, 'Relationship between Ezra
and Nehemiah'.

We cannot explain the phrase *in the twentieth year* (v. 1) by reckoning
from the New Year's Day of Artaxerxes' accession year or of the
first year thereafter. The easiest explanation is that within the palace
they reckoned with complete years from the very date of Artaxerxes'
accession itself, in August 465 (Depuydt 1995b: 193, 196). In that
way, Nehemiah 1 must be situated in the time span between 18
November and 17 December 446.

At the time of the report, Nehemiah holds an important position
at the Persian court in Susa, situated in a fertile valley 150 miles
north of the Gulf, the main city of Elam in the south-west of Iran,
more than 750 miles from Jerusalem as the crow flies. It was the
main winter capital of the Persian Empire. For better control over
the whole empire, different cities functioned as capitals, which of
course lessened the value of such a capital (Boucharlat 1997: 66–67;
Tuplin 1998: 68–69, 82–83). Susa is also mentioned in Daniel 8:2 and
the book of Esther.

Comment
1. Although *the words* is a correct translation of the Hebrew
(*divrê*, plural of *dāvār*), it can also be translated by 'memoirs', or
even 'history'. *Nehemiah* (see Introduction 2i, 'Nehemiah'), *the son of
Hacaliah* (nothing is known about him; his name means 'wait for the
Lord'), is active in *Susa*, which indeed is a *capital* (see *Context*), but
the word rather denotes 'the citadel' (thus NIV, NET), the government
quarter (cf. AV 'the palace'; NASB 'capitol').
2–3. *Hanani* ('[God] is gracious') is a physical brother of
Nehemiah (cf. 7:2); the name occurs often (cf. Ezra 10:20). Had
Hanani with his group made an expedition to Jerusalem in order
to know how things were there? Or was Jerusalem their departure
point, and did they go to Susa for lobbying work? Or just for a
family visit? Whatever the case, Nehemiah does not seem to be the
one who took the initiative. Nehemiah *asked them concerning the Jews
who* had escaped (rather than *who escaped*), *who had survived*, that is,

who had not died in exile but had gone back to Zion. The root of *survived*, however, is more meaningful than that: it shares the same root with the important concept of the remnant, those who in the midst of trials have remained faithful to God. Probably reference is made to the Trans-Euphrates satrapy (not *province*; cf. Introduction 2f, 'Organization of the Persian Empire'; Fensham 1982: 152). While it is obvious that words such as *wall* and *Jerusalem* are frequent in the book of Nehemiah, the word for *broken down* (or more correctly 'with breaches': the walls had not completely disappeared, but they had acquired holes) is frequent too (2:13; 4:3, 7; 6:1), as well as the burned gates (2:13, 17), so that this verse summarizes the basis for Nehemiah's reaction.

4. Nehemiah was upset. This does not mean that Nehemiah was totally unaware of the fact that the building project of about 450 (cf. Introduction 2j, 'Relationship between Ezra and Nehemiah') had led to such a negative result, but a personal report is always more powerful. He remained connected with his fellow believers, notwithstanding his comfortable position. Nehemiah *wept*: see on Ezra 10:1. Mourning does not occur only after a decease, and it takes some time before you are able to act again. For *fasting*, see on Ezra 10:6. In this sorrowful situation, he made the right decision to come before God in prayer.

5. Sources for the elements of the prayer in verses 5–11a can be found in Exodus 20:6; 32:11; Leviticus 26:40–42; Deuteronomy 4:27; 5:10, 31; 6:1; 7:9, 11, 19, 21; 8:11; 9:26, 29; 10:17; 11:1; 12:5, 11; 14:23; 16:6; 26:2; 30:1–5, 16.

With these words Nehemiah stays within Israel's prayer tradition of 1 Kings 8:23, 28–29, 48, 50–51, 53; 2 Chronicles 6:14, 40; 7:14–15; Psalm 130:2; Isaiah 37:17; Daniel 9:4–5; Ezra 9:6; also Baruch 1:15, 17–22; 2:10, 12, 16, 21, 24, 30–34; 3:2, 4; and the Rule of the Community of Qumran (1QS I, 24–25) (Duguid 2012: 262–263; Becking 2018: 172–176).

God of heaven: see on Ezra 1:2. The word *awesome* (or 'who is to be feared') is found several times in the book of Nehemiah (but never in the book of Ezra). The God who is *great and awesome* is the same God who *keeps covenant and steadfast love*. Neither must we see a discrepancy between *those who love him* and those who *keep his commandments.* Finally, we might observe a chiastic structure between the two descriptions through the concepts *love*[2] and *keep*.

6. Some exegetes stumble over the fact that in the first part *ear* (singular!) and *eyes* (plural!) are used and in the second part only *to hear*, but such variations are common in Hebrew and therefore not a problem.[3] For *confessing*, see on Ezra 9:15. In this situation, however, it is also possible that the confession for the community led to a sense of sin in the actual personal circumstances. The *father's house* equals the 'family' (thus NET).

7. Nehemiah is *very*[4] aware of the problem. The reference to Moses (e.g. Deut. 7:11) seems useful only if it is about an old tradition and not if the Pentateuch was created by Ezra (see on Ezra 7:14).

8–9. The request (the imperative must not be regarded as a plain order, especially not with the particle that AV translates as 'I beseech thee' and NET as 'Please'; see Jenni 2002: 5, 13–14) to *remember* is not for a nostalgic return to the past, but for awareness to act in the present (Becking 2018: 175). The same word occurs in 4:14; 5:19; 6:14; 13:14, 22, 29, 31. For *unfaithful*, see Ezra 9:2. The two roles are clearly opposed: *you* are unfaithful, *I* will scatter you.[5]

These two verses are the centre of Nehemiah's prayer (Throntveit 1992: 64). He refers to God's *word* (cf. Exod. 32:13, where Moses pleads for the people of Israel). The first part of the quotation is partially and not literally based on Leviticus 26:33. The second part is a summary of Deuteronomy 30:2–4 ('to gather' is used in a similar context in Jer. 29:14; 31:8; 32:37; Ezek. 11:17; 37:21; Mic. 2:12). In a

---

2 In Hebrew, two different words are used for *love*.

3 The Lucianic tradition within the LXX, sometimes considered to represent the original LXX, has the plural; other LXX manuscripts and the Vulg. have maintained the singular.

4 This word is the representation of a construction in Hebrew that normally asks for an infinitive absolute, but here has an infinitive construct. GKC §113x ascribes it to the 'rapid style'. Indeed, at some places, Nehemiah's Hebrew has particularities that cannot simply be ascribed to its character of Late Biblical Hebrew.

5 The simple juxtaposition of two clauses (notice the cursive '*if*' in AV) may indicate a condition and its consequence: see GKC §159b.

certain sense, Nehemiah no longer needs to pray for the return from exile, but not the whole people of Israel has returned and the restoration is still incomplete. The promise of the possibility of a return is a constant one. As Kidner 1979: 79 formulates it: 'He is empty-handed, but not uninvited.'

10. While in verses 6–7 Nehemiah presents himself as a servant and a sinner, he now speaks about the Israelites as *your servants and your people*. In a certain sense, the fear of the Lord and the joy of the Lord are intensely linked.

11a. When Nehemiah speaks again (cf. v. 6) about himself as *your servant*, this gives the impression of humility, but do not forget that he has used the same word for Moses in verses 7–8. The plural *servants* does not necessarily imply that Nehemiah was praying together with other people.

The context makes clear that *this man* introduces the king. Nehemiah understands well that before God even the king is just 'a human being' (Fensham 1982: 157).

11b. The last words of the prayer (*this man*) create a link with the next section (2:1–20), which is possible through Nehemiah's particular position, mentioned in a form of background information: *cupbearer to the king* (see Introduction 2i, 'Nehemiah').

Meaning
This chapter shows how Nehemiah sympathizes with the Jewish people. Although far away and in a comfortable position, he recognizes the seriousness of the situation and is aware of the way out. He understands that neither he nor Israel has any right to God's intervention, but appeals to God's faithfulness and grace, available for sinners. His prayer is general and comprehensive, but not with all kinds of details, as if it would be a question of magic. The very short prayer of 2:4 is often referred to, but we have to keep in mind that it follows on from a time of prayer. This spirituality does not exclude a down-to-earth approach in the next section.

We too can come, as sinners, to the great God who invites us to ask him to enable us to honour him by doing the right things for the people around us, in his presence.

B. Launch: return, information (2:1–20)

The previous section constituted the introduction; this section constitutes the launching of the main material of the third part of Ezra-Neh., namely the rebuilding of the walls. Like the launching of the building of the temple (Ezra 1:5 – 3:13) and the launching of the purification of the community (Ezra 8), this section mentions the return of exiles, albeit in a very limited way this time (see Ezra 2; 7:1–7; Neh. 2:10). As with the launching of the purification of the community (Ezra 8), this section mentions the gathering of information (see Ezra 8:36; Neh. 2:11–16).

The whole of the section is based on Nehemiah's memoirs.

i. Nehemiah commissioned to rebuild Jerusalem (2:1–20)
Context

It is uncertain whether the beginning of this section should still be situated in Susa. Persepolis is another option: it was the empire's capital during early summer and autumn and a capital where the New Year was celebrated (Tuplin 1998: 73, 76, 83, 86–87, 114). Nisan (v. 1), the month of New Year, in Artaxerxes' twentieth year of government (see *Context* on 1:1–11), was in Julian terms (see Introduction 2b, 'Julian dates') the month from 13 April to 11 May 445. This means that four months had already passed, and that Nehemiah still had not done anything with the information he had received about Jerusalem. Perhaps Nehemiah thought the New Year's banquet (v. 1; Williamson 1985: 178) would offer a good opportunity to ask King Artaxerxes his far-reaching question; perhaps he had not been on duty for all this time: Nehemiah was not the only cupbearer and had to obey his rota.

Nehemiah's arrival in Jerusalem must be dated to July 445 at the latest, that is, including travelling and visiting the governors in Trans-Euphrates (v. 9). This means that his journey was shorter than Ezra's, which can be explained by the different composition of the company (see Ezra 7:7–9).

After the relatively recent troubles with the building activities (see Introduction 2j, 'Relationship between Ezra and Nehemiah'), Nehemiah understood how risky it was to ask for permission to rebuild the walls (vv. 2–8). The explanation Nehemiah gives to the leaders in Jerusalem must be read against the same background (vv. 17–18).

Discussion exists about the extent of the city of Jerusalem; see Introduction 2k, 'Jerusalem' for the viewpoint presumed in the exegesis.

Comment

1. As Nehemiah was the king's cupbearer (see Introduction 2i, 'Nehemiah'), the *wine* was in the first place before him ('before me', thus NET), then Nehemiah tasted it *and gave it to the king*. At the end of this verse background information is provided (see on 1:11b): Nehemiah *had not been*[6] *sad* ('bad, displeasing, unkind') *in* the king's *presence*, or at least, he had always hidden it – personnel were not supposed to bring their private problems to the palace (and perhaps especially in a Iranian context – Fleishman 2012: 250).

2. The king noted that now for the first time Nehemiah's *face* was *sad* (see on v. 1) indeed, and that this was not because he was ill; a correct diagnosis (Batten 1913: 191). Of course, the king desired to count on professional servants; on the other hand, some sympathy made him ask about the background to Nehemiah's state of mind, with exactly the same words as Joseph in Genesis 40:7 (see also Eccl. 7:3). Being confronted with the question, Nehemiah did not know whether it was a form of reprimand or of sympathy. Since the king had observed the problem in any case, the best way out was a full explanation. Notwithstanding Nehemiah's trust in God, the gravity of the moment was very clear: Nehemiah had to ask his question, with no certainty regarding the king's reaction.

3. The salutation *Let the king live*[7] *for ever!* was a normal formula at court and was not felt to be an unacceptable exaggeration (Jenni 2009: 76, 84). Nehemiah tried to explain why his face was *sad*. Through reference to his *fathers' graves* Nehemiah touched the king's

---

6 For the pluperfect, see Joüon and Muraoka 2006: §118d; Lorein 2021a: 24–25.

7 Morphologically the Hebrew has an imperfect, not a jussive, but it might be considered as perlocutive, where the expression of the wish contributes to its realization (cf. Jenni 2009: 86).

Zoroastrian sensitivity; similarly with the fact that the city is *destroyed by fire*, an unholy use of fire, which was so important in Iranian religion (Fleishman 2012: 255, 258). The exact name of *the city* and the situation of the walls are not mentioned because only some years earlier the king had ordered that the restoration of these defensive walls be stopped. The truth may be said, but it is not necessary to do so. Nehemiah did not force the king to answer, but left room, also for himself – in this way being able to find out whether God's time had come to go further (Williamson 1985: 179).

4. The king understood that a request was hiding behind Nehemiah's question and therefore asked for clarification. Thus arose the opportunity for which Nehemiah had hoped and had long been preparing, including in prayer. Now only a quick prayer was possible (and necessary), not with many words or in a specific posture of prayer.

5. Nehemiah asked that the king might finally act upon the decree pending since Ezra 4:21, by giving him a leave of absence in order to *rebuild it* (i.e. the city).[8] He did it in a respectful way: *that you send me ... so that I may rebuild it*.[9] So the plain imperative of some English translations ('send me', 'dispatch me') is unjustified.

6. Probably *the queen* (Zadok 2012: 161; or was it the [most important] queen mother? – thus Brosius 1996: 30–31, 121) was *sitting beside* the king during an informal meeting after the New Year's banquet (for this reconstruction, see Williamson 1985: 178, 180; cf. Briant 2002: 184–186). The name of the queen was Damaspia (Ctesias, *Persica* §44; Briant 2002: 588). The female members of the royal family had no formal authority, but they did have influence (Yamauchi 1988: 685). It is unclear whether this time the king's decision was any different (in procedure or in outcome) because of her presence. Apparently, the king was sympathetic towards a Jew with a religion quite near to his own and from a region with some

---

8   In Hebrew, both the suffix of the verb and *city* are feminine (*pace* Becking 2018: 182).

9   The syntax must be understood as a jussive (*tišlāḥēnî*; optative: Joüon and Muraoka 2006: §163a) followed by a cohortative (*wəʾevnennâ*; indirect volitive: op. cit. §116b), both masked by the suffix.

strategic importance, and who was loyal towards the Persian Empire as well as to his own people (Fleishman 2012: 243–244). The king did not give a direct answer, but by asking about the length of his absence he indirectly gave his permission. We are not informed what this length was, probably because in the end his stay in Jerusalem was longer than expected.

7. Nehemiah asked the king for *letters … for the governors* in Trans-Euphrates (see Introduction 2f, 'Organization of the Persian Empire'). In the Persian period, this kind of letter normally comprised a request for safe conduct and provision of food (Kitchen 2003: 78). English translations vary in their construction and never translate literally (which would be 'may they give letters to me').[10]

8. Another letter was asked for *Asaph* (a Jewish name, '[God] has gathered'), *the keeper of the king's forest* (the Hebrew word used here is based on the Persian word that also produced our word 'paradise'). Perhaps Lebanon is meant here (Högemann 1992: 275), but in Antiquity the Near East counted more woods than it does today. Another candidate is Solomon's domain in Etan, about 5 miles south-west of Bethlehem (Josephus, *Ant.* 8.186), which possibly had passed to the Persian royal domains; in that case the keeper's Jewish identity would be more easily understood.

The timber was needed *to make beams* [or 'rafters'] *for the gates of the fortress* (in Hebr. the same word as 'citadel' in 1:1) which is near to *the temple* (at the north side of the temple, the most open one, allowing watchers to take a higher position to look for attackers; Becking 2018: 197), *and for the wall* [some MSS and most versions have the plural here] *of the city, and for the house that I shall occupy* (lit. 'to which I shall go'; apparently Nehemiah was already thinking of a nice house). It is interesting to see the order in Nehemiah's thinking: the temple, the city, his own house.

9–10. In a 'catching-up report'[11] or flashback, to be translated by a pluperfect, we are informed that Nehemiah went with *officers of the army and horsemen*, this in contrast to the situation in Ezra 8:22.

---

10 An impersonal construction, with the third-person plural masculine as an indefinite subject (GKC §144g).

11 Van der Woude 1985: 11–12, 22, cf. Lorein 2021a: 24–25.

Perhaps this was just the wiser decision. Nehemiah might have already obtained the status of governor (see *Context* on 1:1–11). In this second option, he would have been visiting his colleagues in verse 10 (besides, Judah had no other governor at this moment). Apparently *Sanballat* and *Tobiah* were already informed before Nehemiah actually arrived. The news (namely *that someone had come to seek the welfare of the people of Israel*)[12] *displeased them greatly* (lit. 'it was bad to them with great badness'; cf. the more frequent opposite expression 'it was good in his eyes' / 'it pleased him'). *Sanballat* (or more exactly 'Sanvallat' – Lipiński 2000: 621; '[the moon-god] Sin makes to live') must have been born around 490, as he is also known from Elephantine (an island in the Nile, in Southern Egypt, with many soldiers from Jewish descent; Cowley 1923: no. 30 l. 29) and from a text found in a cave of the Wadi Daliyeh (9 miles north-west of Jericho) but produced in Samaria. This implies that he must have been governor from before 445 until at least 407 BC (Lipiński 2018: 159–160, 180).[13] The name suggests an origin in Haran, a centre of the Sin religion (in Roman times Carrhae; Lemaire 2001: 103–104; Lipiński 2018: 132–133). His children were called names which referred to the LORD (we would say 'good Christian names'), which indicates that he was not negative towards the religion of Israel. He was governor of Samaria.

Both the name *Tobiah* ('the LORD is good') and the name of his son (6:18) refer to the LORD. He is called a *servant*, not in the sense of a slave but as a minister of Sanballat the governor. He is called an *Ammonite*; in the third century BC, one of his descendants became governor of Ammon.

11. Like Ezra (Ezra 8:32), Nehemiah permitted himself a period of *three days*, which gave him the opportunity to get accustomed and informed. We do not know how much time was required by the visits of verse 9.

---

12 Syntactically speaking this is a subject clause introduced by *ᵃšer* (Meyer 1972: §113.1b).

13 Other reconstructions exist (Dušek 2007: 516–549; Lipiński 2018: 167–180), but we need a minimum of different persons when we situate Sanballat II only in the period from 385 to 332. See on 13:28.

12. Nehemiah avoided spreading ideas that were incomplete: he *told no one what*[14] his *God had put into* his *heart.* The verbal form 'was giving' (cf. NET 'was putting'; most English translations here are based on the versions) seems to indicate that God's message became clear to Nehemiah only gradually once he was already in Jerusalem.

No *animal* but Nehemiah's was there, so the people who accompanied him did so on foot. Apparently, the moon was giving its light, but we do not know in which month. It is not clear which animal is serving Nehemiah. The Hebrew only has *animal.* Was it a horse (Fensham 1982: 165)? It is certainly a rather military animal, which had come with him from Persia (cf. v. 9). That would explain why it could not go further in verse 14. Was it a donkey (Fensham 1982: 165; vom Orde 1997: 173)? That is a royal riding animal (Zech. 9:9). Did Nehemiah want to avoid stressing his royal traits (cf. Duguid 2012!)? Was it a mule (Noordtzij 1939: 164; vom Orde 1997: 173)? This would technically be the most able animal, but a bit problematic in view of Leviticus 19:19 (Lalleman 2004: 73, 77–78). But mules do play a role in the days of Ezra and Nehemiah (see Ezra 2:66)[15] and also in the days of King David. And why did even the mule, which could go everywhere, have to stop, as indicated in verse 14? In short: it is not clear.

13. Nehemiah made his tour of inspection on the outside of the wall proceeding anticlockwise. See the map in the Introduction 2k, 'Jerusalem'.

He started at the *Valley Gate*, most probably because he lived there (Simons 1952: 445). This gate had been fortified by King Uzziah in the middle of the eighth century (2 Chr. 26:9; an argument for situating it at the south-western point of the city, not in the middle of the western wall); it leads to the Hinnom Valley. Then Nehemiah went 'in the direction of' (thus NET) the *Dragon Spring,* probably identical with the Rogel Spring (see 1 Kgs 1:9, where we find the

---

14 Syntactically speaking this is an object clause in the form of an indirect question, introduced by the interrogative pronoun *mā* (Lettinga and von Siebenthal 2016: §87D/761, 1).

15 The Greek has 'half-donkeys' (*hèmionoi*), in 2 Esdras 2:66 as well as in 1 Esdras 5:42.

'Serpent's Stone'), which is, however, too far south to really pass by that place. This seems to imply that he followed the wall from a certain distance, perhaps because a thorough inspection was not necessary (Simons 1952: 161–163). The next gate, at the southern end of the Central (Tyropoeon) Valley, is named after the refuse dump near it (cf. NASB 'Refuse Gate'), normally translated by *Dung Gate*, but dung would not be thrown away.[16]

After this first series of geographical indications a verb form is used that emphasizes the continuity of the inspection.[17] The *walls* now had holes in them,[18] while the *gates* had been burned (cf. 1:2–3).

14. The *Fountain Gate* (where the Hebrew has the same word that in v. 13 has been translated by *Spring*; cf. NET 'Gate of the Well') and the *King's Pool* were situated somewhat more to the north, on the eastern side of the city. Further on *the animal* on which Nehemiah was riding could not pass (and this might be a reason to think of a horse [see on v. 12], as a mule could pass almost everywhere).

15. Nehemiah does not give up, but went further that same *night*, apparently on foot. He *went up* (this word is used because of the steepness of the Kidron *valley*; cf. John 18:1), necessarily not near to the wall, doing his utmost to inspect[19] the wall from afar. Then he *turned back*, not necessarily by the same way (Simons 1952: 444), *and entered by the Valley Gate*, where his home was (see on v. 13).

16. Nehemiah had taken only a few men with him (see v. 12), so that the (other) *officials* (see on Ezra 9:1–2, but there translated

---

16 For both items, alternatives are proposed. For the Central Valley (a term also used by Josephus, *Bellum judaicum* 5.136!), Josephus would wrongly have made a connection with 'cheese' (Greek *tyros*), instead of 'Tyrians' in *Bellum* 5.140. On the other hand, what normally is called the Dung Gate (Hebr. *'ašpot*, 'heaps of garbage/manure)' could also be related to *šəfôt*, 'cheese' (Noonan 2011: 290–291). This makes the arguments go in all directions.

17 Imperfect consecutive of *h-y-h* with participle; GKC §116r.

18 For this expression, the basic Hebrew text (cf. n. 25 on Ezra 2:43–54) is problematic. Other manuscripts are not. The meaning of the passage is clear nevertheless.

19 Same construction as in v. 13; see n. 17.

by 'chief men'), *priests* and *nobles* [lit. 'freeborn' – the Hebrew *ḥor* passed into Swahili as *uhuru*; Snell 2001: 28] *did not know … what* he *was doing.* Nobility is nowhere defined but is mentioned from time to time (1 Kgs 21:8, 11; Jer. 27:20; 39:6); Daniel 1 makes us think that some families produced administrators for consecutive generations. Not all commentators are happy with the term *Jews* at this period because of debates about when this term becomes appropriate; see Introduction 2l, 'Samarians/Samaritans – Judeans/Jews'.

17. The situation is really bad (cf. NASB; *trouble* might sound too minimizing; cf. 1:3) and Nehemiah feels involved (*we*). This assessment, a negative one indeed, forms the basis to motivate the people to repair the walls ('go in order that we build'),[20] despite the recent stopping of the rebuilding of the walls (Ezra 4:8–23; Neh. 1:1–3).

18. Both *the hand of my God … for good* (same expression as in v. 8) and *the words that the king had spoken* refer to the favourable change in the king's opinion. Here again two aspects of reality are mentioned in one breath. After hearing the explanation of what had happened in Persepolis (or Susa), the people reacted positively to Nehemiah's appeal, by saying, 'We shall rise up and build' (but *Let us rise up and build* is also a possible translation;[21] this combination of verbs is also used for preparation of the construction of the first temple, 1 Chr. 22:19) and by strengthening *their hands*, an expression of encouragement (Ezra 6:22; for the opposite, see Jer. 38:4).

19. With the information of Ezra 4:19–21, *Sanballat, Tobiah* (see on v. 10) and *Geshem* ('[prosperous through] the rain'; also known as sheikh of the Arabian Kedarites, south of Beth-zur, for which see on 3:16 – Levin 2007: 245–251) understandably thought that the king would not agree to the rebuilding (cf. v. 17). They *jeered* ('mocked at') and asked for an account (cf. Lee and Harper 2019). Mocking is an inappropriate form of humour that hits others to their very core (Becking 2018: 207).

---

20 For the form, see Joüon and Muraoka 2006: §114b; for the syntax, op. cit. §116b.

21 The verbal forms are indicatives, not cohortatives, but form and syntax do not always go together, especially in Late Biblical Hebrew (Fassberg 2016: 12).

20. *The God of heaven*, he *will make us prosper, and we his servants will arise and build*: the different roles of God and human beings are clearly described (he – we). The combination of the verbs *make …prosper* and *build* is also found for the preparation of the construction of the first temple, in 1 Chronicles 22:13 (Duguid 2012: 263). Nehemiah's opponents have no legitimate claim or right or archival record in Jerusalem.

Meaning

Whatever may have been the reason for the four months' delay between Nehemiah 1 and Nehemiah 2, it was never felt to be problematic, which is difficult for often impatient people to understand today.

Nehemiah was prepared with excellent knowledge, explored the possibilities and used the opportunity: at that moment he knew which question should be asked, with the necessary details and motivation. How things developed depended on his interlocutors, obviously when speaking with the king (v. 5), but also in Jerusalem in contact with local leaders (v. 18) (Maciariello 2003: 402). He felt connected with the people (see v. 17: *we*). By informing these local leaders, Nehemiah succeeded in getting them to cooperate (vv. 17–18).[22]

All of this meant that in Nehemiah 2, the conclusion was reached only after some months of reflection (end 446 – July 445), a check on site (vv. 12–16, where the fact that he remained silent at a moment when the information was unclear and investigated before talking must be seen as positive) and after having convinced the officials (vv. 17–18; we need to keep in mind that the relation between the time when an action took place in real history and the pace of the narrative is changing continually).

Every situation has two aspects, and we should never deny either of them: God's sovereignty and human responsibility; this principle becomes very clear in 2:20.

---

22 It is interesting to see how at different points Nehemiah's leadership agrees with the ideas of Leithwood, Jantzi and Steinbach 1999: 30, 71, 76–77, 102, 105, 118 about 'transformational leadership'. Cf. Lorein 2008: 150–154.

C. Core: building the walls (3:1 − 7:3)

This section is about the core of the third part of Ezra-Neh.: rebuilding the walls (together with accompanying problems). Unlike parts one and four, this part does not end with a worship service. The material for this section comes from Nehemiah's files. Nehemiah 3[23] seems to be a copy of the official report sent to the king, as was also the custom in Elephantine (Cogan 2006: 90–91). It might have been written or at least ordered by Nehemiah himself. It is not in chronological order: people were working simultaneously and sometimes aspects are mentioned that were not executed immediately at the beginning of the work. Apparently, some portions have not been repaired by the original candidates, or some vacancies could not be filled in immediately. The report was not redacted in one single flow (Lipschits 2012: 74).

Nehemiah 4 is a description of the difficult circumstances under which the wall had to be built and comes from Nehemiah's files too, more specifically from his memoirs. Even though this chapter belongs to another genre, it presupposes the information of the preceding chapter (in other words, it does not follow immediately on from Neh. 2).

Some discussion exists about the delimitation of the end of this section. In 6:9, 14, 19, we meet three times a form of *to make me afraid* (as ESV translates in vv. 14, 19) or *to frighten* (as ESV translates in v. 9). This points to a threefold structure of chapter 6: verses 1–9, verses 10–14, verses 15–19 (Goswell 2010: 199). On the other hand, the parallel between verses 1–9 and verses 10–14 is much stronger and verses 15–19 seem better arranged together with the unit of the 'final remarks', 7:1–3. Steinmann 2010: 475–485 takes 7:1–3 together with the fourth and last part of the book of Ezra-Neh. Of course,

---

23   For those reading the Hebrew or using translations that follow the
     chapter division in the Hebrew Bible, it is important to understand that
     it adds the first verses of Neh. 4 (vv. 1–6; about Sanballat's opposition)
     to Neh. 3, so that Neh. 3 ends with vv. 33–38 and Neh. 4:7–23 is
     counted as 4:1–17. The grouping together of the Vulg. and English
     translations is more coherent.

the structure suggested by Goswell and Steinmann fits better with
Langton's chapter division (Lorein 2014: 138), but that cannot be
an argument in itself. After all, we should wonder whether biblical authors and redactors always tried to present us with clear-cut
divisions, or rather transitional passages between the larger parts
of Bible books.

i. Brief report of the building activity (3:1–22)
Context
Nehemiah arrived in 445. After he had informed himself, the
construction of the wall started on 12 August 445. The reconstruction
of the walls took only fifty-two days, ending on 2 October 445
(6:15–16). We have no chronological order within the chapter: the
people work simultaneously on the different segments.

For the extent of Jerusalem, see Introduction 2k, 'Jerusalem'.

A historical parallel can be found in Athens, where the Parthenon
temple was built between 447 and 438 on the foundations of a temple
left unfinished due to the destruction of the Acropolis by the Persians
in 480–479 (Nuchelmans 1979: 2144–2145). Some years earlier (449
BC) in Rome the Law of the Twelve Tables had been published.

Comment
   1. With the word *Then* this verse reacts to the last verse of the
previous chapter (2:20): *Eliashib* ('God will restore') *the high priest*
(high priest approximately from 480 until 440 BC [van der Woude
1983: 89];[24] grandson of Jeshua; see on Ezra 2:2) and several other
people understood their responsibility.

The Sheep Gate is near to the temple, where a lot of sheep were
needed for the offerings (Jerusalem's gates appear to have specialized in particular kinds of merchandise; thus Silver 2004: 75), in

---

24 The reconstruction of the list of high priests is as complicated as that
   of the governors. The very well documented reconstruction of Dušek
   2007: 550–591 seems to be flawed by his decision to situate the arrival
   of Ezra in 398 and so cannot be relied on. The reconstruction of
   Steinmann 2010: 51–58 has the disadvantage that it asks for a quite late
   redaction date of the book of Ezra-Neh.

the north of the city, outside the part that had been inspected by Nehemiah during the night. Because of this relationship to the temple, they *consecrated* it. *The Tower of the Hundred* is just west of *the Sheep Gate.* When we read 12:39, *the Tower of Hananel* appears to be still further west, in the direction of the Fish Gate (see on v. 3). They are consecrated too (normally *as far as* includes the term mentioned) as part of the construction, due to their relationship to the temple, not only the nearest tower (the Hundred) but even the other one (Hananel's). The northern side of the Temple Mount being the most open, it needed more fortification and so three towers are mentioned: the Tower of the Hundred and the Tower of Hananel in this verse, and the Tower of the Corner in verses 31–32 when the tour has been made in full, so that while these three towers may be distant from one another in the text of Nehemiah 3, geographically they are very close to one another. In one form or another – unfortunately texts and archaeology do not give a clear picture – this construction formed the citadel (Edelman 2011: 49–53, 63–67; Ritmeyer 2014: 28–29, 63–71).

2. *Next to* Eliashib people were working who had come from some distance: *Jericho* is situated 5 miles west of the Jordan, in the east of the province of Judah. *Next to them Zaccur* ('remembered'; see on Ezra 8:14) was at work.

3. *The Fish Gate,* situated at the north-west of the Temple Mount (much smaller than in Herod's days!), at the northern end of the Central (Tyropoeon) Valley, is restored by the inhabitants of Senaah[25] (see on Ezra 2:35). For the *beams*, see on 2:8. Probably the gate received its name because of a fish market, being on the right side of the city for the import of fish, dried, salted or smoked because of the long distance (cf. Reich, Shukron and Lernau 2007: 157–160).

4. For *Meremoth*, see on Ezra 8:33. The fact that he *repaired* does not necessarily imply that he got dirty hands. It is also possible that he 'organized' the repairs (cf. Cogan 2006: 85–87 for an Assyrian parallel at Dur-Sharrukin at the end of the eighth century BC).

---

25 For other place names with the article, see Joüon and Muraoka 2006: §137b.

Meshullam ('given as a compensation, satisfaction', a frequent name) *the son of Berechiah* is also mentioned in verse 30. According to 6:18, his daughter was a (the?) daughter-in-law of Tobiah, which shows that not all relations were cut between those who worked at the reconstruction of the wall and their opponents. *Zadok* ('[God is] righteousness') is mentioned next.

5. Tekoa is situated 10 miles south of Jerusalem. Apparently, not all *Tekoites* were willing to make these commuting efforts. Exactly what the problem was depends in the first place on the meaning of what in ESV is *their Lord*, that is, God. If this is the correct interpretation, the *nobles* (or 'town leaders', NET; it is not the same word as in 2:16 etc.) of the Tekoite society did not want to commute to serve (lit. 'to give in their necks'; cf. AV) God. This interpretation is less probable if this remark was part of the report sent to the king. The same Hebrew word can, however, also be translated by 'their lords'; in that case, the middle class would not have wanted to support the initiative of the upper class. The problem with this interpretation, however, is that *nobles* are normally the upper class and not the middle class. A third option – this one with a grammatical problem and without parallel, but nevertheless the most acceptable one – is to interpret this word as 'their lord', that is, the governor, Nehemiah (Cogan 2006: 92). In this interpretation, the nobles of Tekoa believed that their competences lay elsewhere than in building activities. 'The poor cannot give anything, the rich do not want to give anything, and the middle class is giving freely,' comments a marginal note on this verse in the first Reformed Bible translation in Dutch (*Deux Aes*, 1562).[26]

6. *Joiada* ('the LORD has known') and *Meshullam* (obviously a different person from the one mentioned in v. 4) *repaired the Gate of Yeshanah*, a quite unimportant city 17 miles north of Jerusalem, in the same direction as Bethel which, as a more important and nearer city, would seem a much likelier name-giver for a gate (Becking

---

26 My translation. The Dutch reads: 'Deux aes en heeft niet, Six cinque en geeft niet. Quater dry die helpen vry', with the image of the dice. The comment itself was already Luther's. See de Bruin 1993: 183–185.

2018: 198), but that might be too rationalistic. Nevertheless, the best explanation for the Hebrew seems to be 'the gate of the old (city)' (Lorein 2021b: 79). For the *beams*, see on 2:8.

7. *Melatiah* ('the LORD saved') came from *Gibeon*, 6 miles northwest of Jerusalem. *Jadon* (probably '[God] has judged') was from Meronoth, probably a village in the same region as Gibeon and Mizpah, but without an exactly known location. *Mizpah* was a city of some importance – the satrap of Trans-Euphrates had a residence there (see Introduction 2f, 'Organization of the Persian Empire'; cf. Jer. 40:10). For the identification Tell en-Nazbeh is mentioned, 7½ miles north of Jerusalem (Lorein 2021b: 72–73).

8. Jerusalem appears to have had a metropolitan function with specialized professions such as *goldsmiths* and *perfumers* (for religious, hygiene and well-being purposes; Carter 1999: 287–288; Bodi 2008: 61 n. 17). The plural in *goldsmiths* (or more generally: 'workers of precious metals'; cf. Judg. 17:4; Prov. 25:4; Isa. 40:19; 46:6; Jer. 10:9) is strange; the Vulgate has a singular, the Peshitta has 'the son of the goldsmiths' (same construction as with the pharmacists), but this does not permit us to determine the original wording. Fensham (1982: 172) thinks that other professions, for example bakers, are not mentioned because they had to do their daily work. *Uzziel* means 'God is my power'; *Hananiah* means 'the LORD has been gracious'. Some commentators have a problem with the translation *restored* (it is not the normal meaning of the verb; once this meaning was based on a rather conjectural homonym, but now it is confirmed by Ugaritic); the alternative ('abandoned') is less attractive. The *Broad Wall* is on the western side of the city.

9. *Rephaiah* ('the LORD has healed') was an official (see on Ezra 9:1), responsible at district level. The province of Judah was divided into (at least) five districts, normally divided again in two halves. Possibly work duties were allotted to these districts.[27]

---

27 In other words, we do not need to discern two Akkadian homonyms *pilku* ('district' and 'labour'); cf. Fitzpatrick-McKinley 2016: 181. Avi-Yonah 1974: 79 reckons with a sixth district, Jericho.

10. *Jedaiah* ('the LORD has known') did not have to travel far: he was working *opposite his house*. The meaning of the name *Hattush* is unknown.

11. *Malchijah* ['the LORD is my king'] *the son of Harim* is also mentioned in Ezra 10:31. The problem mentioned there apparently had no influence on his commitment at this point; or, put positively: his commitment in Ezra 10 was genuine and complete. *Hasshub* ('who has been thought of') was working near to him. It is their second section, but on which section they worked in the first instance remains unmentioned. The *Tower of the Ovens* (or 'furnaces') is situated on a corner at the northern point of the western wall. Towers were specific fortification works (see on v. 1) at points that permitted a good overview at vulnerable locations (see also 2 Chr. 26:9; here the Corner Gate; Simons 1952: 447). The furnaces were not situated within the tower, but immediately outside it (Dalman 1935: 97).

12. *Shallum* ('compensated, satisfied') was the official of the other half of the *district of Jerusalem* (see on v. 9), assisted by his *daughters*. Sons are never mentioned but this does not imply that they never collaborated. Probably as the default situation, their presence did not need to be expressed. Of course, neither does that imply that no other daughters ever assisted.

13. *Hanun* ('who has been given grace to') worked with *the inhabitants of Zanoah*, some 13 miles south-west of Jerusalem. In order to stay closer to the Hebrew, we should follow the translation of the AV, with an adapted punctuation: 'The valley gate repaired [singular; in the sense of 'organized'] Hanun; and the inhabitants of Zanoah, they built [plural] it.' *The Valley Gate* is the gate where Nehemiah had started his inspection tour. Some *thousand cubits* to the east (a good quarter of a mile, indeed a little more) we find the Refuse Gate (see on 2:13). This is the only place where a distance is mentioned, but in combination with the location of the Refuse Gate, which is known, we can calculate where the Valley Gate must have been, of course depending on whether we have a large or a small city (see Introduction 2k, 'Jerusalem'). It is indeed a large section of the wall, perhaps because the problems there were limited (see again on 2:13).

14. In this verse we meet a different *Malchijah* from the one mentioned in verse 11 (and in Ezra 10:25, 31). This official was responsible for the *district* [see on v. 9] *of Beth-haccherem*, located to the south, somewhere between Jerusalem and Tekoa. He *repaired the Refuse Gate*, which indeed opens to the south.

15. A second person called *Shallum* (see on v. 12 and Vulg.; most MSS, however, have 'Shallun', short for 'Salomon'?) was responsible for the district (see on v. 9; only a part of the district, considering v. 19? — but we do not need to change the text for that) of *Mizpah*, already mentioned in verse 7. He *repaired the Fountain Gate*, not far from the Refuse Gate, but already at the eastern side of Jerusalem. Here we have arrived at the most severely damaged part of the wall (see 2:14).

The wall of the Pool of Shelah specifically protected this water supply. These men worked on this wall from the king's garden (southern end; cf. 2 Kgs 25:4; a vegetable garden, as in 1 Kgs 21:2? thus Dalman 1928: 350) *to the steps that go down from the city of David*, that is, a kind of stairway (see on 12:37).

16. In verses 16–26 several smaller parts of the southern half of the eastern wall are discussed, on difficult terrain.

The *Nehemiah* ('the LORD has comforted') mentioned here is not the protagonist of the book of Nehemiah; the name occurred often. The Nehemiah mentioned here has an official function at the head of *half the district* [see on v. 9] *of Beth-zur*, 20 miles south-west of Jerusalem, almost at the southern frontier of Judah. He worked *to a point opposite the tombs of David* [short for 'the tombs of the sons of David' as in 2 Chr. 32:33], *as far as the artificial* [lit. 'the made'] *pool* [outside the wall], *and as far as the house of the* heroes [inside the wall].

17–19. *After him* repaired *Rehum* ('to whom compassion has been shown') and *Hashabiah* ('the LORD has thought of him'), official of *half the district* [see on v. 9] *of Keilah*, 17 miles from Jerusalem, in the south-western corner of Judah. Considering the plural, all men mentioned in verses 17–19 were *Levites*; apparently being a Levite did not exclude one from having a secular position.

It is strange to see the plural *brothers* explained by one person: *Bavvai*. The meaning of this name is unknown, but he is called *son of Henadad*, just like Binnui in verse 24 (see also 10:9 [MT 10]). The difference between the two names is limited, especially if we take only the Hebrew consonants into account. That is why some translations read 'Binnui'. He is the official of the other *half* of *the district of Keilah* (cf. previous verse).

Ezer ('[God is my] help') had a position at *Mizpah*, perhaps not for the district but only for the town (see on v. 15; Steinmann 2010: 431 translates by 'mayor'). He *repaired* a second *section*, presumably having already finished a first section, but its location is unmentioned. Did he work under someone else's responsibility for this first section and is that the reason why his name was not mentioned earlier? The second *section* goes from the *ascent* [stairs] *to the armoury* [cf. Isa. 39:2 ‖ 2 Kgs 20:13; possibly to be identified with the House of the Wood of Lebanon of Isa. 22:8; 1 Kgs 7:2–5; 10:17] *at the* 'turning' (thus AV).

20. *Baruch* ('blessed') worked from this first turning to *the door of the house of Eliashib the high priest*, who himself was working at the Sheep Gate (v. 1) and lived at some distance from the temple itself. The first section for Baruch is unmentioned too, as was the case for Ezer (v. 19).

21. According to verse 4, this was not *Meremoth*'s first section. Now he repaired the wall parallel with *the house of Eliashib*, the high priest, from its *door* [apparently to the south – a bit strange, as this place was most far removed from the temple; perhaps he wanted to separate work and private life] *to the end of the house*.

22. This verse seems to lack at least an object. Moreover, *the priests* are not clearly specified, and two explanations exist for *the surrounding area*: (1) as a proper name this regularly indicates the region around the estuary of the Jordan; (2) understood in a more general way, it might indicate the Jerusalem region. As a translation, 'the priests from the region' would work, but it does not explain anything.

23. *Benjamin* ('right-hand son') and *Hasshub* ('who has been thought of') did not need commuting time. The same applies to *Azariah* ('the LORD has helped').

24. If we read 'Binnui' in verse 18, he was working here at his second section, 'up to the turning, that is',[28] *to the corner* (these last words still belong to v. 24).

25–26. These verses offer some difficulties, but with the following translation the Hebrew is followed as well as possible. *Palal* ['(God) has interceded'] *the son of Uzai* was working *opposite the* turning *and*

---

the high *tower projecting* [i.e. not built within the wall, but (slightly) in front of the wall] *from the* palace *at the court of the* prison (cf. Jer. 32:2; 38:6, 28); *after him Pedaiah* ['the LORD has saved'] *the son of Parosh*. The *temple servants* [see on Ezra 2:43] – they were *living on Ophel* [the hill south of the temple and north of the City of David] – worked *to a point opposite* [strange, as they were working on the wall of which the gates formed part] *the Water Gate on the east and the projecting tower* [like most towers immediately beside a gate] (Lorein 2021b: 75, 80).

27. We arrive here at a part of the wall that seems to have been less damaged, as fewer groups are mentioned, although we must admit that in the second part of the list of Nehemiah 3, other kinds of details are mentioned from those in the first part.

The *Tekoites* (see on v. 5) were doing a second shift (because they were embarrassed by the attitude of their nobles?) *opposite the great projecting tower* until they arrived at *the wall of Ophel*.

28. *The priests repaired* from the top of the *Horse Gate*, situated to the south of the temple. They worked in the same area as where they were living.

29. *Zadok* '[(God is) righteousness'] *the son of Immer* was one of the persons working near to his own house.

Shemaiah ('the LORD has heard') has a special function: he is *the keeper of the East Gate*. This gate is not a city gate, but a temple gate, also known as Shushan Gate and – in later times – as Golden Gate (Ben-Dov 2002: 88; Ritmeyer 2014: 64–66; also mentioned in Ezek. 10:19; 11:1). It is not mentioned here in relation to the building works, but in relation to Shemaiah's function.

30. *Hananiah* ('the LORD has been gracious') *and Hanun* ('who has been given grace to') were doing a second shift, but they had not worked together during their first shift, respectively in verse 8 and verse 13. In this verse the professional activity and the geographical background are not mentioned, but only the names of their fathers. That *Hanun* was *the sixth son* must have been a situation exceptional enough to mention it here. *Meshullam the son of Berechiah* was already mentioned in verse 4 but is not said here to be on a second shift. We have arrived at this point at the temple courts (cf. Ezra 8:29; Neh. 13:7).

31. *Malchijah* ('the LORD is my king'), a frequent name (see on vv. 11, 14 and Ezra 10:25), is here specified as *one of the goldsmiths* (see on v. 8). The *temple servants* were living on Ophel (v. 26) but had their communal quarters within the temple area, together with *the merchants, opposite the Muster Gate* (where the priests were mustered, i.e. organized; cf. Steinmann 2010: 423), a city gate very near to the temple's East Gate. Although the East Gate is *opposite the Muster Gate*, reconstruction of the wall went on a little bit further, around the north-eastern corner of the city, to a tower that can be compared with the Towers of the Hundred and of Hananel (see on v. 1; Ritmeyer 2014: 64–66). The first term (*the house of the temple servants and of the merchants*) is inside the walls, the second term (*the upper chamber of the corner*) is on the wall.

32. With mention of this last portion from the Corner Tower (see on v. 31) to the Sheep Gate, we have arrived at the starting point mentioned in verse 1. Again, the goldsmiths (vv. 8, 31) are active, as well as the merchants, for whom this is apparently the first shift.

Keep in mind that Nehemiah 3 is an overview of the totality of the construction of the walls (including gates and towers) and that at the start of Nehemiah 4 we are at the same chronological point as we were at Nehemiah 3:1.

Meaning

As soon as possible, Nehemiah tried to integrate everyone into his project, not only in order to avoid internal opposition, but especially because Nehemiah knew that conditions could change rapidly, that the government could not be trusted – he knew the system too well (Noordtzij 1939: 171)!

The fact that in this way it was the people's project did not preclude that they needed assistance in order to understand what was important and how to organize themselves. Nehemiah often used natural relationships: many people rebuilt the wall near to where they were living (vv. 10, 23). It is important that people can do what suits them best (cf. Ulrich 2021: 112–113). Such a tactic has practical advantages, creates strong links and reduces internal opposition. Of course, it could not be used for collaborators living outside Jerusalem. When we look at the map of Judah, it is clear that not all villages were represented: Nehemiah did not succeed completely.

Many people are mentioned by name: every individual is important, and this is one of the two reasons why in the *Comment* much space has been given to these names (the other reason being that for the original Hebrew reader the meaning of the names was in most cases immediately clear, a situation 'recreated' by the *Comment*). In this building report, we receive more information about the persons than about the wall. We in our day should also understand the importance of individual collaborators within the church. Unfortunately, we do not succeed either, but it should remain a point of attention.

Such were the facts. But after the facts came the redaction of the report. The list is there, the work is well documented. This information is nice for our understanding of Jerusalem's historical topography, but it also had its importance in Nehemiah's own day: he was able to prove what he had realized as governor, in full collaboration with the people. The facts are important, but so is their documentation: it is an accountability report (Vom Orde 1997: 190), and accountability is most important in today's church.

God is not mentioned in this chapter. Here people are just at work. Of course, this does not exclude prayer: prayer is mentioned in Nehemiah 2 and in Nehemiah 4. In any case, we should not separate work and prayer: they have to form a unity. Prayer must be concerned with what we do and what we do must be in accordance with how we pray. Prayer should neither be an alibi for laziness, nor a closing formula (Vom Orde 1997: 191).

At the end we have some walls, which protect and lock up. Should not we, as New Testament Christians, think of Ephesians 2:14–18 (as Becking 2018: 166 does)? Indeed, the New Testament is still more open than the Old Testament already was. In the Old, belief in the God of Israel was really possible, but always passed through the nation of Israel. In the New, we do not need to become Jews before we can follow the God of Israel. Nevertheless, we should not think that Paul would have disagreed with Nehemiah, and still in our day we need some limits, not in order to lock us up, but in order to protect us from liberalism and spiritualism. Walls (protection) and gates (openness) are both important (Lorein 2021b: 82).

ii. The Samarians try to hinder the building activity (4:1–23)

Context

For this chapter, we follow the division of the Vulgate and of English translations. This implies that what is here called 'Nehemiah 4' is Nehemiah 3:33 – 4:17 in the Hebrew Bible.[29]

Nehemiah 4 must not be situated after the activities of Nehemiah 3 were completed, but shortly after they began, *when Sanballat heard* … (4:1), before the wall had reached half its intended height (4:6).

For the term 'Samarians', see Introduction 2l, 'Samarians/Samaritans – Judeans/Jews'.

Comment

1. The indication *Now when* situates this chapter at about the same moment as the beginning of Nehemiah 3. As what earlier had been only plans was now about to be realized, *Sanballat*, governor of Samaria (see on 2:9–10), reacted more aggressively than in 2:10 (where he was only displeased) and 2:19–20 (where he was only mocking, which he is still doing here: *he jeered*).

2. Sanballat's *brothers* are his colleagues (and his allies); the *army of Samaria* must be understood as local police forces and not as a real army (Noordtzij 1939: 182).

Sanballat's first questions are normally translated by *What are these feeble Jews doing? Will they restore it for themselves?* The problem with the second verb is that it is not its normal meaning (see on 3:8), which would produce the translation 'Will they leave (it) to them(selves)?', in the sense of mocking that they would be unable to do it without help from others (Steinmann 2010: 435). According to the Hebrew, the fourth question must be translated *Will they finish* today?, with the idea being that they would give up if it took more time (because they are *feeble*), and in opposition to Nehemiah's confirmation at the end of verse 6 (Steinmann 2010: 443). The question about the revival of Jerusalem indicates that according to Sanballat the destruction of Jerusalem is something definitive (Becking 2018: 207). In this last question, the word *burned* turns up again (see on 1:2–3).

---

29   See n. 23.

3. *Tobiah* (see on 2:9–10) was just exaggerating in his derision, as a *fox* is a light animal (15 lb, according to Steinmann 2010: 436; it should not be interpreted as 'siege tower'), as is also clear from Nehemiah's reaction (Jenni 2009: 83, 86–87). The *fox* used to hide in ruins during the day (Ezek. 13:4 and Maarsingh 1985: 166; Lam. 5:18).

4–5. Apparently, the ridiculing was not only for internal use, but was also heard by the Judeans. Nehemiah asked God for revenge because *we are* [or rather 'were'] *despised.* And a second reason is mentioned, according to the translations in the line of the AV: *they have provoked you to anger.* Fortunately, AV has put the object in italics (*'thee'*), indicating in that way that the object was added in translation. Newer translations see the builders as the object, as does, for example, NIV: 'they have thrown insults in the face of the builders'. Nehemiah's prayer has some wordplays. For verse 5 Nehemiah quoted Jeremiah 18:23,[30] not without replacing one word by a synonym. By doing that, he created also a second wordplay,[31] as well as the chiastic structure around *guilt* and *sin* (Steinmann 2010: 437, 445; cf. Introduction 4g, 'Literary terms').

6. For the details, see Nehemiah 3. Reference is made here to a certain phase of the building activity; one should keep in mind that (most of) the teams worked simultaneously. In Hebrew, the *mind to work* speaks of the 'heart' (cf. NIV), the seat of decisions: 'the people were committed to act'.

7. *Sanballat* and *Tobiah* represent Samaria, north of Judah; *the Arabs* were ruling in the south; *the Ammonites* were living in the east (cf. Amman, capital of the present-day Kingdom of Jordan); and *the Ashdodites* were west of Judah (Ashdod is the principal Philistine city; see also 13:23–24). The position of the Arabs needs some explanation. Although the region in the south of pre-exilic Judah had been occupied by Edomites (see on Ezra 2:20–35), the Kedarites then occupied a position of power (Stern 1982: 250).

---

30 Mentioning one's source was not required in Old Testament times; chapter and verse numbering occurred only in the thirteenth and sixteenth centuries, respectively (Lorein 2014: 138).

31 Between *təkhas* and *hikh'ísú,* as well as between *búzâ* and *bizzâ.*

8. The enemies went quite far in their actions against Jerusalem (also indicated by *it*, the last word of this verse),³² but they did not dare to contact the satrap. Apparently, Sanballat knew how far he could go without being confronted by an official reference to the king's decision (Fitzpatrick-McKinley 2016: 170).

9. In this verse we find again the two sides of reality, as in 2:20. The one does not exclude the other. The last word in Hebrew should be interpreted as 'because of them' (cf. AV; same expression in v. 14).

10. In addition to external opposition (or rather because of it) an internal tiredness was occurring. *Judah* indicates poetically the community as a whole. Indeed, what follows is considered poetry too, more precisely lament,³³ with its specific rhythm, together with some wordplays.³⁴

11–12. There were also Jews living outside Judah (for Jews in Ammon, see Heltzer 1981: 117; for the term, cf. Introduction 2l, 'Samarians/Samaritans – Judeans/Jews'), which was helpful for Nehemiah's information and made the *enemies'* scheme fail. Verse 12 reads in ESV, *At that time the Jews who lived near them came from all directions and said to us ten times, 'You must return to us'* – or a little more literally: 'they said to us (even) ten times, from all the places:³⁵ "You should return to us"', which might be understood as an appeal to leave the building activities in Jerusalem, either out of fear of repercussions in their own villages, or out of a concern for the safety of their kinsmen staying in Jerusalem (vom Orde 1997: 197). A problem must still be solved with this interpretation: how can

---

32 Grammatically, this is bad Hebrew, but that would not be the first time for Nehemiah. Another option is to read 'to us' instead of *in it* (cf. *we* in the next verse; Fensham 1982: 184); in Hebrew, the difference is limited.

33 Twice three words and two words: *kāšal kōᵃḥ hassabbāl, wəheʿāfār harbê; waʾᵃnaḥnû loʾ nûkhal, livnôt baḥômâ*. See Alonso Schökel 1988: 37 for the theory.

34 Alliteration between *kāšal* and *kōᵃḥ*, end rhyme between *kāšal, sabbāl* and *nûkhal*, perhaps wordplay between *ʿāfār* and *harbê*. Balzaretti (1999: 127) sees also a wordplay between *sabbāl* and Sanballat.

35 For *ʾᵃšer* as introduction to a quote, see GKC §157c.

people outside Judah say that people in Jerusalem should *return* to them, that is, to places outside Judah? AV supposes that a part of the text was dropped, puts 'the places' within the quote and fills the gap with a conjecture ('they said unto us ten times, From all places whence ye shall return unto us *they will be upon you*'); RSV has a smaller supplement, but changes *You must return* into 'where they live', a small change in Hebrew indeed ('From all the places where they live they will come up against us'); NET, normally very close to the Hebrew, even introduces two conjectures here ('warned us repeatedly about all the schemes they were plotting against us'), thus creating – it must be admitted – an easier text. NASB offers here a translation very near to the original: '… told us ten times, "They will come up against us from every place where you may turn"', supposing a quite elliptic Hebrew text indeed, but this time without problems. This might be the best option.

13–14. By stationing everyone away from (Fensham 1982: 186) *the lowest parts … behind the wall* so that they were at the places where they could be seen, Nehemiah gave the impression that the men of Jerusalem were quite strong on a military level (as a kind of Gideon force, suggesting a much larger number of soldiers than actually available; Becking 2018: 212). At the same time, he succeeded in motivating everyone (for *the nobles* and *the officials*, see on 2:16) to continue the work. They should not *be afraid of* the enemies, but rather they should (with marked word order for this second command, with the imperative at the end; cf. Deut. 7:18, also with a marked phrasing) *remember the Lord, who is great and awesome* (for these adjectives, cf. 1:5 and Deut. 7:21), in order to[36] *fight for your brothers, your sons, your daughters* [explicitly mentioned here as a different category, although the plural of 'son' normally should be translated by 'children' – depending, of course, on the concrete circumstances], *your wives, and your homes.* Indeed, the building activity is considered as a kind of holy war (Duguid 2012: 263).

15–17. Even after the *enemies heard that* their scheme *was known* to Nehemiah and *all returned to the wall* (which seems to imply that a pause had occurred in the activities, apparently a short one), he

---

36 With an indirect volitive in *wəhillāḥᵃmû* (Niphal indirect imperative).

continued to watch out. His personal *servants* are working at a fixed
place and therefore can allocate the tasks: *half ... worked on construction*, while the other *half* was engaged in protection. The *coats of mail*
are 'breastplates' (thus NASB), rather heavy protection. Those people
who were moving needed unfortunately to combine both tasks. The
military *leaders* were stationed in such a way that they were able to
oversee the scene.

18–20. An emergency script was worked out. The *trumpet* is the
shofar, made of a ram's horn and fit only to give a signal (no melody;
see Judg. 3:27; 1 Kgs 1:34). For the *nobles* and *officials*, see on 2:16.
How *far from one another* were they? If we reckon with some forty
teams[37] and a wall of 2½ miles (cf. Introduction 2k, 'Jerusalem'), a
distance of 110 yards (roughly a football pitch) would exist between
the different teams. For the combination of commitment and prayer,
see on 2:20; 4:9.

21. They are working from 12 August to 2 October in the northern hemisphere, that is, a working day of on average 12 hours and
48 minutes (with a twilight of about half an hour).

22–23. By workers staying in the city during the night, no commuting time was needed and the risk that people would take a day
off was excluded. So everybody worked hard, but especially the
leader, his (physical) brothers and his staff (Williamson 1991: 50).
Here we must keep in mind that they did so for a project that took
some time, but which was limited.

At the end the Hebrew reads 'each his missile the water', which
is difficult (impossible) to understand. Most English translations
consider the text to be elliptic and translate in the sense NIV does:
'each had his weapon, even when he went for water'; ESV opts for
a conjecture (as do many commentaries) and translates as *each kept
his weapon at his right hand*.[38]

---

37 With some uncertainties: what about the people who worked on a
    second section? What about the composite teams (3:13, 28, 32)?
38 Reading *hayyāmîn*, interpreted as an adverbial accusative, instead of
    hammāyim.

Meaning

This chapter speaks about external opposition. Some elements can be mentioned as a useful guide for parallel situations. In the first place, Nehemiah is open to external information. In the second place, he prays (vv. 4–5) in reaction to the ridicule with its exaggeration of verses 2–3 and so in a certain sense discharges himself of the kernel of the problem. Nehemiah prays for revenge (and so every believer may do) but leaves the revenge to God (and so every believer should do; cf. Pss 44; 58; 74; 79; 109; 137; Jer. 18:23, which is very near to our text; Rom. 12:19; Rev. 6:10; in full consciousness of our own weakness: Matt. 18:33; Luke 23:34). This may disturb us, but absolute passiveness should disturb us too (Noordtzij 1939: 183). Finally, Nehemiah does limit himself to being informed (apparently vv. 1–3, 7–8, 11, 15; certainly v. 12) and praying (vv. 4–5, 9). He is not hindered by the complaint of verse 10, a sign of despondency, or the warnings of verse 12, a cause of nervousness (Noordtzij 1939: 186), but acts, with good arrangements (vv. 13, 16–22) and instructions (vv. 14, 20). It must be repeated that we cannot read here directives for a lifelong rhythm.

iii. The problem of the poor and Nehemiah's commitment (5:1–19)

Context

After the external opposition described in Nehemiah 4, in this chapter we are confronted with an internal problem. Although the problem must have been present for a longer time (Noordtzij 1939: 189), the outbreak described in 5:1–13 must be situated when the construction of the wall was still going on, in a period when the main harvests had come to an end (Yamauchi 1990: 273). The same can be said about 5:14–19, but that passage must be taken in a more general way.

Nehemiah always tried to motivate his people and to be an example, but at the same time we must realize the importance of his official function: governor of the king of Persia (Briant 2002: 585), even though he could hardly use this power against his own population or in his dealings with other governors (Dandamaev 1989: 247).

Comment

1. A new problem led to *a great outcry* [normally to God; Altmann 2016: 249] *of the people and* especially *of their wives*; the mention of the wives' presence seems to highlight the importance of the gathering (see on Ezra 10:1). It is an internal problem, a problem with *Jewish brothers*.

2. *We are* too numerous[39] *to get grain* (or, more generally: 'food') and to *eat and* live.[40]

3–5. These large families needed to borrow in order to get[41] food (either immediately or by intensifying cultivation, which was expensive; Pastor 1997: 17–18) or to pay taxes (v. 4). No interest was paid on loans to poor Israelites[42] – at least, not in theory (see Exod. 22:25; Lev. 25:35–37; Deut. 23:20–21; Prov. 28:8; Ezek. 18:13, 17) – and indeed interest paid by debtors to creditors is not mentioned in this chapter. In that case, however, security was

---

39 While English versions maintain the Hebrew, several commentators change the text (for one consonant in Hebrew) and interpret as 'We are having to put up our sons and daughters as surety in order to …' (Adams 2014: 78). This change to the Hebrew text is unnecessary, as the commentary shows, and so we stay with the Hebrew text.

40 First a cohortative indicating a request for permission (GKC §108c) *wəniqḥâ* (from *l-q-ḥ*, in which verb the *l* is treated as a *n*, GKC §66g) and then two indirect cohortatives indicating the purpose (Joüon and Muraoka 2006: §116b) *wənokhlâ* and *wəniḥyeh* (usually this class of verbs has no cohortative form; see Lettinga and von Siebenthal 2016: §58H/557.3).

41 Same form as in v. 2, but here indirect cohortative without preceding volitive (Joüon and Muraoka 2006: §116c).

42 Things were different with business loans, especially to foreign merchants. In the Ancient Near East a relation existed between risks and percentage. In any case, at least since the Code of Hammurabi §95 (Hammurabi reigned 1792–1750 or perhaps 1629–1586 BC) it was deemed very important to leave no doubt about any details of loans (Maloney 1974: 9–10; Wunsch 2002: 237–238). Written documentation is still important today, especially between Christians, in order to avoid any misunderstanding.

needed. This security could be a utensil, real property (v. 3: *fields*, *vineyards* and *houses*) or *children* (v. 5). If this security is only security and stays with the borrower, there is no problem. If, however, farming land goes as a pledge to the creditor (v. 5), that is, the creditors are using the security as if it were their property instead of just security (*other men have our fields and our vineyards*), then this farming land cannot be used by the debtor any more. It gets even worse when the debtor has to till this land without having the right to use the crop, or when his *sons and daughters* (here indicated by two words, whereas normally – even in the same verse: *children* – the plural denotes both in one word, but according to Fensham 1982: 192 some of the daughters had already been taken as secondary wives) had to work for the creditor as *slaves* (v. 5) (De Vaux 1958: 130, 263; Maloney 1974: 5–10; Wunsch 2002: 232, 238–240).

Of course, it seems rather cruel to force your children to be slaves, but in purely economic terms this was the only viable route, as in that case they kept oversight in order to restore everything (cf. Kreissig 1973: 109; same order for the Near East with Plutarch, *Lucullus* 20).

6–7. When Nehemiah *heard* the *outcry and* the reports (lit. *words*; the same term is used for the book of Chronicles), he became *very angry*, not with those who complained, but with those who were responsible for the problem. We can imagine that he thought he already had enough sorrows with the building project as such and the external opposition, but now he is confronted with a complex internal problem (apparently he had not observed it himself, but needed to be pointed to it). After deliberating within himself, not with others (this may seem strange, but being a governor it was difficult to consult other people – in any case, he did not decide overnight), he concluded that the origin of the problem lay with *the nobles and the officials* (see on 2:16) and *brought charges* against them (this juridical term is a correct translation; 'rebuked' [AV] is too informal and does not take into account Nehemiah's position as a governor), because they were 'seizing the securities'.

And I held a great assembly against them: a people's tribunal is installed (cf. Ezra 10:7), probably because those who were normally the judges were now involved (Fensham 1982: 193).

8. Nothing is known about this buying back of adults. The accusation that the rich would sell their *brothers* confident that the community (*us*) would buy them back should not be taken literally (as only the selling of children was mentioned in v. 5 and this was normally the earlier phase: cf. vv. 3–5). In any case, individual freedom is important for the people of Israel and being set free from slavery plays a role in it (Snell 2001: 120, 135); see also Leviticus 25:42–49 for the instructions and Jeremiah 34:8–22 for a situation shortly before the fall of Jerusalem in 587 BC, where the reproach was made that slavery had been reinstalled (if we may observe a relation between the keeping of slaves and the fall of Jerusalem, it is striking that the problem turns up again at the very moment when the walls of Jerusalem are being rebuilt).

9. The transgressors should have walked *in the fear of our God* (see on 1:5), in order to stay far from the reproaches of *the* heathen *nations*. What was feared in 4:4 is now caused by some of the Judeans themselves.

10–11. Nehemiah's staff (see on 4:22) turned out to be involved in the problem by lending money (v. 4) and food (v. 3), but now a polite suggestion (Dallaire 2014: 114–115) is made: *Let us* please *abandon this* pledge (not 'this interest' as in, e.g., RSV; correctly NET: 'let us abandon this practice of seizing collateral') and please, *return to them this very day their fields, their vineyards, their olive orchards, and their houses, and the percentage.* Some interpreters – for example Becking 2018: 220 – suggest that Nehemiah would cancel the debt itself, but that is incorrect. The *percentage* points to the normal interest (not 'the hundredth part' as in, e.g., AV)[43] that should be paid as compensation for the products of the farming land (see Kidner 1979: 97 for a variant of this interpretation). The words for *wine* and *oil* are specific for recently harvested wine and oil.

---

43 If we suppose that tariffs were constant in the Ancient Near East, this
    means a maximum of 20% for money and 33⅓% for grain (the
    difference to be explained by the difference in risks) per season, i.e.
    from sowing to harvesting, or practically spoken, a year (Maloney 1974:
    3–7, 13, 15–18; Wunsch 2002: 234).

12. Apparently, Nehemiah did not trust his fellows and *made them* (his fellows, not the priests!) *swear* before the *priests*.

The word *promised* (as well as *promise* in the next verse) is the translation of the Hebrew *dāvār*, which has a standard translation 'word', but not in the sense of one term, but as a 'message, communication'.

13. When Nehemiah *shook out the fold of* his *garment*, he lost the important belongings one normally keeps in one's garment (nowadays wallet, phone, keys) and so points to the importance of what he is saying. 'Poverty and excessive differences in wealth are, to Nehemiah, not destined by fate or human failure, but by economic realities in need of being stripped of their sharp and bitter effects' (Becking 2010: 146).

14. The particular story about the debts led Nehemiah to speak *moreover* in his memoirs about his general economic policy. It was not actually mentioned earlier that King Artaxerxes had *appointed* Nehemiah as *their governor in the land of Judah* in the year 445 (see on 2:9−10). Also Nehemiah's first return to the king is mentioned (see 13:6). Governors had the duty to organize the taxes of their province (Tuplin 1987: 146−148; Briant 2002: 585) and the right to eat *the food allowance* [lit. 'bread': the taxes were reckoned in wheat, Williamson 1988: 80] *of the governor*, but we see here that Nehemiah and his brothers had never made use of this right. Probably they were able to do so because they owned substantial personal property (cf. v. 10). We cannot conclude from this, however, that only wealthy people can hold church office: see 1 Corinthians 9:1−14.

15a. About whom is Nehemiah speaking? There was no governor in place when he arrived in Judah − Sanballat tried to act as such, perhaps using Tobiah as a straw man (Williamson 1998: 162) − but Sheshbazzar (see on Ezra 1:8; 5:14), Zerubbabel (see on Ezra 2:1−2), Elnathan, Yehoʿezer and Ahzai (Steinmann 2010: 59) had been governors before. The former governors had taken for[44] food and wine afterwards (ESV: *for their daily ration*, although *daily* is not in the Hebrew text; it does figure in the Vulg.) *forty shekels of silver* (£265 or €290 in 2020; but always recall the reservations mentioned in the comments on Ezra 2:66−69). If this amount is taken per person,

---

44 'In the form of' (Joüon and Muraoka 2006: §133c, *beth* essentiae).

it is incredibly high; if it is from the total population, it would not
have been a problem. If we reckon from the number of meals mentioned in verse 17 and consider the equivalence in today's currency,
the total population seems to be meant. We cannot be enlightened
by other texts about the Persian Empire, as this text is the most
detailed one (Briant 2002: 810).

The *servants* of the former governors behaved as if they were
governors themselves, which could be expected as their salary was
linked with the income of the governor (Williamson 1991: 50).

15b–16. Nehemiah acted differently: *because of the fear of God*, he
persevered 'in this task of the wall' (of course, not by personally taking
the trowel in hand, but by management of the work). He and his
brothers *acquired no land* and his *servants* participated in the work
just like anyone else. What Nehemiah did was very laudable in his
circumstances, but cannot be expected from everyone: see also
1 Corinthians 9:1–14.

17. To the Judeans, namely the *officials* (see on 2:16), altogether
150 persons, were also added *those who came to us from the nations that
were around us*, foreign messengers seeking diplomatic and/or economic relationships, and/or officials coming from the king or the
satrap (Fried 2018: 829). In other words: no room for a quiet meal;
even eating was working.

18. When we reckon with the weight of animals in the (Ancient)
Near East, one ox and six sheep could represent 650 lb (Dalman 1939:
163, 183; Fried 2018: 822 seems to reckon with modern animals). The
birds were probably fattened geese, ducks and doves (Fried 2018: 827).
It is clear that this could feed many more than 150 regulars and some
visitors for one meal (*for each day*!); we might think of 2,400 portions.
Indeed, the Persian Empire was known to have very extended meals,
for the number of participants as well as for the food (Briant 2002:
286–292; for Persian cuisine, see also Amigues 2003). Fried (2018:
827) thinks that guests could take food home in order to feed their
(extended) families too, and of course Nehemiah's staff had also to eat
(Fried 2018: 828). Has the period of *ten days* for the wine something to
do with the Persian partition of the month (cf. Dalman 1932: 211)? In
any case, it is a strange period in a system with Sabbaths.

As a *governor*, Nehemiah had the right to *demand the food allowance*
from the people, but he did not do so, *because the service was too heavy*

on this people. This does not imply that he never used his prerogatives: he had a house, bodyguards and personnel (2:8–9; 4:16) and some projects, not only the ones mentioned in this chapter and the main building project, but also on international (Neh. 6) and internal levels (Neh. 13), as Wright 2010: 350 rightly remarks.

19. *Remember for my good* [this addition is normal in North-West Semitic inscriptions and is indeed not superfluous: see 1 Kgs 17:18], *O my God, all that I have done for this people.* Many commentators criticize Nehemiah for this prayer, because in this way he seems to boast about his good deeds. It is, however, rather the testimony of a conscience that we can present our deeds to God only in full dependence on his grace; see Hebrews 6:10. Ultimately, we cannot go to anyone else, whether we have a spouse and children or not,[45] and with no other attitude.

Meaning
This chapter speaks about internal problems. As in the previous chapter, some elements can be mentioned as a useful guide for parallel situations. When Nehemiah was informed about the societal problems (and we may repeat the words of Williamson 1985: 245: 'There are few issues so divisive of a harmonious community as extreme disparity in personal wealth and income'), he did not react immediately (v. 7), but pondered and incorporated Scripture (cf. vv. 7–8), without specifically quoting it literally (Berman 2017: 151–153).[46] Finally, he had the courage to speak out. Even though he had the authority to enforce a solution, he preferred to mention some arguments (v. 9). Nehemiah did not expect the people to remain silent because a 'higher goal' had to be served (the construction of the walls), but recognized the problems and dealt with them.

Nehemiah's reaction to the problems that were signalled was multifaceted (vv. 14–19): as a governor, towards God, and for the well-being of the people.

---

45 Apparently, Nehemiah had none: see Introduction 2i, 'Nehemiah'.
46 This is also the normal way it is done in Chronicles (Schorch 2013: 2–4).

iv. Attacks on Nehemiah (6:1–14)

Context

Following the external opposition of Nehemiah 4 and the internal problem of Nehemiah 5, we are in this chapter confronted again with the external opposition, still situated during the construction of the wall.

Comment

1. For *Sanballat*, *Tobiah* and *Geshem*, see on 2:19. The use of the prepositions indicates the close relationship between Sanballat and Tobiah. For *breach*, see on 1:2–3. The *I* indicates final responsibility, not handwork (see on 3:4).

2. 'Kephirim' is an unidentified place which has the article (abnormal for a place name) and is translated in both LXX and the Vulgate by 'in the villages' (and thus in many English translations).[47] These three arguments point to an interpretation 'in the villages'. *The plain of Ono* is situated at the crossroads of the provinces Judah, Samaria, Ashdod and Dor, nearer to Samaria than to Jerusalem (27 miles from there; see on Ezra 2:33). Although this region had Jewish inhabitants, it probably did not belong to Judah (see on Ezra 2:33; Lemaire 2015: 86); perhaps Sanballat considered it to be neutral territory. How could Nehemiah know that *they intended to do* him *harm*? Through spies, or because he found this awkward place quite suspicious?

3. However this may have been, Nehemiah replied diplomatically, with a rhetorical question (*Why … ?*, meaning: I am not going to stop the work).

4. The story repeated itself, no-one changed their mind, and no counter-proposal is formulated; Sanballat was not considering going the other way, to Jerusalem.

---

47 Indeed, the difference in Hebrew is very small: 'At (the) Kephirim' (for the article with a place name, cf. n. 25) is written *bakkəphîrîm*; 'in the villages' is written *bakkəphārîm*, if it is derived from the standard noun *kāphār*, but the form *kəphîr* exists too, and then the difference would be nil.

5–7. At the fifth try, *Sanballat sent his servant* [rather 'assistant', NET, NIV] *with an open letter,* allegedly to Nehemiah, but in fact in order to warn many people – as a reasonable degree of literacy existed – about the charge of rebellion against the king. In fact, it was simple gossip.

The letter again highlights the importance of *Geshem.*[48] Sanballat suggests a repetition of the action of Ezra 4:8–16 (some fifteen years earlier); of course, it was he who could arrange for this rumour to reach the king's ears. Indeed, Persian kings had no problem with executing pretenders to the throne, as King Darius reported in the Behistun inscription (§§16–18). It is unclear what advantage Nehemiah could gain by meeting Sanballat.

8. Even though Nehemiah knew that Sanballat himself had created the rumours, he deemed it necessary to react to the charges and to explain the truth. Now, however, any room for negotiation had disappeared.

9. After the presentation of the facts, the reason behind Sanballat's action is mentioned: he and Geshem *wanted* [although this is only concluded from the context; cf. NIV 'trying'] *to frighten* the Jews (see on vv. 10–13; for the term Jews, see Introduction 2l, 'Samarians/Samaritans – Judeans/Jews') so that they would stop the work.

At the end of this verse, we find (as in 4:4–5) a short prayer: *But now … strengthen my hands* (as a clear reaction to *Their hands will drop*). Of course, it is strange that this prayer lacks an address to God (added in ESV), but by interpreting it as a prayer, we keep the parallelism between verses 1–9 and verses 10–14 (cf. Throntveit 1992: 85):

A Chronological situation (v. 1)
  B Attempt to disturb good relations with the king (vv. 2–8)
    C Motivation (v. 9a)
      D Prayer (v. 9b)

---

48 Actually, here the form with the nominative ending is used, as is normal in Arabic: 'Gashmu' (AV); remember that he was an Arabian sheikh: see on 2:19.

A' Chronological situation (v. 10a)
  B' Attempt to disturb good relations with God (vv. 10b–12)
    C' Motivation (v. 13)
      D' Prayer (v. 14)

A different interpretation of the verbal form,[49] in line with LXX and the Vulgate, produces: 'But instead, I then redoubled my efforts' (NAB; more literally: 'But now I strengthened my hands').

10–13. With regard to the visit to *the house of Shemaiah* ('the LORD has heard'; many other persons bear the same name and this one is mentioned only here; probably a priest, because he had no problem meeting in the temple and his father's name is mentioned as a priest's name in 1 Chr. 24:18; Steinmann 2010: 465) – the goal of the visit is not clear – a specific situation is mentioned, but it is unclear which one: he *was confined to his home* (because he felt endangered?) or 'he was very worried' (Williamson 1985: 249). As a good prophet Shemaiah tried to speak in poetry, but the poetical quality is limited to repetition (*temple*; *they are coming to kill you*) and synonymy (*the house of God*, *the temple*). Another meeting is proposed: *Let us meet*[50] (see v. 2!) 'in the middle of the temple'. Apparently, Sanballat and Tobiah wanted to frighten Nehemiah (see his reaction *Should such a man as I run away?*) and to seduce him into sin, so that he would be put to death (Num. 18:7; see his reaction *And what man such as I* – Nehemiah is well aware of the fact that he cannot assume the role of a priest! – *could go into the temple and live?*; Williamson 1985: 259). A different interpretation is suggested by AV and other translations: it is not a good idea to hide in the temple in order to save your life, not so much because of Numbers 18:7 (although a combination might be possible), but because this kind of meeting is not good and because fear for a false prophet is not good (Deut. 18:22; Shepherd 2005: 246–249, but the link with Deut. 18:22 is not as clear as Shepherd would like). Whether because of sin or because of fear, Nehemiah's entrance into the temple would give him *a bad name*.

---

49 Piel absolute infinitive instead of Piel imperative.
50 Morphologically, we have here, unlike in v. 2, an imperfect, but it has the same jussive value: see Joüon and Muraoka 2006: §114b n. 3.

Nehemiah *understood* that Shemaiah was a false prophet and that
Tobiah and Sanballat [in straight cooperation, as the verb is singular]
had hired[51] *him.* This was the last time that *Sanballat* was active: he
had tried many times, by threatening and by negotiating, but here
he understood that he had to stop. Tobiah, on the other hand,
continued his actions, perhaps because he was more engaged on
the local level (Fitzpatrick-McKinley 2016: 172).

14. For this prayer, see on 4:4–5; 6:9. *Remember* in a negative sense
is also used in Psalm 137:7 (elsewhere in the book of Nehemiah
it is in a positive sense). Nothing more is known about *Noadiah*
(for the meaning, see on Ezra 8:33); she is the only false *prophet-*
ess mentioned by name (see Ezek. 13:17 for a general reference);
genuine prophetesses in the Old Testament are Miriam (Exod.
15:20), Deborah (Judg. 4:4) and Huldah (2 Kgs 22:14; 2 Chr. 34:22).
For *wanted to*, see on verse 9.

Meaning
In this section Nehemiah is attacked personally, first in his relation
to the king (vv. 1–9) and then in his relation to God (vv. 10–14).
A common theme of verses 1–14 is that of hired prophecy: while
Sanballat had accused Nehemiah of setting up false prophets (v. 7),
it was after all he (together with Tobiah) who hired false prophets.
It is clear that Nehemiah would have ruined his reputation if he
used false prophets, or if he was used by false prophets. A good
reputation is essential for civil servants and for leaders in the church,
together with their faithfulness and moral standards, in order to
govern effectively. Public sins nullify their effectiveness (Steinmann
2010: 466). Everyone can make mistakes, but when this becomes
structural, measures have to be taken and positions of responsibility
terminated.

A community (or a person) that wants to put its trust in the
Word of God is of course struck at its heart when someone abuses
this trust by false prophecy. False prophecy is recognized when it

---

51 The translation as pluperfect is suggested not only by the context
(Steinmann 2010: 463), but also by postposition of the verb: Lorein
2023b: 60.

contradicts what God has already revealed in his Word. Unfortunately, the abuse of pretended prophecy is not limited to the days of Nehemiah.

When at the end of this unit Nehemiah prayed for retribution, he understood that this concerned something not to be arranged among humans. Nehemiah did not avenge himself but left it to the Lord (Becking 2018: 233–234).

v. Final remarks (6:15 – 7:3)
Context
Here we arrive at the end of the construction of the wall, on 2 October 445.

Comment
15. When we count *fifty-two days* earlier, the work started on 12 August 445. That is very fast, but in the time of Themistocles (beginning fifth century BC) a similar result was achieved in Athens (according to Thucydides 1.93) and in AD 447 the walls around Constantinople were rebuilt in two months (Heather 2006: 309; see Lipschits 2012: 95–97 for other parallels). Besides that, we have to keep in mind that the walls had not disappeared completely (see on 1:3 and Introduction 2k, 'Jerusalem') and that at least some work had been done some years earlier (see Ezra 4:12).

16. The 'holy war' announced in 4:14 ends here. Here again a verbal form can be explained in two ways: *When all our enemies heard of it, all the nations around us were afraid*[52] *and fell greatly in their own esteem* (lit. 'in their [own] eyes'), or alternatively: 'When all our enemies heard of it and all the nations saw[53] it, they fell ...' (thus AV, NET). With the first option, a clear contrast with Nehemiah's courage is created. The *work had been accomplished*: Jerusalem is no longer *in great trouble and shame*, as was the case in 1:3. The expression *with the help of our God* must not be understood in the same way as 'with a little help from my friends'. Although human action is not excluded (see on 2:20), in this verse God's initiative is clearly

---

52   Qal imperfect consecutive third-person plural of *y-r-'*, 'to be afraid'.
53   Qal imperfect consecutive third-person plural of *r-'-h*, 'to see'.

indicated (hence 'was wrought of our God', AV), which marks again the importance of the city (and not only of the temple; Häusl 2013: 102; see on Ezra 1:3).

17–19. What is mentioned in these verses must be situated during the whole period of the construction of the walls. We read that information came not only to Nehemiah, but also to Tobiah through the people of his party among *the nobles* (see on 2:16) and family members. Indeed, Tobiah's wife was a daughter of *Shecaniah* (who was a *son of Arah* – the same as in Ezra 2:5), *and his son Jehohanan* (see on 2:9–10) was married to a *daughter of Meshullam* (who was *the son of Berechiah*; see on 3:4). Not only has Nehemiah been pressured in order *to make* him *afraid*; a positive approach has also been used in order to make him change his mind.

7:1. As Nehemiah simply says that he *had set up the doors*, the passive *had been appointed* seems to indicate that this was not done by Nehemiah himself (but this should not be excluded – De Fraine 1961: 100; in any case, as governor he had the final responsibility). Normally, the *gatekeepers* guarded the gates of the temple, so they had some experience. Mention of *the singers* and *the Levites* may sound strange, but Nehemiah needed trustworthy people. For the three categories, see on Ezra 7:7.

2. For *Hanani*, see on 1:2. The name *Hananiah* is a variant of the first name, but belongs to a second person; the translation 'my brother Hanani, that is,[54] Hananiah', suggested by, for example, Steinmann 2010: 481–482, is hampered by the two different qualifications (*my brother* and *governor of the castle*) and by the plural in the next verse.[55] They became responsible for the city of Jerusalem (the people mentioned in 3:9, 12 were responsible for the district). The qualification *a really*[56] *faithful and God-fearing man* more *than many* (cf. Exod. 18:21; 1 Cor. 4:2) applies only to Hananiah. Apparently,

---

54   *Waw* explicativum: GKC §154 n. 1b.

55   Perhaps it is this person, Hananiah, who had the important task of bringing the Passover Letter to Elephantine in 419 BC (Cowley 1923: no. 21; Muraoka 2012: 98; cf. Tuplin 2017: 656–659).

56   *Kaph* veritatis, expressing his very character: Joüon and Muraoka 2006: §133g.

Nehemiah's brother did not need such a reference. This would be strange in our day (and is indeed a reason for Steinmann saying that Hanani and Hananiah are one and the same person).

The castle is the same word as *the fortress* in 2:8 and *capital* in 1:1, and probably the same structure as in 2:8. Is the 'Tower of Hananel' (3:1; 12:39) named after Hananiah (albeit with the more neutral -el instead of the specific -iah at the end), as Edelman (2011: 68) proposes? Although this is linguistically possible, it would be strange to name it (already in 3:1!) after someone who was still active in those days and was responsible for the whole of the fortress, of which the Tower of Hananel was only a part.

3. It is difficult to understand which schedule Nehemiah had in mind. We meet a first problem when the ESV says *Let not*[57] *the gates of Jerusalem be opened until the sun is hot.* Should we think of the hottest time of the day (noon), or of the moment when the sun has acquired its normal strength (some hours after sunrise)? The first option would be a very late time to open the gates; the second option is not in line with the meaning of 'hot' at other places (see esp. 2 Sam. 4:5; elsewhere, such as Gen. 18:1; Exod. 16:21; 1 Sam. 11:9, 11, both options could be defended, although only the first option normally is) and would be strange in a Near Eastern context. A solution can be found in the interpretation of the preposition, not as *until*, but as 'during', also a possible translation, though infrequent (Zorell 1968: 572). Together with a specific translation of the verbal form ('remain'),[58] we would arrive at the translation 'The gates of Jerusalem will not remain open during the time the sun is hot', that is, during siesta, from 11 am until 2 pm (cf. Dalman 1928: 609; 1939: 134, who nevertheless arrives at a different conclusion). The reason would be that this time of the day the city was specifically subject to attacks (see again 2 Sam. 4:5).[59] *And while they* [the guards] *are still*

---

57   Considering the use of the negation *lōʾ*, a translation 'will not' is needed.

58   Cf. Waltke and O'Connor 1990: §23.3b.

59   For a non-biblical example from the Mediterranean region, see Procopius, *Historia bellorum* 3.2.15–17: in AD 410 Alaric had sent as 'gifts' to the Romans some young people of his army who, on an appointed

standing guard, they will *shut ... the doors* so that[60] you (Hanani and Hananiah) may *bar* them: it seems rather obvious that the guards must close the doors when they are present (remote control not yet being available). Becking 2018: 238 thinks that a rotation schedule is meant. Probably Hanani and Haniah were to verify personally that the gates were closed correctly. Apparently, Nehemiah was afraid of negligence and wanted to have clear measures.

As *some* guards could intervene *in front of their own homes*, it appears that some houses were situated near to the wall (Laperrousaz 1994: 128; cf. Introduction 2k, 'Jerusalem'). As with the construction of the wall itself, here the relation to one's *own* house is exploited too.

Meaning
Of course, the neighbouring peoples did not like Judeans taking their place in the region and they reacted vehemently. Without allegorizing, we can see some parallels with situations where Christians nowadays try to establish their legitimate place in society. Nehemiah's motivation, his respect to uphold the honour of his forefathers who had preceded him (2:3), the intention of taking away the shame of the bad state of Jerusalem vis-à-vis the surrounding nations, his relationship with the Persian authorities, the intelligence with which he built and organized the city – all this can inform many incentives for how we as Christians may live in our society. Trust in God implies this manner of living and working. Nehemiah does everything within his means and is at the same time a witness to dependence on God.

Perseverance is furthered because all are busy with something for which they are specifically engaged (*in front of their own homes*). With such motivation and collaboration, people work together for a common goal in a decentralized way.

---

day at about noon, when their masters had their siesta nap, were to go to the Salarian gate, kill its guards and open the gates.

60 Indirect imperative *ᵉḥōzú* (with *o* in spite of the *ḥ*: GKC §64c) indicating the purpose after the imperfect *yāgîphû* 'they will close' (Joüon and Muraoka 2006: §116e).

4. BUILDING THE COMMUNITY (7:4 – 12:47)

A. Introduction (7:4–5)

This section introduces the fourth part of Ezra-Neh., which is about the reconstruction of the community.

i. A large city with few inhabitants (7:4–5)

Context

Jerusalem had become a well-defended city, so the right moment had arrived to give it also an urban function. Nehemiah looked for people willing to commit themselves to this goal. During that quest, he found an old list (described in the next section, 7:6–73a). This event must be situated between the end of the construction of the walls (see 6:15) and the New Year celebration (see 8:2), that is, between 2 and 8 October 445, even though this is a quite limited period.

Comment

4. *The city was wide and large* [for its description, see Introduction 2k, 'Jerusalem'], *but the people within it were few* [and this fact leads to the next action], *and no houses* were built, that is, they needed to be happy with the houses that were already there. The Hebrew expression behind *wide*, very literally 'broad as far as two/both hands are concerned', means 'broad at both sides' (north–south as well as west–east?) and occurs regularly; it does not seem to have a specific meaning, just 'quite large'.

5. The LORD put it *into* Nehemiah's *heart* to *assemble* the *nobles* (see on 2:16) and the *officials* (see on Ezra 9:1) to enrol them by genealogy, so that they could confirm their relation to the pre-exilic community. This is typically an affair of continuity with the past, and so it is quite evident that Nehemiah continued looking for an earlier *book of the genealogy*, which he did indeed find.

Meaning

Nehemiah's ultimate goal is not to rebuild the city walls: it is about the community, just as his Greek contemporary Thucydides (7.77.7) said: 'Men, they make up the community; and not walls or ships without men within' (my translation). On the other hand, it is impossible to keep people together without structures.

B. Launch: return, information (7:6–73a)

The old list, which is in its place in Ezra 2, found its way into Nehemiah's files and is for that reason published again in Nehemiah 7. Ezra 2:66, however, has no parallel in the text of Nehemiah 7; in English translations it is nevertheless represented as Nehemiah 7:68 (*Their horses were 736, their mules 245*). This causes a difference in verse numbering from this verse on, offering a chapter with 73 verses (with the 'reparation' based on Ezra 2:66) or with 72 verses (without it). See also Introduction 4b, 'Establishing the text'.

We again find four categories: laypeople who do not have any problem with their status (vv. 8–38; cf. Ezra 2:3–35); priests and other temple personnel who do not have any problem with their status (vv. 39–60; cf. Ezra 2:36–58); laypeople without proven relation (vv. 61–62; cf. Ezra 2:59–60); priests without registration (vv. 63–65; cf. Ezra 2:61–63).

As the list is also discussed at Ezra 2, we shall here give attention only to differences. Essentially, the lists of Ezra 2 and Nehemiah 7 are identical, but mistakes easily occur in copying names and numbers.

i. Documentation: the list of returnees (7:6–73a)
Context
We repeat that the list represents the situation of the first return (of the year 537 and immediately after) taken up again at this point by Nehemiah, because of its importance for what was needed in the year 445 (Bodi 2008: 69).

Comment
6–69. The names as such are discussed at Ezra 2. The differences can be resumed in different categories. Strikingly, the differences are most frequent with the laypeople.

Names are written in a variant form in verse 7 (*Mispereth* instead of Mispar in Ezra 2:2), in verse 15 (*Binnui* instead of Bani in Ezra 2:10), in verse 28 (*Beth-azmaveth* instead of Azmaveth in Ezra 2:24), in verse 47 (*Sia* instead of Siaha in Ezra 2:44), in verse 54 (*Bazlith* instead of Bazluth in Ezra 2:52), in verse 57 (*Sophereth* without the article instead of Hassophereth with the article and *Perida* instead of Peruda in Ezra 2:55), in verse 59 (*Amon* instead of Ami in Ezra 2:57), in verse 61 (*Addon* instead of Addan in Ezra 2:59) and in verse 63 (*Hobaiah* instead of Habaiah in Ezra 2:61).

Names are written differently, apparently by errors of copyists,[1] in verse 7 (*Raamiah* instead of Reelaiah in Ezra 2:2 – in Hebrew only one letter is different and probably the transmission in Ezra

---

1   The difference between Lebanah and Hagabah in Ezra 2:45 and *Lebana* and *Hagaba* in v. 48, as well as the difference between Habaiah in Ezra 2:61 and *Hobaiah* in v. 63, is a question of inconsistency in the ESV: these names are written identically in Hebrew. The same applies to *nor their descent* in v. 61 and 'or their descent' in Ezra 2:59, and to *of the daughters* in v. 63 and 'from the daughters' in Ezra 2:61: the Hebrew is the same.

is wrong; *Nehum* instead of Rehum in Ezra 2:2, where the ideas behind the two names are related in meaning), in verse 25 (*Gibeon* instead of Gibbar in Ezra 2:20), in verse 29 (*Kiriath-jearim* correctly for Kiriath-arim in Ezra 2:25), in verse 48 (*Shalmai* instead of Shamlai in Ezra 2:46)[2] and in verse 52 (*Nephushesim* instead of Nephisim in Ezra 2:50, where, however, in both cases Nephisim might be the best reading).[3]

Different names are given in verse 7 (*Azariah* instead of Seraiah in Ezra 2:2) and in verse 24 (*Hariph* instead of Jorah in Ezra 2:18; the meanings of the two names are related).

Names are grouped differently in verses 22–24 (*Hashum, Bezai, Hariph* instead of Bezai, Jorah, Hashum in Ezra 2:17–19) and in verse 26 (*The men of Bethlehem and Netophah* with one number instead of 'The sons of Bethlehem … The sons of Netophah' in Ezra 2:21–22 with two numbers – and a different sum!).

A name is dropped in Ezra 2:2 (*Nahamani* in v. 7), while Magbish (Ezra 2:30), Akkub and Hagab (Ezra 2:45–46) and Asnah (Ezra 2:50) are not mentioned at all in this chapter. In verse 48, Akkub and Hagab are left out, for Akkub perhaps because the same name occurred earlier (in v. 45), for Hagab perhaps because of the consonance with *Hagaba*, two names earlier.

For the differences in numbers two approaches can be used. As far as numerals were transmitted in full (as they are in the medieval Bible manuscripts on which the text we use is based), several resemblances in sound (when orality played a role in the transmission), and so in writing (when copying was fully visual), must be mentioned.[4]

The fact that in Hebrew the words for 'two', 'three', 'six', 'seven(ty)' and 'eight(y)' all begin with the same letter may also have played a role in verse 11, with its *2,818* (instead of 2,812 in

---

2 Where the Qere, however, is correctly Shalmai (see n. 25 at Ezra 2:43–54).

3 Again a Qere problem; see – again – n. 25 at Ezra 2:43–54.

4 Balzaretti (2013: 115–116) studied the Syriac translation, where numbers were also very vulnerable, but not with the same mistakes as in the Hebrew text.

Ezra 2:6); in verse 15, with its *648* (instead of 642 in Ezra 2:10); in verse 16, with its *628* (instead of 623 in Ezra 2:11); in verse 18, with its *667* (instead of 666 in Ezra 2:13); in verse 19, with its *2,067* (instead of 2,056 in Ezra 2:14); in verse 22, with its *328* (instead of 223 in Ezra 2:19); in verse 26, with its *188* (instead of the sum of 179 in Ezra 2:21–22).

The same initial sound of the Hebrew words for 'two', 'three', 'six', 'seven' and 'eight' occurs also in the Hebrew words for 'five' and 'nine', though in a different position. That might explain the situation in verse 13 (*845* instead of 945 in Ezra 2:8), verse 26 (*188* instead of the sum of 123 and 56 in Ezra 2:21–22), verse 38 (*3,930* instead of 3,630 in Ezra 2:35) and verse 45 (*138* instead of 139 in Ezra 2:42).

A number seems to differ completely in verse 10 (*652* instead of 775 in Ezra 2:5), but here we have a combination of the problem just mentioned and the position of 'five', which is in both cases the same, in verse 10 as 'fifty' and in Ezra 2:5 as 'five'.

The fact that in Hebrew the words for 'twenty' and 'forty' begin with the same letter may have played a role in verse 44, with its *148* (instead of 128 in Ezra 2:41).

Another factor is that Hebrew has a dual form, for which the ending is not very different from the singular form. This may explain verse 17 (two thousand in *2,322* instead of one thousand in 1,222 in Ezra 2:12) and verse 32 (*123* instead of 223 in Ezra 2:28).

In verse 17, the dual occurs also for the hundreds in Ezra 2:12, but then we have in verse 17 'three hundred', written in two words. This situation occurs also in verse 22 (*328* instead of 223 in Ezra 2:19).

We know, however, that numerals could be written with a symbol system (in ciphers) and we must reckon with this system at some phase in the transmission of the Bible text (already in Nehemiah's files, just before the writing of the medieval manuscripts text or somewhere between these two extremes). Two systems are known: the system with symbols for 1, 3 (a proper group), 10 and 20 (see Cowley 1923), occurring already in the eighth century (Meyer 1982: §7.4), and the alphabetic system, based on the Greek system and occurring from the second century at the latest (Lettinga and von Siebenthal 2016: §2L/31).

With the cipher system, small differences can easily be explained, for digits, tens and hundreds as well as for thousands.

A number differs by one in verse 18 (*667* instead of 666 in Ezra 2:13), in verse 19 (*2,067* instead of 2,056 in Ezra 2:14), in verse 20 (*655* instead of 454 in Ezra 2:15), in verse 23 (*324* instead of 323 in Ezra 2:17), in verse 26 (*188* instead of the sum of 179 in Ezra 2:21–22), in verse 45 (*138* instead of 139 in Ezra 2:42).

A number differs by three in verse 38 (*3,930* instead of 3,630 in Ezra 2:35).

A number differs by twice three in verse 11 (*2,818* instead of 2,812 in Ezra 2:6) and in verse 15 (*648* instead of 642 in Ezra 2:10).

A number differs by ten in verse 19 (*2,067* instead of 2,056 in Ezra 2:14), in verse 26 (*188* instead of the sum of 179 in Ezra 2:21–22) and in verse 62 (*642* instead of 652 in Ezra 2:60).

A number differs by one hundred in verse 13 (*845* instead of 945 in Ezra 2:8), verse 17 (*2,322* instead of 1,222 in Ezra 2:12), verse 22 (*328* instead of 223 in Ezra 2:19), verse 32 (*123* instead of 223 in Ezra 2:28).

A number differs by one thousand in verse 17 (*2,322* instead of 1,222 in Ezra 2:12).

The difference between *655* in verse 20 and 454 in Ezra 2:15 is indeed quite large and requires a combination of errors. Nor can the difference between *721* in verse 37 and 725 in Ezra 2:33 be explained in one single movement. In verse 67 we clearly have the complete number (*245*), while in Ezra 2:64 the tens and units must have fallen out. Is there a connection with the fact that verse 68 (*Their horses were 736, their mules 245*) is lacking in most manuscripts?

When we write out in alphabetic numerals the numbers with differences between Ezra 2 and Nehemiah 7, we cannot explain any set of problems. So that system does not seem to have played a role.

It cannot be excluded that transmission of the text occurred in one phase by fully written numerals and in another phase by ciphers, and that errors occurred in different systems. We must also keep in mind that a copyist of numbers (or names) would never have the spontaneous reaction that what he was writing was not plain Hebrew.

Table 4.1 presents all the differences, with the devices that can explain them. More than one explanation may be valid. Some differences remain unexplained. It is clear that we cannot speak of one big solution.

confusion of sound		confusion of sound (ś)	confusion of sound (')	singular/dual	units/tens	in ciphers
Ezra 2	Neh. 7					
v. 5: 775	v. 10: 652	2/7 and 6/7			50/5	8/2
v. 6: 2,812	v. 11: 2,818	2/8				800/900
v. 8: 945	v. 13: 845	8/9				8/2
v. 10: 642	v. 15: 648	8/2				
v. 11: 623	v. 16: 628	8/3				
v. 12: 1,222	v. 17: 2,322			2,000/1,000		2,000/1,000 and 300/200
v. 13: 666	v. 16: 667	7/6				7/6
v. 14: 2,056	v. 19: 2,067	7/6				60/50 and 7/6
v. 15: 454	v. 20: 655					5/4
v. 19: 223	v. 22: 328	8/3				300/200
v. 17: 323	v. 23: 324					4/3
vv. 21–22: 123+56	v. 26: 188	9/8 and 8/7				80/70 and 8/9
v. 28: 223	v. 32: 123			100/200		
v. 33: 725	v. 37: 721					
v. 35: 3,630	v. 38: 3,930	9/6				3,930/3,630
v. 41: 128	v. 44: 148		40/20			
v. 42: 139	v. 45: 138	8/9				8/9
v. 60: 652	v. 62: 642					
v. 65: 200	v. 67: 245					40/50

Table 4.1: The differences between the lists in Ezra 2 and Nehemiah 7

70–72. As in these verses the donors are different from those mentioned in Ezra 2, a comparison cannot be made.

The Hebrew text has 'priests' garments: thirty and five hundred' (cf. AV); ESV, probably because of the strange order of the numerals (and because of Williamson [1985: 266–267]) has split the numeral and supplemented the minas.

73a. At least the first half of this verse is still referring to the situation of Ezra 2 (for the second half, see the introductory comments on the section 7:73b – 10:39).

Meaning
Nehemiah found this list in the registers and found it interesting enough to quote it here in full. He was conscious of his work being a continuation. In order to go on with this existing tradition, he was interested in history, showing respect for those who had committed themselves by moving from Babylonia to the land of the ancestors.

For the list itself, see *Meaning* for Ezra 2.

How does this list, with all its problems, relate to our belief that Scripture is faultless? We should repeat here that we do not have something magical – or gnostic, with an immediate approach to ultimate reality – and that we always have to be careful and assiduous in our study of Scripture.

C. Core: building the community, commitment to the Law (7:73b – 10:39)

Although we find at least the first half of 7:73 also in Ezra 2:70, at the end of the list found in the archives, the second half is also (almost) identical with Ezra 3:1. Nevertheless, the setting in the seventh month applies as well to the event reported in Nehemiah 8 (see *Context* below). English versions do not change the verse numbering but they differ in putting verse 73b together with Nehemiah 7 (AV, ESV) or together with Nehemiah 8 (NIV, NET).

We find another verse-numbering problem at 9:38: while never considered as 10:1 in English versions, it is placed together with Nehemiah 10 in NIV and NET, which concurs better with the story structure.

While the previous section only launched the main subject of the fourth part of Ezra-Neh. (7:4 – 12:47), now we find the core of this part in this section: building the community, again with reference to the past, as when building the temple (see introductory comments on Ezra 4:1 – 6:15), but differently from there in the second part, because now it is not about purification of the community but about teaching it. It will be followed by a description of a worship service, which we will consider as a new section (11:1 – 12:47), in order to highlight its parallelism with the first part of Ezra-Neh. (Ezra 1:1 – 6:22). As in all parts, we have here also a return, albeit a return to Jerusalem. The New Year celebration is a perfect occasion to do so.

We can divide this section into three descriptions of meetings with the same elements, as shown in Table 4.2.

	7:73b – 8:12	8:13–18	9:1 – 10:39
Time indication	7:73b, 8:2	8:13a	9:1a
Gathering	8:1	8:13b	9:1b–2
Meeting the Law	8:2–5	8:13c	9:3
Application	8:7–10	8:14–15	9:4–37
Reaction	8:12	8:16–18	9:38 – 10:39[5]

Table 4.2: Three meetings with their elements

The prayer of 9:5b–37 has a concentric structure (Throntveit 1992: 102; see Introduction 4g, 'Literary terms'), implying that it is not just an improvised list of thoughts.

A Praise (9:5b)
  B Confession – retrospective (9:6–31)
    X Request (9:32)
  B' Confession – present (9:33–35)
A' Lament (9:36–37)

---

5 For the different verse numberings, see Introduction 4b, 'Establishing the text'.

The section is probably based on Ezra's files, partly on his memoirs (Neh. 8:1 – 9:5a), partly on documents (9:5b–37).

i. The gathering of the first day (7:73b – 8:12)
Context
Although the narrative order is not always identical to the order in which the facts took place historically, such occurrences are normally indicated in one form or another. In Nehemiah 8, we have the impression of the text just following the discovery described in 7:4–5, which simply followed the building of the walls. This implies that, even though a reshuffle is often proposed, one is not indicated (Bänziger 2014: 174–177). It remains surprising, however, that Ezra again plays an important role – now together with Nehemiah – while after Ezra 10 he was not mentioned any more. We suppose that after the events of Ezra 10 Ezra had left Jerusalem (cf. Introduction 2j, 'Relationship between Ezra and Nehemiah'), that Nehemiah as a governor was mainly engaged in rather material and political matters, and that now the time had come to focus again on content. For that focus Ezra, as priest and scribe (see Introduction 2h, 'Ezra'), was better equipped. Apparently, he had come back to Jerusalem, but this does not mean that Nehemiah disappeared completely (Neh. 8:9). Of course, you could cut his name out of the text and then produce a new reconstruction of history, but for this approach no basis exists in the manuscripts.

Even if Nehemiah 7:73b has been quoted from Ezra 3:1, it still serves a double function: the events of Nehemiah 8 – 10 also must be situated in the seventh month, more precisely of the twentieth year of King Artaxerxes, starting on 8 October 445. The start of the seventh month (of course reckoned according to a year starting in spring) is the New Year celebration for an autumn year (cf. Lev. 23:24).

Comment
7:73b – 8:1. It is important to see here *all the people gathered as one man* asking for education in the Law. They are gathering on *the square* between *the Water Gate*, a city gate in the eastern wall of the city, and the south-eastern part of the temple. The gathering is not on the

Temple Court, because women were not allowed there (Fensham 1982: 216). Women did assist at main gatherings: see Deuteronomy 31:12; Joshua 8:35. The people wanted to know more about God's teaching and for that reason made an appeal to someone who knew God's Word. Ezra is mentioned here without any introduction (see *Context*). *The Book of the Law* is presented here as a fixed entity, ascribed to Moses. This would be difficult to combine with the often-mentioned hypothesis that the Pentateuch would only have been written during these days (see Introduction 2n, 'Ezra's Law'). Just as the people had gathered in 537 on the first day of the seventh month for the burnt offerings (Ezra 3:1–2), they now gathered for the study of Scripture (which does not imply a replacement of offerings by study in Nehemiah's day).

2. Mentioning the *women's* presence seems to highlight the importance of the gathering, as in Ezra 10:1; Nehemiah 10:28–29; 12:43 (Williams 2002: 64). Young people *who could understand what they heard* were present too (cf. Deut. 31:12–13).

3. This verse can be considered as an introductory summary (Williamson 1985: 288). *Morning* started shortly after half-past six; *midday* is at noon. The initiative to read the Law came from the people, Ezra apparently had made a good choice of Scripture passages and the Levites were able to explain them to everybody. The result: they *were attentive to the Book of the Law* (lit. 'their ears were directed to the Book of the teaching'; cf. AV).

4. Literally, the *platform* is a 'big thing'. The usual translation of the word is 'tower' (cf. NET: 'towering wooden platform'); AV has 'pulpit', functionally correct. A (more expansive) parallel can be found in 2 Chronicles 6:13.

To the right of Ezra stood *Mattithiah* ('gift of the LORD'), *Shema* ('[God] has heard'), *Anaiah* ('the LORD has answered'), *Uriah* ('the LORD is my light'), *Hilkiah* ('the LORD is my share') and *Maaseiah* ('works of the LORD'); to his left stood *Pedaiah* ('the LORD has saved'), *Mishael* ('who belongs to God'), *Malchijah* ('the LORD is my king'), *Hashum* ('broad nose'), *Hashbaddanah* ('the strong one has thought of [me]'?), *Zechariah* ('the LORD has remembered') and *Meshullam* ('given as compensation, satisfaction'). These men probably came from the different categories (priests, Levites, laypeople).

5. *Ezra opened the book*, in those days in the form of a scroll (the codex, the precursor of our book form, was used from around the turn of the era for authoritative texts because a codex permitted easier consulting than a scroll). *The people stood* during the reading of the *book*. Before, they probably sat on their heels (Noordtzij 1939: 210).

6. Where the Hebrew uses the same word for God's action towards humankind and for human action towards God, many English translators tend to use 'to bless' for the first situation and 'to praise' for the second (cf. NIV: 'Ezra praised the LORD'). *Amen* can be translated by 'truly, that is right'.

7–8. *Jeshua* ('the LORD has saved'), *Bani* ('[God] has built'), *Shere-biah* ('the LORD has heated', i.e. born on a hot day), *Jamin* ('right hand', i.e. lucky), *Akkub* ('protected'), *Shabbethai* ('born on a Sabbath'), *Hodiah* ('the LORD is my splendour'), *Maaseiah* ('works of the LORD'), *Kelita* ('dwarf'), *Azariah* ('the LORD has helped'), *Jozabad* ('the LORD has endowed'), *Hanan* ('[God has been] gracious') and *Pelaiah* ('the LORD has acted wonderfully'; the name occurs also in a stamp for someone responsible for levy or taxation – Altmann 2016: 247 – but whether it refers to the same person is uncertain) were *Levites*[6] and made *the people … understand the* teaching.[7] At this point, the *Levites* have obtained an important function. They read God's teaching (not necessarily Moses' *Law*) paragraph by paragraph, not restricted to a summary (cf. the Aramaic equivalent in Ezra 4:18), apparently with some explanation (cf. ESV *clearly*), possibly in Aramaic (cf. NASB 'translating'; as a kind of precursor for the Targum, which in any case was always an explanatory translation).[8] The explanation was for everyone on his or her level, *so that the people understood the reading*. Understanding is more than knowing the exact text; it is about application in daily life (Becking 2018: 248).

---

6 *Waw* explicativum: GKC §154a n. 1b.
7 In *lattôrâ* the preposition indicates the second object of the verb 'made … understand'.
8 This verse does not say that the people did not know Hebrew (cf. 13:24), because this verse does not necessarily speak about *translation*. Of course, Bible translation is permitted, but one cannot base that on this verse.

9. The two main characters are mentioned with their roles: *Nehemiah … the governor* (lit. 'the reverend, his excellency'; cf. Ezra 2:63) and *Ezra the priest and scribe* (see *Context* for Ezra 7:1–10). The declaration came from the political leader, the religious leader and those who in practice spread the teaching.[9]

10–12. Understanding is fundamental; action just follows (v. 12; see also vv. 16–18 and the commitment of 9:1 – 10:39; Duggan 2001: 295–296). The *fat* is in Hebrew not the word for the forbidden fat of Leviticus 3:17 but another word (Kidner 1979: 107). For the food, see 2 Samuel 6:19; Isaiah 25:6. Expository preaching first led to emotion (v. 9; because they realized their falling short; Becking 2018: 249) and then to *great rejoicing*.

Only a short time after the reconstruction of the walls, Ezra and Nehemiah taught the people that they should not be sorrowful, because *the joy of the LORD is your strength*. The words are well known (also from the 1971 earworm song by Alliene G. Vale, repeating it four times, which does not help much to understand it), but is this the right translation? And what does it mean? Does the LORD rejoice in believers as suggested by Zephaniah 3:17b (Wong 1995: 383–386)? Or is it the other way around, as in Psalm 9:3 (ET 2); 32:11? Without denying the LORD's rejoicing, the second option seems the most appropriate, also in view of the *śimḥat Tôrâ* 'the joy over the Instruction'.[10] When our joy is not superficial but based on what God has done and still does, it is a real 'stronghold' (better translation than ESV *strength*, which is possibly influenced by the LXX [Loiseau 2016: 90]; see Ps. 27:1; Jer. 16:19; Nah. 1:7 where the same word is indeed translated by 'stronghold'), a fort where we can take refuge, dependent neither on our own feelings or acts, nor on those of our family, church or professional environment.

---

9 The singular *wayyo'mer* must be explained by its position before the subjects (GKC §145a).

10 The word *ḥedwâ* used here is parallel to *śimḥâ*, introduced in Late Biblical Hebrew, probably from Aramaic (Polak 2006: 615).

Meaning
Here is an early example of what the church today still has to do. The Book as such is not what is most important; it is about reading and understanding the Book.

We cannot say that sacrificial service has been *replaced* by a study of the Scriptures (Neh. 8 versus Ezra 3:1): observe that the reading of Scripture again will lead to concrete commitment in the temple in Nehemiah 10.

Feasting is a good thing when it is for the right reason. On this occasion, the people for whom nothing has been organized are not forgotten (vv. 10, 12), and we should still see what can be done for people who are not able to provide for themselves (by their situation or by their character), whether through social security or by charity.

See also *Meaning* for Nehemiah 9:1 – 10:30.

ii. The gathering of the second day (8:13–18)
Context
The second meeting took place on 9 October 445, with a smaller audience. For the first meeting, see *Context* on 7:73b – 8:12.

Comment

13. Now only *the heads of* the families, *the priests and the Levites* are present and we find a Bible study instead of a sermon. The idea of 'theocratic democracy' does not exclude more restricted meetings (Stiegler 1994: 164–165).

14. The leading people read *in the Law* [or more general: the 'instruction'] *that the LORD had commanded by Moses* [which seems to imply that the Pentateuch was known as a whole, as an old text and as connected with the historical figure of Moses; see on Ezra 3:2; Neh. 1:7] *that*[11] *the people of Israel* [here the comprehensive term occurs again] *should dwell in booths*: this Feast of Booths took place from the fifteenth to the twenty-first day of the seventh month (Lev. 23:34;

---

11 Instead of the Hebrew behind this second *that*, not *'ašer* but *kî* would be expected (it is repeated at the beginning of v. 15). Aramaic would have in both cases *dî* and this is probably the cause of the confusion (Polak 2006: 616).

22 to 28 October 445), which still left enough time for preparation. Living in booths reminded people of the fragility of life during the exodus, but also of God's care. This was not the only feast in that period: *the feast of the seventh month* consisted of several days.

15. This new contact with Scripture led to action too. Of course, *Jerusalem* had not been mentioned in the Torah, but many people are implied in this new application (Williamson 1985: 295).

Instead of the more general description of Leviticus 23:40, we find here a list of specific trees that have branches suitable for making booths: *olive*, oleaster, *myrtle* and *palm*. The expression *as it is written* indicates a reference to God's Word, not a verbal quotation (see Introduction 5g, 'Some specific terms').

16. Roofs of Ancient Near Eastern houses were constructed in such a way that you could stay on them (which is why they needed to have a railing: see Deut. 22:8). For the *square at the Water Gate*, see on 8:1; *the Gate of Ephraim* must be situated in the west, near the Broad Wall. This use of public places was necessary to accommodate all the people who did not live in Jerusalem.

17. *The assembly* indicates not only those who physically had made the journey from Babylon, but also those who were spiritually on the same line.

The Jews had already celebrated the Feast of Booths, at least according to Ezra 3:4 (and that can hardly have been the only time; for a much earlier celebration, see 1 Kgs 8:2, 65). Why then do we read here that [*in fact,*] *from the days of Jeshua* [new spelling for the fifteenth-century person; see on Ezra 2:2] *the son of Nun to that day the people of Israel had not done so*? The accent must lie on the word *so*: they had not done it with the attitude they had at this moment, that is, dependence on God for the journey and for staying in the land. Their joy was greater still (*very great rejoicing*) than at the first meeting (v. 12).

18. The reading *from the Book of the Law of God* can be compared to Deuteronomy 31:10–13, although what is described here is not a regular event but unique (van der Kooij 2009: 35, 39, 43; so it does not imply that this year was a sabbatical year). On the twenty-second day of the seventh month (29 October 445) followed *a solemn assembly*, as prescribed in Leviticus 23:36.

Meaning
See *Meaning* for Nehemiah 9:1 – 10:39.

iii. The gathering after the Feast of Booths (9:1 – 10:39)
Context
On 31 October 445,[12] after the end of the Feast of Booths, a third meeting[13] took place. For the first meeting, see on. 7:73b – 8:12; for the second, 8:13–18.

Comment
1–3. The people are attending in large numbers, apparently on their own initiative. Use of the term *Israel* in verse 1 points to a spiritual unity, not limited to physical descendants of Jews. Can verse 2 be interpreted as a separate ceremony for genealogical *Israelites* (lit. 'the seed of Israel'), because those who did not physically belong to this group could not confess the sins of their ancestors (Steinmann 2010: 531)? This interpretation is hindered by the word used for *foreigners*, which points not to the foreigner living in the country as a guest but to the foreigner not belonging to the group, mostly with the sense of 'hostile' (see on Ezra 10:2).

After a period of feasting, room can now be given to other emotions (although they were already announced in 8:10). The twenty-fourth day of the month Tishri was probably the remembrance day for the murder of Gedaliah (2 Kgs 25:25; Jer. 41:2; cf. Zech. 7:5; this date [and not the third day of the same month] is maintained by the Karaites [Lorein 2011a: 63]). Or had the Day of Atonement – not mentioned elsewhere in this story and typically a day of humility (Lev. 23:27–32) – moved to this day (Blenkinsopp 1989: 32)? Whatever the case, they are now *fasting and in sackcloth*. A

---

12 Of course, we may think of 31 October 1517, the date when Martin Luther published his 95 Theses, which eventually led to the Reformation, but that is mere coincidence. Cf. Lorein 2021d: 250.

13 Although ESV has, respectively, *gathered, came together* and *were assembled* in 8:1, 13; 9:1, the Hebrew has the same form three times.

sackcloth coat was made from rough black (cf. Isa. 50:3; Rev. 6:12) goat hair and worn to express grief in a physical way (Carpenter and Grisanti 1997: 1270).

In the first instance, only Ezra read (8:3); then the Levites read (8:8); at this moment they all read (Duggan 2001: 296) *from the Book of the Law* [better: 'Instruction'] *of the LORD*. This Scripture reading led to confession of guilt. The wording *they stood up in their place* gives the impression that they had received a fixed place. This would not be correct, however; it is rather about not moving all the time (as in 8:7; cf. NIV 'they stood where they were', not a literal translation, but indicating well what is meant). They read for some three hours and confessed and worshipped for another three hours, possibly divided into smaller units.

4. Having such a large audience, the Levites again receive a specific role. Even when everyone is engaged, a task continues to exist for those who in a more specific way have committed themselves to understanding God and his Word. Kidner (1979: 110–111), with reference to Mishnah (Middot 2:5), thinks that the *stairs of the Levites* were part of the temple domain, fifteen in total (see Pss 121 – 134), going from the Court of Women to the Court of the Israelites. They might also be understood as a part of a building where the Levites were located.

Jeshua [for most names, see on 8:7], *Bani, Kadmiel* ['God is before me'], *Shebaniah* ['the LORD has come near'], *Bunni* [short for 'God has built'], *Sherebiah, Bani, and Chenani* ['(God) has arranged'] uttered a plaintive cry for help.

5. Almost the same Levites, albeit in a different order, without Bunni and Chenani, but with *Pethahiah* ('the LORD has opened') and *Hashabneiah* ('the LORD has thought of us'), took the lead and made an appeal to the people (*Stand up and bless* [see on 8:6] *the LORD your God*) and then – passing by a verbal form that indicates the purpose: 'so that they praise' – directed themselves to God (*your glorious name*). The words *from everlasting to everlasting* indicate the desired period of praising, as in Psalms 41:14 (ET 13); 106:48 (cf. Pss 72:19; 89:53 [ET 52]).

6. Ezra's prayer starts in this verse (as the LXX explicitly states: 'and Ezra said'). The first words refer to Deuteronomy 6:4 (without quoting that verse literally), against every form of polytheism or pluralism.[14] This God has created everything and sustains everything, an idea with which Hezekiah's prayer starts also (2 Kgs 19:15; Isa. 37:16). The *heaven of heavens* indicates the place where God lives (although not exclusively: 1 Kgs 8:27). The *host of heaven* (the angels, not the stars) are also created and worship God.

7. Ezra goes further along in history, mentioning God choosing Abram and bringing him out (cf. the exodus!) of Ur in Southern Mesopotamia to Canaan (passing by Haran, like Ur a centre of the worship of the moon-goddess Sîn; Lipiński 1994: 173; Millard 2001: 52–53, 57). In addition, the name change (see Gen. 17:5) is considered important enough to mention in this overview. In this way, Ezra refers not only to the promise of the land but also to that of being a great nation (Gen. 15).

8. After God had chosen Abram (v. 7), he *found his heart faithful*, a term that is cognate of the word for 'endorsement' that occurs in verse 38. For the description of God keeping his promise we find the same expression in Daniel 9:12. The period of the patriarchs is finished with the common closing formula *for you are righteous* (Rendtorff 1997: 112).

9. Here the overview continues to the time of the exodus, when the Israelites cried for help. See Exodus 3:7; 14:10.

10. The translation according to which the Egyptians *acted arrogantly against* the Israelites is too soft; the translation 'insolently' (RSV) goes in the right direction. The verb recurs in verses 16, 29. The idea of God making a name for himself is also found in Daniel 9:15 and Jeremiah 32:20–21.

11. This verse corresponds mostly with Exodus 14:21; 15:5, but *the depths* may refer to the location of the dead (also in Jon. 2:4 [ET 3]; Ps. 68:23 [ET 22]). The element *went through* comes from

---

14 i.e. against pluralism in the sense that all faiths are equal at a theological level and that indifference is a virtue. Most of us live together with people who have other opinions (a pluralist society) and we should be committed to living together in a peaceful way and with rights not dependent on the question whether someone is religious or not. In any case, we cannot force other people to believe that the LORD is their God, the LORD alone. Cf. Lorein 2020.

Numbers 33:8 (where ESV has 'passed through', which is a more standardized translation of the underlying Hebrew); *the midst of the sea* is mentioned several times: Exodus 14:16, 22, 27, 29; Numbers 33:8. The idea of *dry land* occurs not only in Exodus 14:22, 29 (and its remembrances in Exod. 15:19; Josh. 4:22; Ps. 66:6), but also in Jon. 2:11 (ET 10).

12. See Exodus 13:21.

13. God *spoke*[15] and gave good laws, meant not as punishment but as protection. This verse also stresses the fact that no new ideas are mentioned here, but everything is in the line of the Sinai covenant, mentioned in verses 8 and 32 (Bänziger 2014: 60–62, 90–91).

14. For the importance of the *Sabbath*, see on 10:33. Moses is called God's *servant*, an honorific he shares with Abraham (Gen. 26:24), David (2 Sam. 3:18), Job (Job 1:8), Isaiah (Isa. 20:3), Nebuchadnezzar (Jer. 25:9) and Zerubbabel (Hag. 2:23).

15. God gives, even ten times in verses 6–31 (Duggan 2001: 294; Oeming 2006: 574; Vermeylen 2006: 92–95, 101–102). The *bread from heaven* refers to Exodus 16, mentioned also in Psalms 78:24; 105:40 as an example of God's faithful care. Jesus develops this theme in John 6:32–33. Finally, it is mentioned in Revelation 2:17 in an eschatological perspective. God *had sworn* [lit. 'had raised his hand': hence NIV 'had sworn with uplifted hand'; lifting the hand was the gesture when taking an oath] *to give* the Israelites the Land.

16. With *But they* a new subunit (vv. 16–21) confronts the sins of the Israelites with God's mercy (Rendtorff 1997: 113). The Hebrew behind [*they*] *acted presumptuously* is the same form as that referring to the Egyptians in verse 10: only a thin difference exists between Israel and the Gentiles.

17. The translation *appointed a leader* should be maintained: the translation 'determined' (Fensham 1982: 225) might be possible here, but not in Numbers 14:4, and consequently should not be accepted. Most manuscripts (and the Vulg.) offer the reading 'in their rebellion' (thus AV, NIV), but some manuscripts (and the LXX)

---

15 The form *dabbēr* is an absolute infinitive, as is *kārōt* in v. 8; indeed the absolute infinitive occurs more frequently after a regular verbal form in Late Biblical Hebrew (GKC §113z).

have *in Egypt*, different by only one letter in Hebrew. While God taught in several ways, the people were rebellious in several ways. God is *ready to forgive* (lit. 'a God of pardons', plural!; cf. Dan. 9:9). The confession that God is *gracious and merciful* occurred also in Exodus 34:6 (in the inverse order in older texts: Fassberg 2013: 66) and 2 Chronicles 30:9 and will come back in verse 31; that God *did not forsake them* occurred also in Ezra 9:9 and will come back in verses 19 and 31 (and in 4Q504 XVI, 10, around 175 BC; Lorein 2011b: 373).

18–19. 'Sin abounds, grace superabounds' (Kidner 1979: 112).

20. The *good Spirit* is a typically Persian (Avestan) religious term, but the combination occurs also in Psalm 143:10. It is interesting to see how this verse was one of the influencing elements of the Qumran Community, which in turn influenced the choice of the term 'Holy Spirit' (also found in Isa. 63:11; Lorein 2011b: 379, 395).

21. For the wearing out of their outer *clothes* and so on, see Deuteronomy 8:2–4.

22. God *gave* the Israelites *kingdoms and peoples and allotted* [the kingdoms] *to them* [the Israelites] a share up to a *corner* (i.e. completely; cf. Steinmann 2010: 527–528 for a more elaborated discussion).

Most translations simplify the redundant Hebrew text of the second half of the verse, which more literally translated would be: 'So they took possession of the land of Sihon, that is,[16] the land of the king of Heshbon and the land of Og, the king of Bashan', respectively a city (now Tell Hesban, 12½ miles south-west of Amman) and a region (much more to the north, at the height of the Sea of Galilee) in Transjordan (see Num. 21:21–35 and Josh. 12:1–5, where Sihon is called the king of the Amorites).

23. This verse does not contain astronomical information (indeed, you can see far fewer stars than the number of Israelites, but many more stars exist than their number).

24. The *Canaanites* had been warned (and individual exceptions were possible), but as an example to others they met the consequences of their gruesome sins (which normally do not lead to punishment on earth, but can do so, because there is not only God's

---

16 *Waw* explicativum: GKC §154a n. 1b.

love but also his righteousness). We can never apply their specific case to any other (Ford 2017; Zehnder 2018: 9, 13).

25. Much of this verse reminds us of Deuteronomy 6:10–11. Seven elements are mentioned (see on vv. 29–30a). A *rich land* is literally a 'fat land' (thus AV). Fat indicates prosperity (as in Gen. 27:28) and good health (a contrast with modern society). To a large extent, this is conditioned by the presence of water ('oil of the earth' is a synonym of water: Job 29:6; Lorein 2011a: 66). The presence of *cisterns* is very important because it is too risky to be dependent on wells, which can easily become unreachable (Dalman 1928: 71, 526, 654). With *delighted themselves* reference is made to the garden of Eden.

26. According to Oeming 2006: 582, mention of the *prophets* contains a reaction against the Samarians, who had only their 'Samaritan Pentateuch', but we should keep in mind the distance between the Samarians in Nehemiah's day and the Samaritans of the New Testament period (see Introduction 2l, 'Samarians/Samaritans – Judeans/Jews'). The expression [*they*] *cast your law behind their back* is another image of rebellion and rejection. See also Matthew 5:12.

27. Here we have a wordplay: *you gave them into the hand of their* oppressors, *who* oppressed *them. And in the time of their* oppression *they cried out to you.*

28. *But* as soon as they had rest (cf. NIV; Steinmann 2010: 529), *they did evil again.*

29–30. Israel's rebellion is expressed seven times (see on v. 25). The verb of verse 10 (about the Egyptians) and verse 16 (about the Israelites) is repeated here. The body part *shoulder* represents the whole: the Israelites were completely *stubborn* (the NIV replaces the Hebrew image by another image).

The confession that *if a person does them, he shall live by them* is also found in Leviticus 18:5; Ezekiel 20:11; Romans 10:5; Galatians 3:12.

Although the combination of *Spirit* and *prophets* does occur in biblical times, as here, it becomes particularly successful from the days of the Targum onwards (Lorein and van Staalduine-Sulman 2005: 45–47).

31. Again, in this verse, God's *great mercies* are mentioned, as in verses 19, 27 and 28.

32. The words *Now, therefore* (lit. 'And now') indicate an important new stage in the prayer (Vermeylen 2006: 79; cf. Throntveit's

structure [see introductory comments on 7:73b – 10:39], which
Vermeylen 2006: 78, however, does not like). Between confession
of faith (vv. 6–31) and confession of guilt (vv. 33–35) comes sup-
plication about the actual problems. For God's qualities, see also
Deuteronomy 7:9; Nehemiah 1:5; and Daniel 9:4; for *God ... the
mighty* we have the same term as in Deuteronomy 10:17; Isaiah 9:5 (ET
6); 10:21; Jeremiah 32:18. The expression *let not all the hardship*[17] *seem
little to you* asks God not to be indifferent. Tiglath-pileser (in the OT
also called Pul) III (reigned from 744 to 727) was the first Assyrian
king to intervene on Israelite soil: see 2 Kings 15:19; 1 Chronicles
5:26. That the start of the *hardship* is situated with *the kings of Assyria*
indicates that again the whole of Israel, including the North, is taken
into consideration (Bänziger 2014: 91).

33. The confession of guilt (vv. 33–35) is linked with the confession
of faith (vv. 6–31): awareness of sin leads to a better understanding
of God. Brown 1998: 151 states:

When we sin, all is not lost if the experience of personal repent-
ance and assured cleansing heightens our understanding of God. It
is forgiven people who are most sincere in worship, most devoted
in service and most effective in witness.

God's righteousness (see also 2 Chr. 12:6; Jer. 12:1; Dan. 9:7,
14) is the basis for confidence to continue believing and praying
(Rendtorff 1997: 116–117).

34. The series *kings, princes* and *fathers* occurs also in Daniel 9:6.
For the continuous sinning, see on 13:18.

35. The words *your great goodness* are introduced in Hebrew by the
preposition that in AV just becomes 'in'; ESV is a bit more colourful
with *amid* and in NIV we find the interesting translation 'enjoying'.
It indicates anyway a concession: 'in spite of your great goodness'.

---

17 The word *hardship*, although not the object, is preceded by what
normally is an 'object marker', *nota accusativi*, which consequently must
be called here a 'subject marker', *nota nominativi*, probably because it is a
non-active subject (Kroeze 2008). The same applies to 'the column' in
v. 19 and *our kings* in v. 34 (although these kings are 'non active' in a
very specific way). It is unclear why this rare phenomenon appears
three times in this prayer.

For *rich land* ('fat land'), see on verse 25. The forefathers *did not serve* God and, as a result, became *slaves* (v. 36, using the same root).

36–37. While the king of Persia supports the Jews and their governor is at their side, they nevertheless need to recognize (*Behold*; see 1 Sam. 25:41) a lack of freedom (as in Ezra 9:7–9), at least if we translate by *slaves* (which seems the most reasonable option, especially in the context of the remembrance of the murder of Gedaliah: see on vv. 1–3). Oeming 2006: 582 translates in the more optimistic sense of

> We, we are today (your) servants, in the land that you promised our fathers. Look, we are (your) servants on it. And it multiplies its fruit for the kings that you (legitimately) placed over us because of the sins of our fathers. They reign over our bodies and over our livestock with benevolent care. Yet we are now in great distress (because we once again are close to rejecting your Torah).

Oeming is right in positing that an anti-Persian policy was not a priority for Israel. In both interpretations a link with *did not serve* of the previous verse is present, but ultimately an ambivalent approach (not anti-Persian but not happy either) best serves the text (Lorein 2011a: 67–68).

9:38 – 10:1. The transition verse can be considered as the conclusion of Nehemiah 9 or as the introduction to Nehemiah 10. English versions have it as 9:38; the Hebrew edition (and translations in other languages) have it as 10:1 (see Introduction 4b, 'Establishing the text'). Either way, insight (expressed in the prayer) leads to action: on their own initiative they make an 'endorsement' (not the word usually translated as *covenant*; it is related to the word *faithful* in v. 8). Eighty-four persons (divisible by twelve: see Ezra 8:35) are mentioned. That would require many seals, which is technically impossible. Perhaps one single seal was used (of the Jehud-style; Avigad 1976: 4, 10), or the term *sealed document* might be considered as 'a legal record'. And then the names were written (most people in Israel were able to write, at least their name; Millard 2023: 215) of *our princes, our Levites, and our priests*, here not as witnesses, but as real parties. On other occasions the seal could close one copy, which made any tampering with the document impossible because the seal could not be broken (cf. Isa. 29:11; Rev. 5:1–5), while a second copy remained open (cf. Jer. 32:11) for consulting the agreement; or the seal simply confirmed the importance of the document (cf. Esth. 8:8); but here neither of these seems to be the case (Duggan 2001: 257–260).

Nehemiah is again called 'his excellency', as in 8:9a. *Zedekiah* ('the Lord is righteous') is mentioned together with him in the second half of 10:1; according to Steinmann 2010: 557, he is mentioned with a shorter form of his name as 'Zadok the scribe' in 13:13 and would have been the secretary for this text. Ezra is not mentioned at all, because he was not a representative of any group.

2–8. Then follow the priests (the order is the inverse of that occurring in 9:38): *Seraiah* ['the Lord is ruler'], *Azariah* ['the Lord has helped'; in 12:1 the shorter form 'Ezra'], *Jeremiah* ['the Lord has founded'; not the prophet, of course], *Pashhur* [Egyptian, 'portion of (the god) Horus'], *Amariah* ['the Lord has spoken'], *Malchijah* ['the Lord is my king'], *Hattush* [Akkadian, 'his sceptre'?], *Shebaniah* ['the Lord has come near'; in 12:3 'Shecaniah': in Hebrew writing, the difference is minimal], *Malluch* ['(God) is king'], *Harim* ['dedicated'; in 12:3 'Rehum', 'to whom (God) has been merciful', probably the right form], *Meremoth* ['elevations'; in 12:15 'Meraioth'], *Obadiah* ['little servant of the Lord'], *Daniel* ['God is my judge'; not the prophet, of course], *Ginnethon* ['little gardener' (Lipiński 2001: §29.11, §29.38); in 12:4 'Ginnethoi', probably a written error: Vulg. has 'Genthon'], *Baruch* ['blessed'], *Meshullam* ['given as a compensation, satisfaction'], *Abijah* ['the Lord is my Father'], *Mijamin* ['from the right side'], *Maaziah* ['the Lord is a refuge'; in 12:5 'Maadiah': in sound almost equal but with the meaning 'ornament of the Lord'], *Bilgai* ['brightness'; in 12:5, 18 the variant form 'Bilgah'], *Shemaiah* ['the Lord has heard']. Because these names represent families, the historical overview of 12:1b–6a presents mostly the same names (Steinmann 2010: 557–559).

9–13. The Levites follow the priests, in two subgroups: in the first place *Jeshua*, *Binnui* and *Kadmiel* (it is not clear whether *of the sons of Henadad* defines *Binnui* or *Kadmiel*) and then *their brothers*, all individuals (no family names for the priests). Most names have been explained at 8:7; *Binnui*: 'built'; *Kadmiel*: 'God is before me'; *Shebaniah*:

'the LORD has come near'; *Mica*: 'who is as (God)'; *Rehob*: 'spacious';
Hashabiah: 'the LORD has thought of (him)', easier to explain than
the form in 9:5; *Zaccur*: 'remembered'; *Beninu*: 'our son'. *Shebaniah*
and *Hodiah* are mentioned twice (v. 10 and vv. 12–13), accidentally
or as namesakes.

14–27. About half of these names are also mentioned in Ezra
2:1–19. Other names also occurred elsewhere, but clearly not for
the same persons (because they belong to the category of priests or
Levites). *Bunni*: '(God) has built'; *Adonijah*: 'the LORD is my master';
Azzur: 'helped'; *Hodiah*: 'the LORD is my splendour'; *Anathoth*:
'(from) Anathoth' (see on Ezra 2:23); *Nebai*: unexplained, unless
the Ketiv 'Nobai'[18] is correct: then 'from Nob' (for Nob, see on
11:32); *Magpiash*: unexplained; *Meshullam*: 'compensated, satisfied',
a frequent name; *Hezir*: 'swine' (strange in a Kashrut society, but
occurring more than once; Yamauchi 1988: 739–740); *Meshezabel*:
'God saves'; *Zadok*: '(God is) righteousness'; *Jaddua*: 'known (by
God)'; *Pelatiah*: 'the LORD gives deliverance'; *Hanan*: '(God) has
been gracious'; *Anaiah*: 'the LORD has answered'; *Hoshea*: 'may (God)
save'; *Hananiah*: 'the LORD has been gracious'; *Hasshub*: 'who has
been thought of'; *Hallohesh*: 'the charmer'; *Pilha*: 'harelip'; *Shobek*:
'who precedes'; *Hashabnah*: '(God) has thought of us'; *Maaseiah*: 'the
works of the LORD'; *Ahiah*: 'the LORD is my brother'; *Hanan*: '(God)
has been gracious'; *Anan*: 'cloud' (as announcement of beneficent
rain; Lipiński 2007: 197); *Malluch*: '(God) is king'; *Harim*: 'dedicated'.

28. For *gatekeepers* and *singers*, see on Ezra 7:7; for *temple servants*, see
on Ezra 2:43–54. With *all who have separated themselves from the peoples
of the lands to the Law* [teaching] *of God* are indicated all who had
committed themselves to the Jewish faith, whether or not of Judean
origin, whether or not returned from Babylon (cf. Exod. 33:16; Lev.
20:26; Ezra 6:21): this identification concerns faith in God's instructions, not physical descent: room for newcomers certainly exists
upon the condition of conversion, as Zehnder (2005: 433) states
(see also Lau 2009: 366, 369, 371–372; Hagedorn 2015: 306; Lorein
2021d: 250–251):

---

18   Also in LXX. For 'Ketiv', see n. 25 at Ezra 2:43–54.

The interdiction is in fact limited to those cases in which the spouse is not willing to separate himself from the 'impurity of the peoples of the lands', and, on the contrary, it must be feared that heathen elements would rub off on the Jewish spouse and/or the children.[19]

Mentioning the wives' presence seems to highlight the importance of the gathering, as in Ezra 10:1; Nehemiah 8:2–3; 12:43 (Williams 2002: 64). All these people are summarized at the end as 'everyone who knows understanding' in a way which stresses the individual commitment.

29. In this verse a general principle is mentioned that is elaborated in the next verses as three subjects: mixed marriages, the keeping of the Sabbath and material support for service in the temple. The combination of *a curse and an oath* seems to refer to the end of Deuteronomy: everyone declared that a curse such as in Deuteronomy 28:15 would rightly hit them if they did not stick to the endorsement.

At the end of the verse the elements appear in pairs: *to walk / to observe and do*; *in God's law / all the commandments … and his rules and his statutes*; *that was given by Moses the servant of God / of the LORD our Lord.* The importance of Moses' historical legislation is clear.

30. To stay far away from mixed marriages is considered the most important point (see *Meaning* on Ezra 9:1 – 10:44). At this point relations are not dissolved but a line of conduct for the future is decided, put in more general terms than in older texts that mentioned peoples who did not exist any more (see on Ezra 9:1; Lorein 2011a: 68–69).

31. The commandment concerning the Sabbath is very old (Gen. 2:2–3; Exod. 20:8–11) and had already been mentioned as a sign for foreigners who joined the Jewish faith (Isa. 56:6–7). Nevertheless, it received a more prominent place during the exile, probably because keeping the Sabbath had become the clearest sign of Jewishness

---

19 My translation; the German reads: 'Das Verbot [ist] wohl auf die Fälle beschränkt, in Denen der Ehepartner nicht bereit ist, sich von der "Unreinheit der Völker der Länder" zu trennen, und im Gegenteil befürchtet werden muss, dass heidnische Elemente auf den jüdischen Ehepartner und/oder die Kinder abfärben.'

at a time when making sacrifices had become impossible. This is also documented for Egypt in the year 475, some thirty years earlier than this chapter (Lindenberger 2003: no. 14, 22, 26). On the other hand, a new social situation requires a new specification: is it permitted to buy on the Sabbath from people who were not under this commandment? The faithful of Nehemiah's day decided that they would *not buy*. Indeed, not only professional but also private activities were forbidden (Exod. 35:3) – insofar as this division can be made in an agricultural society. This agreement was developed in the later history of the Jews and its specifications have become stricter and stricter.

The second part of this verse treats the sabbatical year. While the Sabbath is in the first place a religious institution on an individual or family level, the sabbatical year functions rather as an economic institution in society (Deut. 15:1–4) and nature (Exod. 23:10–11). The rest for the soil and exemption for debts (lit. 'the burden of every hand') did not necessarily follow the same schedules. The first cycle was perhaps even different for every parcel of land: this might explain why nowhere in the Bible is there mention of its application.[20]

32–33. What was the cause of this promise? Had King *Artaxerxes* stopped sustaining the Jewish religion in these days as his predecessor Darius (see Ezra 6:9–10) and he himself previously had (Ezra 7:21–24; Neh. 2:8 – but that was for a specific goal)? After all, a royal allowance never implies that the congregation does not have to add anything of its own, and its contribution cannot imply that royal funding was rejected (contra Goswell 2011: 197). The congregation, however, was not very rich (taxes were high) and in that way could easily have been tempted to economize on the temple service, for example by giving less than expected (Mal. 3:8) or by offering lame animals (Mal. 1:7–8).

---

20 It was known, however, to Tacitus, *Historiae* 5.4 ('through pleasing laziness the seventh year too was given to idleness'; my translation). It is also mentioned, for a specific place, in 1 Maccabees 6:49, 53, as is the case with Flavius Josephus, *Ant.* 14.202, if the Latin version is followed.

The amount of *a third part of a shekel* (£2.02 or €2.39 in 2021; for the calculations, see the comments at Ezra 2:66–69; 7:22) seems to be lower than in Exodus 30:13, but it is not clear whether the currency and frequency of the contribution were the same. According to Exodus 30:12, 14; 38:26; and 2 Kings 12:4; 2 Chronicles 24:6, 9 (at the end of the ninth century) the census tax was levied regularly (but perhaps not every year) upon every individual (cf. Matt. 17:24) and brought to Jerusalem. After the destruction of the temple in AD 70 it was transformed into a tax of the Romans on the Jews (Josephus, *Bellum judaicum* 7.218).

The *showbread* was stocked in two piles of six loaves in the temple sanctuary; they were renewed every week (see Lev. 24:5–8). The *regular … offering* was brought in the morning and in the afternoon (in general, see Josephus, *Ant.* 3.237; for the hour of the afternoon, see on Ezra 9:4); it consisted partly of a *grain offering* and partly of a *burnt offering* (Num. 28:1–8). On the last day of every week, the first day of every month and other festival days specific offerings were brought (Num. 28:9 – 29:38; see on Ezra 3:5). A *sin offering* was brought if a group (here *Israel*) or an individual had sinned inadvertently (Lev. 4:1 – 5:13). Becking (2018: 290) discerns three kinds of offerings (calendrical, course of life and crises) and observes that the second category (course of life offerings) is absent here. While *the service of the house of our God* (v. 32) refers to the liturgy, *the work of the house of our God* refers rather to the technical infrastructure (Batten 1913: 377).

34. 'Contribution' (thus NIV; the Hebrew word is close to the word for *offering*; hence ESV) of *the wood* had not been previously arranged this way, but the principle of continuity of the altar fire had been established in Leviticus 6:12 (Hebr. 6:5). This means that we find here a practical elaboration of an existing principle. The Mishnah (Ta'anit 4:5) reports some of the *times appointed*, most of them in our months July and August (see further Lorein 2011a: 70).

35. For the liturgy of the *firstfruits*, see Deuteronomy 26:1–11.

36. What is mentioned in this verse had already been detailed earlier: Numbers 18:15–18; Deuteronomy 15:19–23.

37. For the vegetables no quantity had been defined (Exod. 23:19; 34:26; Deut. 26:2), which could imply a certain generosity.

The first term refers to an early stage in the production of *dough* (Dalman 1933: 271), probably based on barley, in one term: 'barley grits' (it seems difficult to bring dough to the temple). For the second term Fensham (1982: 241), basing himself on the context, opts for 'products', but this translation lacks an etymological basis. For Williamson (1985: 338), it is an explanation of the first term, the prime portion (not the first, but the best) of grain, '*that is*, our sacred contribution'. The problems with both terms are apparently old: the first is translated in a very general way in both LXX and the Vulgate, and the second is absent from the LXX and translated clumsily by Jerome ('firstlings of our firstlings').

For these regulations we can refer to Numbers 18:11–12 and Deuteronomy 18:4–5, but now what will go to the priests and what will go to the Levites is better defined. The regulations are also referred to in Judith 11:13, to be situated in 150 BC. They are further elaborated in some circles (for the Essenes, see Jubilees 32:2, about the same period; for the Pharisees, see Luke 18:12).

The practical arrangement of *the tithes* is easier than in Deuteronomy 14:23–25. Generally, the tithes had a religious as well as a social aspect and could be distinguished in three categories: (1) the yearly tithes for the Levites, who in turn gave their tithes to the priests (Num. 18:26 and here in this verse); (2) the yearly tithes to have festival meals before God in Jerusalem (Deut. 12:17–18; 14:26–27); (3) the triennial tithes for the poor (Deut. 14:28–29; 26:12). See also Tobit 1:7–8; Flavius Josephus, *Jewish Antiquities* 4.240; and Lorein 2010b: 348–349.

While many English translations think of agriculture, the Hebrew is more general: 'the towns of our work'.

38. What is given to the Levites is verified by someone in another category, that is, *the priest* (as this applies to anyone in this category, a translation 'a priest' would be correct too; cf. NIV, NET). The Levites pay *the tithe of the tithes*, so they also contribute to the good working of the cult based on what they have received. The *chambers* (as well as the storerooms) were probably situated near the entrance, easily accessible, well protected and away from the area of worship activity (2 Chr. 31:11; Noordtzij 1939: 239; Boda 2010: 198, 396).

39. The *vessels* are receptacles used for storage of the contributions brought in for sacred use (Batten 1913: 379). They do not want to *neglect* the temple, the text using the same word as for God's mercy in 9:17, 19, 31 (there translated by 'forsake'): they want to make concrete their gratitude for God's benefactions.

Meaning

Scripture and interpretation
The assembly of 9:1 – 10:39 is seen as the basis for the synagogue worship service and thereby for our worship service (but see already 2 Chr. 17:9; cf. Lorein 2011a: 73). This service is based on Scripture and should lead to a desire for greater understanding of truth. Without a basis in the exposition of Scripture, worship easily leads to meaningless repetition and insincerity (Brown 1998: 130).

We have no new spoken prophecy or any other form of new revelation, but existing texts of Scripture speak with great authority in new situations. The Pentateuch (for the importance of Moses' written instruction, see Bänziger 2014: 178–182), as well as the prophetic and historical books and the Psalms have been referred to in the *Comment*. The number of sources cited as well as their evident authority here counter the view that most biblical books were composed only in post-exilic times.

This makes the task of interpretation more important. We do not find a systematic treatise on theology, but instead (as theology should always do) the text forces a reflection on new circumstances in which we have to understand the basic principles very well, in order to be able to apply the text in an appropriate way. At 9:6 we noticed the way Deuteronomy 6:4 is used with variation, because Scripture does not contain set words but principles, expressed in words.

The reading of Scripture is based on a grateful understanding of history (9:6–31, esp. vv. 6–8, 13–15, 20), calls for a testimony in the present (8:15) and leads to a faithful commitment for the future (9:38; 10:28–29), a commitment much larger than that of a few years earlier (Ezra 10:12–14) or even of a few months earlier (Neh. 5:12; Duggan 2001: 292).

Sacrificial service has not been *replaced* by a study of the Scriptures: in this unit we see that the reading of Scripture leads to concrete commitment in the temple: there is no contrast between the two.

Our faith is not based on one general principle. Rather, God has constantly intervened in history (9:6–31, esp. vv. 6–8, 13–15, 20; Introduction 2a, 'Rootedness'). In this way, historical overview and confession of faith go together.

Not all aspects of the history are mentioned; some selection has occurred in this overview. For example, David is not named (this does not mean that his story was not known to Ezra: see Neh. 3:15–16). On the other hand, some elements are repeated.[21] Even though other interpreted summaries of the past exist, this one, together with that of Psalm 136:5–22, is the most important in the Old Testament (for the New Testament, see Acts 7:2–47; Heb. 11:3–33).[22]

Theology is based on this historical overview and leads to a practical application, as Williamson 1985: 340 states: 'Neither Old nor New Testament has any place for confessions of faith that leave life-style and practice unaffected.'

In these new circumstances (with Persian benevolence in their own country, but not completely free), the community is obliged to define itself again, in line with God's earlier revelation, but in a non-legalistic way, 'creating what space they could for their own unique self-expression and in a generally unfavourable environment' (Blenkinsopp 1989: 31).

Clines (1981) is right when he says that practical regulations can be changed or added and that temporary regulations can become fixed or generalized. Perhaps he is even right when he says that apparently contradicting regulations can be followed together by being as strict as possible. He is, however, wrong when he says that faith needs to become more and more rigorous because the

---

21 Vermeylen 2006: 84–85, 87–88, 92–95, 97, 103: fathers in vv. 9, 16; Egypt in vv. 9, 17; insolence in vv. 10, 16; pillar of cloud in vv. 12, 19; good commandments/Spirit in vv. 13, 20; manna in vv. 15, 20; water in vv. 15, 20; not abandoning in vv. 17, 19, 31; rebellion in vv. 26, 29; great mercies in vv. 27, 28, 31; beginning again twice in v. 28 (always without accepting Vermeylen's general conclusions!).

22 In the intertestamental period we have Sirach 44 – 50; Damascus Document II 17 – III 20; Judith 5:6–19; 1 Maccabees 2:52–60.

synthesis of all earlier variations means that now all the details have to be followed. This legalistic application in New Testament times (also earlier and later) is a wrong way of dealing with Scripture which does justice neither to the Pentateuch nor to Ezra. It is constantly about principles, including in the Pentateuch. The very word *tôrâ*, 'teaching', points to the fact that it is not about legalism, just as in the Mesopotamian and the Athenian standard legal systems of the same period (Lanni 2006: 37–70, 170; Lorein 2011a: 74–75; Berman 2017: 111, 177–178), but here the principles are God-given and canonical.

What started as a practical measure to respond to a principle in a specific situation continued to be part of the rules of behaviour, although in new situations perhaps other measures would have met the original principle (Bänziger 2014: 99).

Scripture is not only a piece of literature, but also reports history that appeals to us in new circumstances, in order that we may continue with the principles and renew their application, at the right midpoint between a life without principles and blindly following the rules. This is possible because God has given us his good Spirit, guiding us when we read Scripture (9:20).

Theocratic democracy
The lists in 8:4, 7; 9:4–5; 10:1–27 point to the importance of individual responsibility (which is not the same as individualism!). Belonging to the community is also a personal decision. Not the leaders but the people as a whole are mentioned at pivotal points (8:1, 15; 9:1; 10:39). Stiegler (1994: 164) uses the term 'theocratic democracy'. The people have taken the initiative to read Scripture (8:1, 3, 5, 6, 9, 11, 12; 9:1; Duggan 2001: 294). We must also observe where all this takes place: believers are active, as believers, in the city, not the temple (Häusl 2013: 105; see on Ezra 1:3).

This democracy does not exclude persons having specific responsibilities: Ezra (Neh. 8:1–3), the presidium (8:4) and the Levites (8:7, 9, 11, 13; 9:5, 38; 10:28, 34, 37–39) are mentioned: we still need persons who study administration or theology, but this must lead to maturity and understanding for all individuals (Lorein 2008: 151–152, 154). And so the Levites, who at the start were not eager to go with Ezra (Ezra 8:15b–17), nevertheless come to exercise an important role. Later on, the Pharisees will take over this role, but from the moment their advice to the people turns out to be fixed rules, it becomes a yoke instead of a help.

This development from centralization to democracy can also be observed in the Old Testament as a whole, at least within the Hebrew canon: where in the Torah God himself continually teaches, in the Nevi'im the prophets usually speak in God's name to give correction, and eventually in the Persian period the people have to live without prophecy or miracles, using only the means which we also have today (cf. Grosheide 1963: 192; Lorein 2023a: 1167–1168). We see a similar transition in the New Testament: where elders are first appointed by the founder of a church, in churches with a larger scriptural basis because of Jewish influence we find teamwork, and eventually more democratic tendencies appear (Erickson 1983–85: 1084–1087). That is how faith develops in prayer and the reading of Scripture, and we try – with our abilities as well as piety (Whybray 2002: 127)[23] – to reach the good for ourselves and our fellow citizens, in an uneasy relationship to the government, which partly supports us, but on the other hand is obviously unchristian. This 'independence', however, does not hinder a broad and deep view of God, as is sufficiently proven by Nehemiah 9 (Whybray 2002: 128–129).

D. Worship service and measures for continuation (11:1 – 12:47)

After the optimizing of habitation some lists are attached by the final redactor. They come from different periods, perhaps partly from Nehemiah's (or Ezra's) files, but after all, they can come from anywhere. Apart from the lists, most of the time Nehemiah is speaking. In 12:44–47, he is spoken of in the third person, which does not make it impossible that these verses also came from his files, but this is less sure.

This last section of the fourth part (7:4 – 12:47) ends with the structuring element of a worship service (cf. the last section of the first part) to celebrate the repopulation of the city.

---

23 For this combination in the intertestamental period, see Lorein 2022.

i. Repopulating Jerusalem (11:1–2)

Context

After the special gatherings of the previous section, we continue with the problem mentioned in 7:4–5: Nehemiah wants to corroborate Jerusalem's urban function. This problem needs to be solved first (Fensham 1982: 255: 'to safeguard Jerusalem … was a higher priority than the dedication ceremony'). The migration must have taken some time, and if the dedication indeed took place during winter (see *Context* on 12:27–43), we must situate it in the period from autumn 445 to the winter of 444.

Comment

1. Despite the presence of the temple, Jerusalem is not attractive enough and a specific policy of decentralization turns out to be necessary (Kreissig 1973: 108). The Hebrew does not make clear whether *the leaders of the people lived in Jerusalem* (because they needed to?) or 'settled' there as a first group (thus NIV), giving the right example. When 'one out of the ten' went to *Jerusalem*, 'the nine (other) wedges' *remained* where they were. Even though the situation at *Jerusalem* is problematic, it is called *the holy city*, a rather rare description in the Old Testament (see nevertheless besides v. 18 Isa. 48:2; 52:1; later on Tobit 13:10 [ET 9]; 4Q504 XV, 12; 1 Maccabees 2:7; and in the New Testament, Matt. 4:5; 27:53; Rev. 11:2), perhaps because it is to a significant degree populated by human tithes (Klement 2011: 69; Häusl 2013: 105).

2. Apparently other cities were more attractive than Jerusalem. Do those who were 'willing' form a supplement to the 10% indicated by casting lots? Did they change places with the conscripts? Are they persons who themselves chose to be part of the 10%? Were all of the 10% happy to be selected? None of these options can be excluded.

Meaning

Nehemiah did not have specific ideas about who should live in Jerusalem but only about a suitable social and economic partition between capital and country, so he left the decision to the casting of lots (see Prov. 16:33). In that way he avoided being suspected of interfering in private matters. We must not underestimate the weight of such (or any) removal and it is a good thing that the people concerned are appreciated for their commitment (Ulrich 2021: 145).

ii. Documentation: several lists (11:3 – 12:26)
Context
The lists, which do not take time within the actual storyline of this section, treat a very long period. In addition to the situation in Jerusalem, that in Judah is mentioned (11:25–35).

Comment
3. This verse starts by mentioning the heads *of the province* in so far as *they lived in* the capital and then represents the situation before the reorganization (7:73). For the *temple servants*, see on Ezra 2:43–54; for *the descendants of Solomon's servants*, see on Ezra 2:55–58.

4–6. In verses 4–19 the new inhabitants of Jerusalem are mentioned. A parallel list is found in 1 Chronicles 9:2–17. Differences between the two could be ascribed to copying errors, but it is more probable that different extracts were made from the archives for different definitions.

The elaborate genealogies of *Athaiah* ('the LORD's help') and *Maaseiah* ('the works of the LORD') mark them as important personages (Batten 1913: 268). Only a total for *the sons of Perez* (a son of Judah and Tamar: Gen. 38:29) is given here: *468 valiant men* (normally 'men of quality' but here indeed in a military sense).

7–8. *Sallu* ('who has returned'; also situated by a genealogy) and *his brothers* were Benjaminites, together *928 men*.

9. *Joel* ('the LORD is God') and *Judah* ('praise') had some responsibility over Judahites as well as Benjaminites. It seems that they took on the responsibility of Hanani and Hananiah (see 7:2, four chapters earlier, but in time only weeks before), but possibly it is another kind of responsibility. English versions consider *Judah* to be *second over the city* (see on v. 17) but he may also have been responsible for the Mishneh, the 'second quarter' of the city (Kidner 1979: 118).

10–14. The *priests* are divided into several subcategories: *Jedaiah* ('the LORD has known'), *Jachin* ('may [God] establish'), *Seraiah* ('the LORD is leader') and *their brothers*, totalling *822 men*, *did the work of* *the house.* In spite of *Seraiah*'s long genealogy it is not complete (see 1 Chr. 6:4–15). He was the *ruler of the house of God*, that is, the high priest (Williamson 1985: 351; vom Orde 1997: 272–273). One of his namesakes was high priest at the beginning of the exile (see 2 Kgs 25:18–21).

Adaiah ('the LORD has adorned') and *his brothers*, totalling *242* men, were *heads of fathers' houses*, that is, 'family heads'. *Amashsai*[24] ('the LORD has carried'), *and their*[25] *brothers*, totalling *128* men, were probably soldiers of priestly origin (Williamson 1985: 352; Vom Orde 1997: 273; Schaper 2000: 243; differently Steinmann 2010: 568, with reference to Ruth 2:1: strong in their faith); they served under the direction of *Zabdiel* ('gift of God').

15–18. *Shemaiah* ('the LORD has heard'), *Shabbethai* ('born on a Sabbath') and *Jozabad* ('the LORD has given') were, as *Levites*, responsible for the infrastructure and tools (vom Orde 1997: 274). It is important to notice that the Bible also mentions people responsible for maintenance, work behind the scenes. Often church history does not notice these kinds of people, but, as Brown 1998: 200 states, 'their loving service is not forgotten in the place where the best records are kept'.

Other Levites were *Mattaniah* ('gift of the LORD'), literally 'the leader (who) at the beginning would praise[26] at the prayer', *Bakbukiah* ('bottle of the LORD'; see on Ezra 2:51), who was *the second*, perhaps leading those who sang in reaction to the first group in antiphony (Noordtzij 1939: 243), and *Abda* ('[God's] servant'). *All* these *Levites* totalled *284* men.

19. Besides the general category of Levites we find also *Akkub*

---

24   Probably the variants *s* and *ś* are both represented, while *ś* is also
     changed into *š*, which altogether produces the spelling *Amashsai*.

25   *Whose* brothers? It is too easy to change the possessive pronoun to 'his',
     but this is what has already been done by the LXX. Vulg. has 'their'.
     Yamauchi (1988: 746) interprets *brothers* as 'associates'. It must be kept
     in mind that the excerpt from the archives was always partial in these
     lists.

26   *Yəhôdeh*: Hiphil imperfect third-person singular masculine; for the
     unelided form, see GKC §53q.

('protected'), *Talmon* ('bright') and their brothers as *gatekeepers* (see on Ezra 7:7).

20. With the exception of these 3,044 men, the people lived in *Judah*, more precisely, on their ancestral property.

21–24. What is the function of these verses? Apparently, the final redactor had found other lists and had no better place to integrate them than at this point. So these people must not be situated at the same time as those mentioned in verses 4–18.

A first notice contains a remark about the *temple servants*, who in verse 3 were situated in Judah. In this notice, they are mentioned as living on *Ophel*, the mountain south of the temple. They were directed by *Ziha* (Egyptian, '[the god] Horus has spoken') and *Gishpa* (looking at Ezra 2:43 the identity with Hasupha is suggested, but some phonological issues oppose this hypothesis).

If the *Mattaniah* of verse 22 is the same person as the one in verse 17, this list goes on for three more generations, at least fifty years later, that is, around the year 395 (see on 12:10–11), which would be an important indication for the date of the final redaction. Of course, if verses 17 and 22 are just speaking about namesakes, nothing can be concluded about dates.

Uzzi ('[God] is my strength'), belonging to the category of the *singers*, is in this list *the overseer of the Levites*. The *command from the king* is the same as[27] *a fixed provision for the singers*. The phrase *as every day required* (lit. 'of the matter of the day on its day') occurs also in Ezra 3:4. Does this *provision* regard their allowance by *king* Artaxerxes I (465–424; was strongly engaged in the worship of the peoples of the Persian Empire – see Ezra 7:23)? Or does this *provision* regard the schedule of *king* David (not all singers were constantly in office)? Whatever the case, in verse 24 it is about *king* Artaxerxes.

Pethahiah ('the LORD has opened') represented the Jews at the Persian court (Heltzer 1994).

25–30. Another list mentions cities and their *villages* (places without walls: see Lev. 25:31), where the Judahites lived, not necessarily within the 'official' frontiers of Judah, but at quite a

---

27   *Waw* explicativum: GKC §154a n. 1b.

distance from Jerusalem (Dibon, Beersheba, Lachish, Ono, possibly the Valley of Craftsmen), perhaps because their families
had lived there earlier (cf. 7:6; Janzen 2002: 500–507). In any case,
Hadid, Lod and Ono most probably belonged to Samaria (see on
6:1–2; Lemaire 1994: 21). In the south, interference with Idumea
existed.

Unfortunately, many places cannot be located. Even for those
with a description below, localizations are often uncertain. *Kiriath-
arba* (Hebron, 16 miles south of Jerusalem), *Dibon* (probably an
unknown place in the Negev; perhaps the famous city of Moab,
39½ miles south of Amman and 2½ miles north of the Arnon River),
Jekabzeel (7½ miles east of Beersheba), *Jeshua*, *Moladah* (halfway
between Beersheba and the Dead Sea; Lipiński 2006: 399), *Beth-pelet*
(modern Tell el-Farah, 7 miles north-east of Beersheba), *Hazar-shual*
(3 miles east of Beersheba), *Beersheba* (typically the most southern
city of Judah; in the Negev), *Ziklag*, *Meconah*, *En-rimmon* (11 miles
north-east of Beersheba, mentioned in Zech. 14:10 as the most
southern place of the mountains of Judah; van der Woude 1984:
261), *Zorah* (17 miles west of Jerusalem, 2½ miles north of modern
Beth Shemesh, in the Shephelah), *Jarmuth* (3 miles south-west of
modern Beth Shemesh; 16 miles west of Jerusalem), *Zanoah*, *Adullam*
(9 miles north-east of Beth Guvrin), *Lachish* (Shephelah, halfway
between Hebron and Ashkelon) and *Azekah* (just over the frontier
of the region of Ashdod; 5½ miles north-east of Beth Guvrin). All
these places are situated between the south of the city of Jerusalem
(*the* southern *Valley of Hinnom*) and the most southern city of *Beersheba*
(v. 30).

31–36. The Benjaminites stay more within the frontiers of
Judah, more specifically in the north of this region, in the cities
(for most of them see on Ezra 2:20–35) of *Geba* (mentioned as a
northern frontier place in Zech. 14:10), Michmas (as in Ezra 2:27
‖ Neh. 7:31), *Aija* (probably identical with Ai, as in Ezra 2:28 ‖
Neh. 7:32), *Bethel*, *Anathoth*, *Nob*, *Ananiah*, *Hazor* (3½ miles north
of Jerusalem; not the famous city north of the Sea of Galilee),
Ramah, *Gittaim* (25 miles north-west-west of Jerusalem), *Hadid* (3
miles east of Lod), *Zeboim* and *Neballat* (3½ miles north-east of
Lod). It is unclear whether *the valley of craftsmen* (see 1 Chr. 4:14;
craftsmen work with metal or wood: Kreissig 1973: 59) is a place

north of Jerusalem (Keil 1873: 90–91), the region of Ono (Kidner 1979: 121) or a place near Jaffa, on the way to Jerusalem (Noordtzij 1939: 246). Some *Levites* who formerly lived in *Judah* now went to *Benjamin* (Keil 1873: 265); the AV ('And of the Levites were divisions in Judah, and in Benjamin') may seem more logical but is farther removed from the Hebrew.

12:1–7. Another list is inserted, of priests who returned in the year 537, as is indicated clearly both at the beginning (v. 1) and at the end (v. 7), possibly in two subcategories: verses 1b–6a of families still active in the time that is the main theme of these chapters, and verses 6b–7a of families who were no longer active (they are not mentioned in 10:2–8). For the meaning of the names of verses 1b–6a, see on 10:2–8. *Joiarib*: 'the LORD will do justice'; *Jedaiah*: 'the LORD has known (me)'; *Sallu*: 'who has returned'; *Amok*: 'deep'; *Hilkiah*: 'the LORD is my share'.

8–9. Most of these Levites also occur in other lists (see on 8:7; 10:9–13; 12:24–25), but it is not clear what the function of this list is at this point. *Judah* ('praised') may be a variant of Hodiah (8:7; 10:13), even if it is not immediately related. *Unni* ('[God has] answered') is mentioned only here. We may think of a writing error for 'Uzzi', but the person mentioned in 11:22 was active only much later (if our reconstruction of that verse is correct). The first group was responsible for the music; the second group too, but in an assisting role, for antiphonal singing (see on 11:17; 12:24).

10–11. Within the context we receive the impression that the Jeshua of verse 8, a Levite, is now situated in his genealogy. The names of the genealogy, however, are those of the high priests, from the days of the first return to three generations (just as in 11:22) after the reconstruction of the walls. This list is confirmed by several extra-biblical sources. *Jeshua* (see on Ezra 2:1–2) was high priest from 550 to 510 (all dates according to van der Woude 1983: 89; cf. n. 24 at Neh. 3:1); *Joiakim* ('the LORD will raise') was high priest from 510 to 480; *Eliashib* was high priest from 480 to 440 (thus also during the construction of the walls; see on Neh. 3:1); *Joiada* ('the LORD has known [me]') was high priest from 440 to 425; Johanan (high priest from 425 to 390, mentioned for the years shortly before 407 in Cowley 1923: no. 30 l. 18) remains unrecorded in this list (but see on vv. 22–23),[28] which continues with *Jonathan* ('the LORD has given'), Joiada's son, but never a high priest himself (because he was the son-in law of Sanballat? see 13:28; Kidner 1979: 154) and *Jaddua* ('known [by God]'). *Jaddua* must have started his ministry as high priest in about 390 (van der Woude 1983: 89), which then gives an indication for the date of the final redaction of Ezra-Neh. (see Introduction 3a, 'Components and redaction'). For earlier high priests, see on Ezra 7:1b–5.

12–21. Still another list, now with the successors of the priests mentioned in verses 1–7. Family names are mentioned first, and then the name of the individual active during the days of the high priest *Joiakim* (cf. v. 10). *Meraiah* ('the LORD), *Hananiah* ('the LORD has been gracious'), *Meshullam* ('satisfied'), *Jehohanan* ('the LORD is gracious'), *Jonathan* ('the LORD has given'). For Hattush (see v. 2), no successor is mentioned, probably accidentally, as the family was still functioning in the days described in 10:4. *Joseph* ('may [God] add'); *Adna* ('pleasure'); *Helkai* ('[God] is my share'); *Zechariah* ('the LORD has remembered') is the prophet (see *Context* for Ezra 5:1 – 6:15); *Meshullam* ('satisfied'); *Zichri* ('my remembrance'). While *Miniamin* himself is mentioned, accidentally the successor stayed unrecorded. *Piltai* ('deliverance'); *Shammua* ('heard'); *Jehonathan* ('the LORD has given'). Then starts the part of the list with the priests who had no successors in the days of 10:1–8 (see above on vv. 1–7): *Mattenai* ('gift of the LORD'); *Uzzi* ('my strength'); *Kallai* (unexplained); *Eber* ('from the other side'; some manuscripts and the LXX read 'Ebed', '[God's] servant'); *Hashabiah* ('the LORD has thought'); *Nethanel* ('God has given').

22–23. For *the Levites* an official registration was made from the middle of the fifth to the beginning of the fourth century, one

---

28 It is suggested that 'Johanan' and *Jonathan* refer to the same person according to Ockham's razor – 'Numquam ponenda est pluralitas sine necessitate'; but in fact there is some necessity to see two persons here. Even if we were to condone the difference of the names themselves in v. 11 and v. 23 as a scribal error (a same confusion between these names [not these persons!] is hinted at in the Babylonian Talmud, Shabbat 54b), we have different biographies.

long period[29] (cf. vv. 10–11). The expression *in the reign of Darius the Persian* is unclear, for two reasons. In the first place, the preposition translated *in* is normally translated 'on' (including 'for the sake of'; Becking 2018: 304) or possibly 'until'. In the second place, more than one *Darius* was a *Persian* king. This leads us to the main options: *priests* had been registered (1) 'because of Darius' kingdom' (i.e. since Darius I, who reigned from 522 to 486, also in the days of the reconstruction of the temple); (2) 'until Darius' *reign*' (i.e. until Darius II, who reigned from 424 to 405). The family *heads* were registered in the temple *Chronicles* (the same word as used for the Bible book Chronicles), until the time of the high priest *Johanan*, Eliashib's son and Joiada's brother, who was in charge from 425 to 390.

24–26. This list first presents the leaders of the *Levites* in *the days of Joiakim* (high priest from 510 to 480) and *in the days*[30] *of Nehemiah* (largely 445–425) and *Ezra* (458–457 and 445–444), so taken together the middle of the fifth century: *Hashabiah* ('the LORD has thought'); *Sherebiah* ('the LORD has heated', i.e. born on a hot day); *Jeshua* ('the LORD has saved'); and probably Binnui and Kadmiel (lost from the members of the list through misreading 'Binnui' as 'son of'; the difference in Hebrew is small; cf. v. 8 and 10:9). *Their brothers* who assisted them in singing antiphonally (cf. v. 9) are not mentioned. For *the commandment of David*, see 1 Chronicles 6:31–32; 16:4; 23:30; 2 Chronicles 29:25. The expression *the man of God* characterizes David as a prophet (Boda 2010: 279; cf. Lorein 2022: 28).

The list continues with *Mattaniah* ('gift of the LORD'), *Bakbukiah* ('flask of the LORD'), *Obadiah* ('servant of the LORD'), *Meshullam* ('satisfied'), *Talmon* ('bright') and *Akkub* ('protected'), who guarded *the storehouses* situated within *the gates* (see on 10:38).

---

29 Because it is one (long) period, the phrase *in the days of* is not repeated in v. 22; cf. Isa. 1:1 (Joüon and Muraoka 2006: §129b; *pace* Steinmann 2010: 579).

30 The phrase *in the days* of is repeated in v. 26 (as in v. 47) because two different periods are meant (Joüon and Muraoka 2006: §129b).

Meaning

The genealogies show again that we do not speak about an unorganized band, but about people with a structure and a history: organization and archives are important. The history of the main characters and changes is here somehow balanced by mentioning extended lists (Kidner 1979: 117, 121). These lists underline again the importance of individuals, within their families (without denying the possibility of God starting new lines of grace; Exod. 20:6: '[I, the LORD, am] showing steadfast love to thousands of those who love me and keep my commandments'). Through the mention of place names, it is also clear that these things really happened. Christians have a spiritual message grounded in God's acting in concrete situations.

On the other hand, while a well-documented genealogy was necessary for Old Testament priests and Levites, this is no longer necessary in the New Testament: not for priests, Levites or believers in general. The way is open.

iii. Dedication of the wall (12:27–43)

Context

Although no date is mentioned the dedication must have taken place sometime in 444, in order to create enough time for the migration (see *Context* for 11:1–2) and to make preparations (12:27–30), and possibly during winter. Perhaps this interval is also suggested by the insertion of the lists at this point.

The idea of winter is often based on 2 Maccabees 1:18 (e.g. De Fraine 1961: 129; cf. 1 Maccabees 4:36, 54), but this text is at least not completely trustworthy (see Introduction 4f, 'The afterlife of Ezra-Neh. in Antiquity'); it is applied in the interpretation of verses 28–29 and verses 40–42. In this way we arrive nevertheless at a realistic hypothesis.

A clear disadvantage of this chronological reconstruction is the lapse of time between the end of the work on the walls and their dedication. Of course some preparation time is needed, but so long? This drawback can be met if we do not think of the winter as being at the end of the year 444, but at the beginning.

Comment

27–29. Only when an optimized habitation of Judah has been arranged can time be given to the official *dedication of the wall* of Jerusalem. The word *dedication* was also used for 'the dedication of this house of God' at the end of part 1, in Ezra 6:16–17; earlier the word appeared for the dedication of the tabernacle (Num. 7:10, 11, 84, 88) and the dedication of the first temple (2 Chr. 7:9; Ps. 30:1); a Greek equivalent will appear, with the same musical instruments, in 1 Maccabees 4:36, 54 at the rededication of the temple after its desecration by Antiochus IV Epiphanes, 14 December 164, the basis of the Jewish Hanukkah festival. What is prepared in these verses will eventually be carried out in verse 43. *The Levites* were sought *to celebrate the dedication with gladness*, literally 'to make a dedication and joy', a hendiadys (see Introduction 4g, 'Literary terms') generally accepted in English versions. The next words may also form a hendiadys (NIV 'with songs of thanksgiving') but here such a literary device is not applied in most English versions. It is not problematic that now all *singers* are brought together in *Jerusalem* (contrary to the rule hinted at in 11:23), because in winter less agricultural work needs to be done.

For *cymbals*, see on Ezra 3:10. *Harps* are stringed instruments with a resonance body in the form of a pot and with curved yoke arms, easy to place on the ground, and with a rather large number of strings (made of sheep's gut; Keel 1972: 324–325). *Lyres* (Hebr. *kinnôr*) are stringed instruments with a smaller resonance body and almost straight yoke arms, portable, and with a smaller number of strings (made of bird's gut). Even though the same name for *district* occurs in 3:22, it is now specified by *surrounding Jerusalem* and so can be situated within a short distance. *The villages of the Netophathites* may be found 7½ miles south of Jerusalem (cf. Ezra 2:22). *Beth-gilgal* is situated 12½ miles from Jerusalem, not far from Jericho; *Geba* 6 miles north of Jerusalem; *Azmaveth* 5 miles north-east of Jerusalem.

30. See Exodus 19:14–15 for the purification of *people*, Numbers 19:18 for that of constructions.

31–37. The starting point of the processions is located to the south of the city, probably at the Valley Gate (if not, this important gate would not be mentioned at all; see Introduction 2k, 'Jerusalem'), near Nehemiah's house (Simons 1952: 445, 447). There it must have been possible to get on top of the wall. The wall was wide enough to have three persons walking side by side (vom Orde 1997: 289). The two processions are equivalent, both counting officials, priests and levitical musicians.

The Hebrew of verse 31b is elliptic ('and I made stand two big thanksgivings and processions to the right on the wall to the Dung Gate'), needing to be filled in by translations. The first procession, under Ezra's direction (v. 36b), went anticlockwise, for some yards to the south-east, then to the east by the *Dung Gate* (the Refuse Gate) and then to the north by the *Fountain Gate* and the steps to where in earlier days David's palace was situated (south of Ophel) until the *Water Gate* (cf. Simons 1952: 449–450). At that moment, they had not yet arrived at the temple, but apparently from that point on they just went through the city to the temple. Probably it was too dangerous to continue on the wall, considering the important difference in height from the eastern side.

Even though many names have been mentioned before, we have never seen the same group. *Hoshaiah*: 'the LORD has saved' as leading layperson; *Azariah*: 'the LORD has helped'; *Ezra*: '(God's) help'; *Meshullam*: 'satisfied'; *Judah*: 'praise'; *Benjamin*: 'right-hand son'; *Shemaiah*: 'the LORD has heard'; *Jeremiah*: 'the LORD has founded'. Other priests went with *trumpets* (or rather, 'clarions'; see on Ezra 3:10): *Zechariah* ('the LORD has remembered') as leading musical priest, *Shemaiah* ('the LORD has heard'), *Azarel* ('God has helped'), *Milalai* ('the LORD has spoken'?), *Gilalai* ('the LORD has committed'?), *Maai* (unexplained), *Nethanel* ('God has given'), *Judah* ('praise') and *Hanani* ('[God] is gracious'). *The musical instruments of David* were probably (see 1 Chr. 25:1) cymbals, harps and lyres (cf. v. 27).

38–39. The second choir went clockwise, along a longer but much easier track. Here the leading layperson is Nehemiah (*I*). They *went to the north* (thus ESV, factually correct and with only one letter different from the Hebrew text, which has 'in the opposite direction', as NET and NIV have) by the south-western extremity of the city, *the Tower of the Ovens* (see on 3:11), *the Broad Wall* and *the gate of Ephraim* (apparently considered as a whole), *the Gate of* the old city (see on 3:6), *the Fish Gate* (see on 3:3), *the Tower of Hananel and the Tower of the Hundred* (see on 3:1). At the latest at *the Sheep Gate* they must have come down from the wall *and they came to a halt at the Gate* *of the Guard* (the Muster Gate, see on 3:31), where the two groups met each other.

40–42. Now the group who went with Nehemiah is specified: *the priests Eliakim* ['God will raise'], *Maaseiah* ['works of the LORD'], *Miniamin* ['from the right hand'], *Micaiah* ['who is as the LORD?'], *Elioenai* ['my eyes are on the LORD'], *Zechariah* ['the LORD has remembered'], *and Hananiah* ['the LORD has been gracious'], with clarions (see on Ezra 3:10); probably with other instruments (cf. v. 36) the priests *Maaseiah* ['works of the LORD'], *Shemaiah* ['the LORD has heard'], *Eleazar* ['God has helped'], *Uzzi* ['(God is) my strength'], *Jehohanan* ['the LORD has been gracious'], *Malchijah* ['the LORD is my king'], *Elam* ['(coming from) Elam'], *and Ezer* ['(God is my) help']; and lastly the *singers* with *Jezrahiah* ('the LORD will appear') as leading musical priest.

Psalm 147 is often mentioned as very appropriate for this occasion (Ps. 147:2 referring to the building of the walls, v. 13 referring to Neh. 7:3 and vv. 16–18 being congruent with the season of the dedication; cf. Delitzsch 1871: 397–399, 402), but its use here must remain hypothetical.

43. The existing positive atmosphere – after all the preparations – is now underlined by the fivefold use of the stem for 'joy' (*rejoiced … made rejoice … joy … rejoiced … joy*). *Great sacrifices* befit God's greatness (Becking 2018: 310). The *sacrifices* were *offered* by the priests: the layperson Nehemiah kept the proper distance (differently from Uzziah's behaviour in 2 Chr. 26:16–18; cf. Duguid 2012: 266). Mention of the wives' presence seems to highlight the importance of the gathering, as in Ezra 10:1; Nehemiah 8:2–3; 10:28–29 (Williams 2002: 64). The volume of the rejoicing had the same effect as in Ezra 3:13, but this time no weeping is mentioned.

Meaning

The importance of an official celebration, with a large group of participants, a concrete programme and music, is made clear in this unit. It leads to joy (see v. 43; cf. 8:10, 17). The joy is not empty: it follows on from the confession of sin (Neh. 9) and commitments (Neh. 10). The whole celebration leads also to another commitment (see the next unit). All this cannot be achieved without proper preparation (vv. 27–30).

iv. Arrangements for the temple service (12:44–47)
Context
Even though far-reaching references are given in verses 46–47, the actual setting must have an immediate relation (*On that day*, v. 44) with the dedication of the wall.

Comment
44. The positive atmosphere must be consolidated. *The storerooms* were situated within the temple complex (see on 10:38). For the *contributions*, see on Ezra 8:25. The need to pay for *the priests and for the Levites* is realized. This happened *according to* the potential of *the fields*.

45. For *the singers and the gatekeepers*, see on Ezra 7:7–9. *The command of David and his son Solomon* is not mentioned explicitly anywhere. For *Solomon*, see on 13:26.

46. In this verse the Hebrew consonantal text has the singular (AV 'chief'), but the Masoretes wanted to read[31] the plural (ESV *directors*). Although the combination *songs of praise* generally occurs in English translations (and in the BBC programme *Songs of Praise*), the Hebrew has the singular.

47. This verse speaks about quite different periods: *the days of Zerubbabel* (mid sixth century; see on Ezra 2:2) and *the days of Nehemiah* (mid fifth century), but the action remains the same: they continued to give and to set apart.[32] For the contribution of the *Levites* to the priests, see on 10:38.

Meaning
Ultimately, not much has happened in this section: earlier decisions have been worked out (for which some lists were needed) and a ceremony has been celebrated. At the same time, we should realize the importance of 'practical arrangements' (people changing their living circumstances) and celebrations, which can have a lasting impression on those who participate.

---

31 Cf. Ezra 2:43–54, n. 25; Ezra 3:7, n. 31.
32 This is also indicated by the participle.

Practical arrangements make it clear that in addition to a certain benevolence some structural measures are necessary in order to perpetuate good intentions.

The Torah led the people to a consciousness of their limitations, but also to community building (absolute liberty cannot give that) and joy. These things are important enough to spend money on salaried church personnel (Becking 2018: 240).

5. CODA: RECALCITRANT REALITY (13:1–31)

Until now, no repartition has been proposed that puts this chapter in a nice literary structure. We might think of a structure that starts with Zerubbabel, who is a little bit alone, and ends with a coda which does not have the same ingredients as parts one to four.

A		Part 1	*Zerubbabel* arrives	Ezra 2 (537)
	B	Part 2	Ezra arrives	Ezra 7 (458)
		C	Part 3	Nehemiah arrives	Neh. 2 (445)
	B'	Part 4	Ezra returns	Neh. 8 (445)
		C'	*Coda*	Nehemiah returns	Neh. 13 (430)

This section actually describes six incidents that occurred after the happy ending of the procession (12:27–43) and the introduction of the contribution system agreed upon in Nehemiah 10 (12:44–47). Chronologically it is situated in the right place (explained by v. 6), but it makes the story end in a minor key: we are still living in an imperfect world (cf. *Meaning* for 13:1–3). The six incidents are all related to aspects treated earlier in Nehemiah 10:

- lack of obedience to God's Word (vv. 1–3; cf. 10:28–29);
- Tobiah's office in the temple (vv. 4–9; cf. 10:37–39);
- poor payment for the Levites (vv. 10–14; cf. 10:32–37);
- disturbance of Sabbath rest (vv. 15–22; cf. 10:31);
- non-Jewish education of the children (vv. 23–27; cf. 10:28, 30)
- desecration of the priesthood (vv. 28–29; cf. 10:28–30).

For this chapter, Nehemiah's memoirs are used.

A. Lack of obedience to God's Word (13:1–3)

Context
Probably all six incidents took place after Nehemiah's visit to the Persian court, that is, after the year 430, with antecedents in the period 433 to 430.

These six incidents form the last piece of history described in the Old Testament. What is described in the book of Malachi must be situated between Nehemiah 12 and Nehemiah 13. While the redaction of Chronicles is later, the facts described in it are not.

For the first incident, the expression *On that day* does not offer a precise context (see on v. 1).

Comment
1–2. *On that day* (not necessarily a precise indication, according to Kidner 1979: 128), reading was performed[1] *from the Book of Moses* [see on 8:1] *in the hearing* [lit. 'in the ears'] *of the people*. The *Book* must have had quite a large extent because they seem to have been surprised about an item that *was found written*; most probably this was what we now call the Pentateuch. Reference is made to Deuteronomy 23:3–6. We do not find a story about the Ammonites being unwilling to sell *food and water*; certain elements are found about the Edomites in Numbers 20:17–21. The story about the Moabites hiring Balaam against the Israelites is mentioned in Numbers 22 – 24. Because two different peoples are meant, the translation *they did not meet ...*

---

1   Impersonal Niphal. Cf. Gen. 17:17; Isa. 53:5 in the light of Joüon and
    Muraoka 2006: §152f–fa; *pace* Steinmann 2010: 596). Cf. Vulg. and LXX.

but [they][2] *hired* is not correct: the Ammonites did not meet, and the Moabites hired. Both peoples traced their origin to Lot and his daughters (Gen. 19:36–38; Deut. 2:9, 19). The last phrase (*our God turned the curse into a blessing*) also comes from Deuteronomy 23:5.

3. While this subject matter was treated earlier (cf. Ezra 9 – 10; Neh. 10:30), the people seem here to discover the principle anew. Scripture reading brought them to *separate ... all* of 'mixed form', perhaps 'syncretists', *from Israel*, as earlier in the religious sense, that is, 'the believers'). The idea of 'mixed form' is too easily translated by *those of foreign descent*; the word also occurs in Exodus 12:38, where it might be used in a positive way – for a sort of proselyte – but not necessarily so (see Cole 1973: 113; Houtman 1986: 141). It is not clear which form it took on this occasion. No action of the leaders is mentioned here.

Meaning
It would have been nice if our text had ended at 12:47 (or 12:43), but the redactor keeps himself to reality – as always in Scripture – and so a coda follows. Even though Ezra and Nehemiah have done their utmost and people's willingness was genuine at a certain moment, acquisitions were never definitive. We can consider this as a comfort for us when the same happens in our own lives or in the life of the church around us. We have, indeed, no room for optimism in that sense. Our optimism is grounded rather in God's presence through all difficulties. That can also be our reason to continue to strive for biblical ideals, especially at moments when they are far from attained.

According to Bedford 2002: 150, these verses are about stopping infiltration from a foreign cult. Blenkinsopp (2017: 192–195, 200) sees them as excommunication in order to restore the balance of largeness and strictness proper to the Judeo-Christian faith. The prohibition is based on Deuteronomy 23:3–6, but it is clear that stable principles are applied with consideration for the actual

---

2   Actually third-person singular, referring to the king (see Num. 22:4–6). The other side is also third-person singular, referring to Israel (Steinmann 2010: 596–597).

situation (Lorein 2008: 148–149; Zehnder 2018: 8). What we read in these verses is not the full story, but apparently this reaction was needed with these individuals.[3]

B. Tobiah's office in the temple (13:4–9)

Context
This incident occurred already before the one of verses 1–3 (see v. 4). It is in this unit that Nehemiah's return to King Artaxerxes is mentioned, from 433 to 430 (see Introduction 2e, 'Persian kings').

Comment
4–5. It is often said that *Eliashib* was a namesake of the high priest, because his function is not mentioned, and the high priest would not work on the organization of the temple in person (e.g. Williamson 1985: 386). On the other hand, we must remember that many things are said to have been done by the king, while he had only ordered those things or even just agreed to them. *Eliashib … was appointed over the chambers,*[4] that is, the storerooms of the temple (see on 10:38). He *was related to Tobiah*, not necessarily as a kinsman. *Tobiah* has been mentioned earlier (2:10, 19; 4:3, 7; 6:1, 12, 14), never with a positive attitude towards the Judeans. In any case, an office on the temple premises is not suited for someone with this reputation, even though there would be no problem of space, in view of the lack of contributions.

The grain offering, normally[5] stored in these rooms, is a sacrifice of flour in combination with *oil* and *frankincense* (see Lev. 2:1) often accompanied by a drink offering of *wine* (Num. 15:4–10) (Averbeck

---

3 Indeed not everything the Bible describes is approved by that mere fact, but Ulrich's (2021: 151) suggestion that the reaction was wrong gives too much place to an unsupported interpretation.

4 The Hebrew reads a singular. It is perhaps too easy simply to change it into a plural. Here the word needs rather to be interpreted as a collective, as 'he was appointed over the accommodation … and prepared large accommodation'.

5 As indicated by the participle.

1997a: 983; 1997b: 1020). For the handling of offerings at the temple, see on 10:37–39.

6–7. For the characterization of *Artaxerxes* as *king of Babylon*, see on Ezra 5:13; perhaps this description is triggered by the fact that the king was residing in Babylon at that very moment. We speak about the year 433 (see 5:14; possibly, if it was at the end of *the thirty-second year*, in 432). The text does not mention why Nehemiah *went to the king* and so only guesses are possible. Noordtzij (1939: 260) suggests Nehemiah thought he had brought his mission to a good end; Batten (1913: 291), with reference to some LXX manuscripts,[6] that his term as governor was over. *After some time* he *asked* for permission for himself[7] to go back *to Jerusalem*, apparently again with large powers, if not as governor. Unfortunately, when exactly Nehemiah returned to Jerusalem is not mentioned. It is generally accepted that he was absent for some years. Only in that way can the regression[8] in Jerusalem be explained. We also have a historical parallel: the satrap of Egypt was called back by King Darius II at the court from 411 to 408 (Yamauchi 1990: 246). That Persian kings took their time is also illustrated by the duration of visits by foreign delegations to the Persian court (Hofstetter 1972: 101). We conclude that 430 was the year of Nehemiah's return to Jerusalem, where he probably stayed until 425 (Briant 2002: 585).

8. Udjahorresnet (for whom see on v. 31b) did the same in an Egyptian temple (albeit not with furniture but with foreigners), including a consequent purification (Naoforo Vaticano ll.18–21; Posener 1936: 15, 167, 169–170). See also John 2:13–17.

---

6 After *I went to the king*, the Lucianic recension (represented in a few MSS) adds 'eis to kairon tôn hèmerôn hôn ètèsamèn para tou basileôs', interpreted as 'at the expiration date of the days I had asked permission for from the king', but this seems to be a doublet (thus also Janz 2010: 333) and probably there was no fixed date at the start (see on 2:6).

7 Niphal with the meaning of 'for oneself': GKC §51e.

8 Perhaps it was a conscious action by those who were opposed to Nehemiah's reforms. Thus Fitzpatrick-McKinley 2016: 170, 172.

9. While Tobiah had used only one office, several *chambers* need to be cleansed. Impurity is – alas – contagious, as is also illustrated in Haggai 2:10–19.

Meaning
It seems that Nehemiah gives much attention to outward appearances. We have to keep in mind, however, that in a time when belonging to Israel physically was no longer the criterion, it needed to be clear who belonged to Israel spiritually. The idea of being clearly Christian is also put forward in the New Testament, even though there some of the externalities have been dropped (cf. 2 Cor. 3:3). Ultimately, this gives us a larger task to discern what really matters. We find an example in this unit: to let out a surplus room in the church building is not forbidden, but what is really holy cannot be frittered away for lucre.

C. Poor payment for the Levites (13:10–14)

Context
The third incident also has its origin during the period when Nehemiah was staying at the Persian court.

Comment
   10. Nehemiah *found out*[9] that the whole system had collapsed: contributions (see on Ezra 8:25) were no longer given and the persons in charge *had fled* to their private business. The fact that the tribe of Levi did not have a tribal territory (Deut. 18:2) does not exclude the possibility of land being owned by Levites (Thompson 1974: 207–208). The priests were less hindered by the lack of tithes because they also received a part of the sacrifices (Steinmann 2010: 607).
   11. What is here translated by *I confronted* should have been translated 'I brought charges against', as in 5:7. For the *officials*, see on Ezra 9:2. Apparently, in spite of the sincere enthusiasm depicted

---

9 Lit. 'began to know', inchoative of *y-d-ʿ*, 'to know'. Hence, NIV 'learned'.

in Nehemiah 8 – 10, strong leadership is needed, especially when we realize that the combination of all the royal taxes and temple contributions indeed constituted a heavy burden (Briant 2002: 585). Nehemiah *gathered* the Levites *and set them* again *in their stations*, even before the problem of the tithes was solved (see next verse). Sometimes you have to arrange things before all conditions are met.

12. Now *Judah* does again what it ought to do. Since Tobiah no longer occupied the room intended for the tithes (see vv. 5–9), this could be done without any problem.

13. Nehemiah installed a well-balanced bookkeeping department: *Shelemiah* ['the LORD has given satisfaction'] *the priest, Zadok* ['(God is) righteous'] *the scribe* [Ezra was not the only scribe and operated on a different level from this committee], *and Pedaiah* ['the LORD has saved'] *of the Levites. Hanan* ('[God has been] gracious') is joined to the team as a general *assistant* (lit. 'at their hand'), so probably it was he who did the work, while the others formed rather a board of supervisors/trustees (Becking 2018: 320). The trustworthiness of these four persons is essential.

14. For the general meaning of this verse, see on 5:19. Here the usual addition 'for good' is lacking. The translation 'my acts of loyal love' (Kidner 1979: 130) makes it easier to understand that the Hebrew word for *good deeds* is the same as the one translated in, for example, Ezra 3:11 by 'steadfast love', because in that verse it refers to God's loyalty. For material writing, 'wiping out'[10] text was possible on clay as well as on papyrus, so the image for this immaterial book must have been clear. In Hebrew we have the same verb as in 4:5 (some translations use 'blotted out', others use the same translation in both places). The correspondence with Malachi 3:16 is striking (cf. Ps. 139:16; Isa. 65:6; Dan. 7:10; Rev. 20:12; on the other hand, Exod. 32:32; Ps. 69:29 [ET 28; both texts with the same term as in this passage!]; Ezek. 13:9; Dan. 12:1; Luke 10:20; Phil. 4:3; Rev. 20:15 seem to speak about election, not about particular deeds).

---

10 The form *temaḥ*, a Hiphil jussive second-person masculine singular from *m-ḥ-h* (probably *tamḥ* > *temeḥ* [Lettinga and von Siebenthal 2016: §58P/565] > *temaḥ* [influenced by guttural]).

Meaning

We may conclude from these verses that the appointment of different people in charge of material matters (here the storerooms, v. 13) reduces the possibility of corruption, which is often the basis of a malfunctioning society and much discontent and instability. And of course, every individual should be trustworthy (cf. 1 Cor. 4:2 on the spiritual level).

Even though in rabbinic literature Nehemiah is blamed for the prayer in verse 14 – as if he boasted of his deeds – we can read this prayer as the testimony of a conscience that we can present our deeds to God only in full dependence on his grace (see on 5:19) and of a votive offering of our professional life (Mathys 2015: 356).

D. Disturbance of Sabbath rest (13:15–22)

Context

The fourth incident is situated at the time of the grape harvest, in October (Dalman 1928: 162), but without reference to a specific year.

Comment

15. Nehemiah did not limit himself to Jerusalem but also visited the countryside. Heavy labour is mentioned here, especially *treading wine presses*, hewn out in the rock, in order to get the wine (normally red wine; Dalman 1935: 369–370) out of the grapes with one's bare feet. The forms *treading*, *bringing* and *loading* indicate that this happened repeatedly (Becking 2018: 322).

16. *Tyrians* came from Tyre (Noonan 2011: 282 stresses the fact that we should not translate 'Phoenicians' here) on the Mediterranean coast in Phoenicia, present-day Lebanon, and were active everywhere in Cisjordan (Lemaire 2015: 35) and were thus living *in the city* (as explained by ESV, i.e. Jerusalem; 'Judah', however, is also an option: Kreissig 1973: 69). In their quality as seafarers and traders they traded especially in *fish*, an important food in the Jewish kitchen (cf. Lev. 11:9; Num. 11:5; Brown 1998: 237). It must be noted that Nehemiah did not address the Tyrians directly, because they were not under Sabbath law; nor was trading with them as such problematic (Altmann 2015: 116).

17–18. These verses start with the same verb as that in verse 11, which again should be translated by 'I brought charges against'. For the *nobles*, see on 2:16. Already early in his ministry Jeremiah had warned against working on *the Sabbath day* (Jer. 17:20–23, 27). But despite the lessons of the destruction of Jerusalem, the importance of consecration of the Sabbath in Egypt some fifty years earlier and the agreement of 10:31 (see there), people lapsed into their old patterns when they regained a safe life in Jerusalem. This stressing of the people's continual sinning occurs often: not only here and in 9:34 but also in Ezra 9:7; 1 Kings 8:46–47; Psalms 78:8, 17, 32; 106:6; Jeremiah 3:25; Lamentations 5:7; Daniel 9:5, 15–16.

19. This verse starts a new phase of the affair (AV: 'And it came to pass'), with Nehemiah passing from persuasion to obligation (as often in this chapter). Nehemiah had concluded that, even though the Sabbath rules strictly speaking were applicable only to the Jews, he needed to make them compulsory for everyone if he was to obtain any practical results (see on 10:31) and avoid unfair competition for the Jews (Williamson 1985: 395; Altmann 2015: 113–114).

Even though the exact translation of the expression at the start of this verse is unclear,[11] we can say generally that *it began to grow dark at the gates* and so officially *the Sabbath* was about to start, because festive days were also observed on the evening of the preceding day (Cassuto 1961: 28–30).

20. *The merchants* hoped to be able to continue their work immediately *outside Jerusalem.*

21. Nehemiah does not want to act without warning that he would *lay hands on* them (the same expression as in Esth. 8:7)[12] and apparently that was impressive enough to be effective.

---

11 The *gates of Jerusalem* forms the grammatical subject (cf. AV: 'when the gates of Jerusalem began to be dark'), but the verb seems to be related to 'shadow' (cf. NET: 'When the evening shadows began to fall on the gates of Jerusalem'). Moreover, it is possible that it did not become dark *within* the gates, but that the gates *threw* ever-longer shadows so that it became dark (cf. Vergil, *Eclogae* 1.83: 'longer fall the shadows from the hill heights'; my translation). For the inchoative aspect ('began to'), see Cook 2012: 191–192.

12 To express the laying on of hands for blessing, the Hebrew uses another verb.

22a. For *the Levites*, working on *the Sabbath day* in order to keep it *holy* was part of their duty (Steinmann 2010: 610).

22b. Here we find one of Nehemiah's short prayers; see on 5:19.

Meaning
We see that before using his governor powers, Nehemiah started by repeating the teaching of olden times (vv. 17–18), which can be the most efficient way (Altmann 2015: 115). When problems continue to exist by people not complying with convened rules, drastic measures may be necessary, but always starting with self-evaluation (see e.g. Matt. 7:3–5 ‖ Luke 6:41–42) and warnings (see Matt. 18:15–16), applying strict procedures (see e.g. John 7:51) and never with self-willed action (see e.g. Acts 15:2). Nehemiah seems to have become tired (v. 22b). Nehemiah's reaction teaches us that when we are tired, we can pray to God for lighter burdens (or stronger shoulders).

E. Non-Jewish education of the children (13:23–27)

Context
The fifth incident is related to the first one. See the *Context* for 13:1–3.

Comment
23–24. If the children spoke only Ashdodite (spoken west of Judah, on the Mediterranean coast), we can conclude that they had had no religious education. Because the children were able to speak, there must be a certain distance in time vis-à-vis the promises of Nehemiah 10. The mention of *the language of each people* implies that the children of Ammonite women spoke only Ammonite and the children of Moabite women only Moabite. This may not have been so problematic, as Ammonite (spoken around what is nowadays Amman) and Moabite (spoken east of the Dead Sea) were also Semitic – more precisely Canaanite – languages, not too distant from Hebrew (here referred to as *the language of Judah*: cf. 2 Kgs 18:26, 28 ‖ 2 Chr. 32:18 ‖ Isa. 36:11, 13), but nevertheless really different (Lipiński 2001: §7.7–8). What can be said about Ashdodite is purely hypothetical. Lemaire 1995: 158–162 supposes that in spite of the Indo-European origin of the Philistines in the second millennium,

their language in Nehemiah's time was also (as for Ammonite and Moabite) a variant of Canaanite.

25. After having seen (v. 23) and heard (v. 24), Nehemiah brought charges (see on vv. 11, 17) against the men (clearly masculine in Hebrew – the women and still less the children cannot be held responsible for this). For *cursed*, see on 10:29. The action of beating and pulling out hair was a usual humiliating Persian sanction (see, however, also Isa. 50:6). At a given moment, Artaxerxes I, Nehemiah's king, replaced it by a symbolic act, probably reserved for the higher classes (Stolper 1997: 347–350). Often reference is made to Ezra, who pulled hair from his own head (Ezra 9:3), followed by the conclusion that Nehemiah had a worse character than Ezra. Generally, however, the person of Nehemiah gives us the impression of someone with a much more retiring character than Ezra. We should also take into account that this chapter is situated – even though we do not know in exactly which year – after Ezra's actions described in Ezra 9 – 10 and after the agreement mentioned in Nehemiah 10:30. Teaching and agreements have thus been in vain, which can explain Nehemiah's vehement reaction. It must be stressed that this verse is not speaking about separating from actual partners (as in Ezra 10), but about a promise concerning the coming generation (as in Neh. 10:30).

At the end of this verse two constructions are mixed: it starts *I made them swear* ('that they should not give their daughters' or 'we shall not give our daughters') and continues with (I told them:) *You shall not give your daughters*. The grammatical problem does not impair our understanding of the verse.

26. It is typical for biblical historiography that in one single sentence both someone's importance and faults are mentioned, from both a divine and a human perspective, that is, in the fullness of reality. Nehemiah's reference to Solomon would be meaningless if Solomon was not a historical figure (see on 12:45). For God loving Solomon, see 2 Samuel 12:24–25; for Solomon's sinning, see 1 Kings 11:4–8.

27. This verse speaks again (as does Ezra 10:2–3) about making strange (see on Neh. 9:2) *women* dwell with them (not a marriage!). For acting *treacherously*, the same root is used as with 'faithlessness' in Ezra 9:2.

Meaning
Whereas Nehemiah in different respects corresponded with King Solomon (leader of the army, building activities, temple administration, jurisdiction and diplomatic contacts – even though the problems mentioned clearly show that he was not completely successful), he was still closer to the ideal of Israel's king as described in Deuteronomy 17:15–20 (a Judean, with only functional horses, his opinion about marriage, use of his own properties, his knowledge of the Law and the common obligation to keep the Law). Nevertheless, even though Nehemiah exercised functions like a king, he clearly was not a king,[13] but rather a quietist, convinced that God was able to work provisionally through the Persian kings and their system. This did not mean that he did not see any need for improvement (for some drastic measures taken, see *Meaning* for 13:15–22). Nevertheless, while working in gratitude, he stressed the need for obedience to God's Law while awaiting his sovereign intervention (cf. Duguid 2012: 263–269; Karrer 2021: 110–116).

F. Desecration of the priesthood (13:28–29)

Context
Even though the sixth incident is immediately related to the previous one, it need not have taken place at the same time.

Comment
28. A grandson of *Eliashib the high priest* was married to a daughter of *Sanballat*, who had given so much trouble to Nehemiah (see 2:19). For the identification of Eliashib's grandson, see on 12:10–11. The priests (probably as well as the rest of the aristocracy) were not too happy with Nehemiah's approach to marriages, because in this way they were separated from the neighbours' elites and thus from means of influence (Schaper 2000: 241). Power was more important to them than good religious family life. This parting of the ways between power-oriented priests and the pious population continued

---

13   Some kind of continuity existed nevertheless, an idea welcomed by the Hasmoneans (Duguid 2012: 268; Fitzpatrick-McKinley 2016: 194).

in history with the Hasidim (third century BC) and later on with the Pharisees (non-priestly) and the Qumran Community (priestly, but separated from the Jerusalem temple; also second century BC), with all its consequences in New Testament times (Lorein 2016: 303–307).

Most translations have *I chased him*, but also possible is 'I made him flee from me', which ends with the same result. According to Steinmann (2010: 611), this must be interpreted as a banishment from Judah, in order to avoid the risk that this son might possibly become high priest, in opposition to the commandment of Leviticus 21:14.

Although not explaining this Bible passage, it is useful to mention here that probably about a century later another Sanballat was involved with a high priest Jaddus (Josephus, *Ant.* 11.302–303, 306–312). Despite elements common to both stories, the two Sanballats should not be confused,[14] and neither should Jaddua in 12:11 be confused with this Jaddus.

29. For Nehemiah the attitude of Eliashib and Jehoiada is clearly unacceptable. Nevertheless, it was tough for Nehemiah, otherwise this prayer would not have been necessary. Probably reference is made to the *covenant* of Numbers 25:11–13 (van Eeken 2002: 66–67). For the prayer, see on 6:14.

Meaning
Even though every act of corruption is serious, it has a leveraging effect with people who have a responsibility to lead within the church (cf. Steinmann 2010: 612).

G. Final verses (13:30–31)

Context
Although verses 30–31a are sometimes interpreted as Nehemiah's summary of his realizations (Bedford 2002: 157), it would have been strange in that case to leave unmentioned the construction of the walls. So it is better to consider this action as a new measure in order to safeguard the Levites' position (cf. vv. 10–12; Schaper 2000:

---

14 See on 2:10 (n. 13).

245) and thus as a consequence of incidents that occurred during Nehemiah's visit to the royal court.

Comment

30–31a. Nehemiah *cleansed … priests* as well as *Levites* (both groups mentioned somewhat later in the sentence) *from everything foreign* (see on 9:2). Nehemiah *established the duties* and organized provision *for the wood offering … and for the firstfruits* (see 10:34–35). *Priests and Levites* should not be contrasted too much.

31b. See on 14. For Mathys (2015: 326, 353, 356, 362), with this prayer Nehemiah placed himself into the centre, thus making the book of Nehemiah into a votive inscription, not written in stone on the temple walls but written in a form that could be copied, so that Nehemiah's prayer is not just kept once in a museum (as is the 519 BC entreaty of Udjahorresnet, the Egyptian physician of the Persian king Cambyses [Posener 1936: 1–2,166], which ends with: 'O great gods at Sais, remember all the meritorious things the chief medical officer Udjahorresnet has done, and may you then do for him every useful thing and solidly establish his good reputation in this country for ever';[15] Naoforo Vaticano ll.47–48) but in innumerable Bibles, even though Nehemiah and Udjahorresnet lived in similar circumstances, sandwiched between the Persian king and the interests of their own people. This is undoubtedly an interesting reconstruction but mixes up how things went historically and what at the outset was Nehemiah's intention.

Meaning

For the idea of Nehemiah as a king, see *Meaning* for 13:23–27.

Final question: did the exile produce a better attitude among the Judeans? Not as a final solution (according to 2 Chr. 36:21, it brought some reparation for specific sins). Did Nehemiah's efforts bring improvement? Again, not a final improvement. A better attitude arrives only with sanctification brought by salvation through Jesus Christ.

---

15   My translation of the French translation by Posener 1936: 26.